Oral traditions and the verbal arts

A guide to research practices

Ruth Finnegan

London and New York

First published 1992
by Routledge
11 New Fetter Lane, London EC4P 4EE

Simultaneously published in the USA and Canada
by Routledge
a division of Routledge, Chapman and Hall, Inc.
29 West 35th Street, New York, NY 10001

© 1992 Ruth Finnegan

Phototypeset in Times by Intype, London
Printed and bound in Great Britain by
Mackays of Chatham PLC, Chatham, Kent

British Library Cataloguing in Publication Data
Finnegan, Ruth
   Oral traditions and the verbal arts: a guide to research practices.
   1. Social anthropology
   I. Title   II. Series
   306

Library of Congress Cataloging in Publication Data
Finnegan, Ruth H.
   Oral traditions and the verbal arts: a guide to research practices / Ruth
Finnegan.
   p.   cm.–(ASA research methods in social anthropology)
   Includes bibliographical references and index.
   1. Ethnology–Field work.   2. Oral tradition–Research.
   3. Ethnology–Methodology.   4. Folklore–Field work.   5. Folklore–
Methodology.   6. Folklore–Performance–Research.   I. Title.
   II. Series.
   GN346.F56   1991
   306′.072–dc20
                                                                    91–16746
                                                                    CIP

ISBN 0–415–02875–2
        0–415–02841–9 (pbk)

Oral traditions and the verbal arts

Oral literature, oral tradition, verbal folklore, folk literature, oral performance, popular culture – these areas of human communication and performance are now attracting increasing attention from social anthropologists. Professor Ruth Finnegan has played a key role in developing an anthropological approach to the study of these areas, and this book clearly reflects her personal involvement and authority.

Designed as a guide both to the practicalities of fieldwork and to the range of methods by which oral texts and performance can be observed, collected or analysed, *Oral Traditions and the Verbal Arts* takes the reader through all the stages of preparing for, conducting and following up research. Particular emphasis is laid on the recent interdisciplinary work on performance, on the *processes* involved in the creation and analysis of texts, and on related ethical issues. The book is distinctive in its comparative perspective, with examples taken from both historical and modern cultures, ranging from African and South Pacific forms to those from contemporary Europe. Theoretical controversies about approach and terminology are clarified, and the kinds of topics discussed are relevant to current anthropological work on, for example, memory, the emotions, artistic expression and individual creativity. A full and up-to-date bibliography is included.

Oral Traditions and the Verbal Arts provides helpful background and stimulus for all those exploring this rich and expressive area of human culture. Invaluable to students and researchers in anthropology and cultural studies, it will also be immensely helpful to folklorists and oral historians.

Ruth Finnegan is Professor in Comparative Social Institutions at the Open University. She was editor of the anthropological journal *Man* from 1987 to 1989, and is the author of many books and articles, including *Literacy and Orality*, *Oral Literature in Africa* and *Oral Poetry*.

ASSOCIATION OF SOCIAL ANTHROPOLOGISTS

ASA Research Methods in Social Anthropology

Panel of Honorary Editors:-
A.L. Epstein   James J. Fox   Clifford Geertz
Adam Kuper   Marilyn Strathern

Series Editor:
Anthony Good,
University of Edinburgh

To those who taught me, a generation apart,
Limba story-tellers and their audiences in
northern Sierra Leone in the early 1960s
and
friends and colleagues at the University of
Texas at Austin in 1989

Contents

Figures

Series editor's foreword

Anthony Good

This is the fourth volume in the '*Research Methods*' series initiated by the Association of Social Anthropologists (ASA), and the second to have been published by Routledge. Its immediate predecessor, *Observing the Economy* by C. A. Gregory and J. C. Altman, covered classic social anthropological territory, but the present book deals with a topic in which British anthropologists, at any rate, have only become interested rather more recently, although it is just as fascinating and important.

For this is a book about the study of human communication, or, to be more precise, of that aspect of it which involves the performance of songs, myths, stories, folktales, and similar forms of verbal artistry. Folklorists have always had to face the theoretical and methodological issues posed by collecting, transcribing, and analysing such material, of course, but there can surely be no social or cultural anthropologist who has not also grappled with similar problems, and few indeed who would not say with hindsight how much they would have benefited from this clear, thought-provoking statement of how best to go about it.

Such subject-matter raises distinctive moral dilemmas too. Who – if anyone – can be said to 'own' the data in question, and what artistic, legal, or financial responsibilities do fieldworkers bear towards those whose verbal performances they 'collect'? Dr Finnegan does not shirk such questions, though she shows that they allow of no easy answers.

Like its predecessors, the present volume serves two related purposes. First and foremost, as part of a series on research methods, it is of course designed to help anthropological fieldworkers be more explicitly aware of the constraints and implications of the various possible methods which can be used to study oral literature.

In order to achieve this first objective, however, it is also necessary to address the theoretical controversies generated by research on these topics. This makes the book an invaluable guide for students and general readers who are interested in enjoying oral literature for its own sake, or in finding out what its study can tell us about human society in general, rather than in carrying out such research for themselves. Its usefulness in this second respect is in fact much enhanced by the practical focus and 'close-to-the-ground' style of exposition required by its primary aim.

Ruth Finnegan has played a key role in developing a distinctive social anthropological approach to the study of oral literature, and her personal involvement and authority comes over clearly throughout the present volume.

Preface

As part of the 'Research Methods in Social Anthropology' series, this book is directed in the first instance to anthropologists, and contributes to the general series aims by concentrating on a particular area of human action and expression. As with other volumes in the series it is designed as a practical and systematic introduction to the processes and problems of researching in this area rather than a comprehensive textbook covering its history and theory. However, since theory and method cannot be fully separated in this area any more than in any other, the book also has to get involved in critical assessment of wider issues that others have found illuminating or problematic in the conduct of research on these topics, and their relation to comparative findings or controversies.

The study of oral traditions and verbal arts leads into an area of human culture to which anthropologists are now increasingly turning their interests, whether for its own sake or as part of research on other topics, linking up with developing work on such subjects as performance, text, memory, the emotions, the ethnography of speaking and the anthropology of artistic action more generally. It is thus now timely to have a volume of guidance for anthropologists as to the possibilities and problems of researching in this area and to the developments in related disciplines which bear on this. At the least this pulling together of some existing experience of research practices should be a useful aid for graduate students eager to work on the kinds of topics discussed here, and perhaps for their supervisors too. I hope it will also be helpful to anthropological colleagues and fellow students more generally, whether or not specialists in particular topics, as well as to those who are as yet relative beginners in this area.

Although the book is first and foremost written for anthropologists, it is impossible to enter this area of study without also drawing on work in many related disciplines and touching on wider interdisciplinary concerns. For this reason if nothing else the questions discussed here will be of interest across several other disciplines besides anthropology. Many of the issues are directly relevant to questions pursued within folklore, for example (a discipline which nowadays often overlaps with anthropology), or in literary and linguistic study, as well as for area or period specialists interested in the rewards and pitfalls of studying the oral forms within their own areas. For some studies, the discussion here will be all the more pertinent in that it points not just to field procedures but also to broader issues underlying the analysis and processing of texts, and comments on theoretical viewpoints that cut across disciplinary divides. Oral historians may also find much of interest here. For though the book is not intended as a specialist historiographical manual on how to use oral sources to deduce historical facts or construct a history of the past (on which there are already excellent guides such as David Henige's *Oral Historiography* or Paul Thompson's *The Voice of the Past*), it will certainly be relevant for at least the new breed of oral historians interested in a wider look at social context, social and psychological roles, and the structuring of textual formulations.

In other words, the book is intended for all those who for whatever reason are interested in research into verbal art and oral traditions. These are terms which, however elusive in detail, point in a general way towards a significant area of human communication and performance covering such topics as stories and story-telling, narrative, myth, song, poetic expression, oratory, riddling, and the many forms of heightened verbal expression – and, not least, how these are performed and constructed. It is not designed as a textbook about speech and language as a whole, but merely as a practical guide for researchers involved in, or embarking on, ethnographic or analytic research relating to some aspect of oral traditions or the verbal arts in their broadest senses – indeed for all those who are working or intending to work in this general area whether formally and in conjunction with some educational institution, or informally on their own.

In this area of research, even more than in many other fields of anthropology, there is a great deal of earlier work, drawn from many disciplines. The researcher needs to have some acquaintance with this. So another aim of the book has to be to give some preliminary guidance on the voluminous literature and its related controversies. It is impossible to give a full bibliographic account, for the literature is huge and constantly enlarging, but I have attempted to provide at least a start into it by including some key references in most of the major sections. I have tried to be balanced, but naturally have tended to concentrate on my own favourites or those most easily accessible. Specialists will know many others and can take them further – my suggestions are merely to provide some entry points for those as yet new to the literature on particular topics.

Despite being convinced of the importance of having a book like this – if only to help others to avoid many of the mistakes I made – I have found writing it far from easy. Among the many problems I met, one was the 'simple' matter of the title. The first working titles and sub-titles included – in varying metamorphoses – 'oral traditions, oral literature, the verbal arts, performance, narrative, folk literature, oral texts'; and that was only some of them. *Whichever* I tried to settle on carried hidden and often intensely controversial implications about definitions and approach. I had to start somewhere and, after much soul-searching and discussion with others, decided that the present title was slightly less contentious than some and did give some indication of the kinds of topics covered. But issues over terminology don't go away, and are tackled in the first chapter.

I began by thinking that preparing this book would be a small 'service' task on a limited subject. But, though it is still intended that way rather than an original contribution to theory or knowledge, it soon became clear that it inextricably touches on the whole of culture, the whole of human life, and, if the deadlines for publication hadn't fortunately arrived, could have gone on for ever. Dividing it up neatly under different headings was near-impossible too; whichever way I tried meant either lack of due context or unacceptable repetition. I didn't solve this problem either, but have tried to cope with it a little by the many cross-references within the volume. As I proceeded I also became increasingly aware of the book's gaps. Probably the biggest are specialist linguistic questions and music – both essential to certain topics, but given the focus and contents of this book (too long already) as well as my own lack of expertise, not covered here. Eventually, I hope, companion ASA volumes on music and perhaps on visual anthropology will be forthcoming as essential complements to the more 'oral' elements which it is my brief to concentrate on here.

Finally, I need to mention the embarrassing fact that preparing this book has shown up my own failings as fieldworker and analyst even more sharply than I had anticipated. My apologia is that perhaps I would have avoided some insensitivities or omissions if I had been able to consult a volume of this kind. And that, to extend this further, no handbook can really ever provide a comprehensive guide, even if it can help up to a point; in the end perhaps we all have to face our own problems and learn from them. The suggestions here, in other words, will no doubt provide helpful background and stimulus for those exploring aspects of this rich and expressive area of human culture, but, as with other volumes in the series, they cannnot constitute a mechanical guide and will have to be interpreted in the light of personal aims and circumstances.

Acknowledgements

Obviously this book could not have been written without the active assistance of many others, so without I hope implicating them in my errors, may I express my sincere gratitude to all those who helped, whether specifically named here or not. For advice and support – sometimes explicitly related to plans for this book, sometimes more general but equally helpful – may I particularly thank Roger Abrahams, Karin Barber, Dick Bauman, Dan Ben-Amos, Pamela Buckley, Alan Dundes, John Miles Foley, Henry Glassie, Liz Gunner, Michael Herzfeld, John W. Johnson, Józsi Nagy, Jeff Opland, Venetia Newall, Marilyn Strathern, Elizabeth Tonkin, and Marta Weigle. I owe a special debt to Lauri Harvilahti, Bengt Holbek, Lauri Honko, Senni Timonen, Anna-Leena Siikala and others who encouraged and instructed me during and following my visit to Finland and Scandinavia in 1988; and to Stoianka Boiadzhieva, Dimitrina and Nikolai Kaufman, Liliana Daskalova, and their colleagues at the Bulgarian Institute of Folklore in Sofia. I also particularly remember John Blacking's long encouragement and inspiration over the years – alas that his volume on music, planned as a mutual complement to this one, could not be completed. Many thanks too to Michael Branch, Stuart Hall, Dell Hymes, and anonymous reviewers for the press for reading and commenting on parts of the manuscript or its initial outline, and to Tony Good, a model series editor in his meticulous commentary and welcome improvements on successive drafts of the whole manuscript.

The dedication of the volume is not just empty words for I have unrepayable debts, different but equally profound, first to the Limba storytellers and audiences of Kakarima, Kamabai and Kabala in northern Sierra Leone who taught me about performance and text (as well as about some of the many complications a fieldworker and a tape-recorder could get tied up in); and second to those generous friends and colleagues at the University of Texas in Austin during the fall semester 1989 who disciplined and extended my gradually formulating ideas. Without the first the book would never have been started. It is equally true that without the second it could certainly not have been finished: I really need to thank everyone there, but special thanks to graduate students in the 'Orality and Literacy' seminar in Austin for our joint intellectual explorations, and to Steve Feld, Aurolyn Luykx, Glen Perice, Tom Porcello, Greg Urban, and, especially, Joel Sherzer and Katie Stewart for their advice and challenges, and for going well beyond the usual calls of duty and of friendship in helping me fight my way through that first amorphous mash of badly word-processed draft.

Among my more formal debts – sincerely appreciated too – are those to my own institution of the Open University for the support it has always given me, not least through the library and its marvellous inter-library loan service; and also to those other libraries I have drawn on, specially the British Museum (as I persist in calling it), the Finnish Literature Society's Library in Helsinki, and the many libraries at the University of Texas at Austin, from the great Perry-Castaneda Library to that small jewel of a reading room at the Center for Intercultural Studies in Folklore and Ethnomusicology. For permission to reproduce various figures and diagrams etc. I gratefully acknowledge the following:

Norwood Editions for Figure 4.1; University of Tennessee Press for Figure 4.2; Mrs Berta Bascom and the American Folklore Society for Figure 7.1; Mouton de Gruyter, a Division of Walter de Gruyter and Co., for Figure 7.2; University of Texas Press for Figure 7.3; University of Pennysylvania Press for Figure 8.1; Gallimard for Figure 8.2; Collins and Co. for Figure 8.3; Harvard University Press for Figure 8.4; Suomalainen Tiedeamatemia, Helsinki for Figure 8.5; Boston University Scholarly Publications for Figure 9.1; Dennis Tedlock and Doubleday and Co. Inc. for Figure 9.2.

Finally, I am most grateful to those who helped in processing the text – a phase of whose importance I am now even more aware than when I started on this book. My thanks in particular to Katy Wimhurst of Routledge, and to Margaret Allott, Molly Freeman, and, most of all, Maureen Adams whose forgiving and cheerful professionalism in dealing with the horrible task of processing my constant revisions and getting the whole into a suitable state for handing over on disc had to be experienced to be believed. And in the same breath may I thank my husband David Murray not only for his usual unmatched moral and intellectual support but also for lending me his Macintosh.

1 Introduction: scope and terminology

1.1 PREVIEW

The study of verbal arts and oral traditions has long seemed a Cinderella subject within British social anthropology, in the past often treated as more a matter for folklorists, oral historians or linguists rather than mainstream anthropology. But this position is changing. This book reflects both these developing interests within anthropology and their links with concurrent intellectual trends in related disciplines.

Anthropologists have in fact always taken some interest in patterned communication and tradition, in myth, and in ritual – even if British anthropologists have in the past focused less than their American or European counterparts on the artistic or performance elements of these processes. The anthropological tradition of combining in-depth fieldwork with a comparative perspective has also influenced work in this area. This has become increasingly important as older divides between anthropology and such other disciplines as oral history, literary study and, in particular, folklore are now narrowing.

More specifically, recent moves in anthropology have led to more interest in the kinds of topics covered in this volume. Besides the longer-term and often-cited shift 'from function to meaning', which has helped to heighten the visibility of verbal formulations and artistry, there is also now keen anthropological discussion of theoretical ideas relating to performance and to the ethnography of speaking. Older emphases on the primarily cognitive aspects of the 'rationality debate' or on the proclivities of the human mind – themselves not unrelated to the topics covered here – have been broadening to include analysis of artistry and emotion, and their manifestation in words and in action. Perhaps the most influential development has been the increasing attention to personal creativity and experience, part of what Peter Rivière sums up as 'the reinstatement of the individual as a thinking and feeling subject who is the creator of his society and culture' (1989: 22). The social – and often political – construction of such processes as memory, speech, literacy, myth, or the control of knowledge is also increasingly appreciated, issues now moving to the centre stage in modern anthropological thinking.

Not that the subjects discussed here are easy to define or delimit. Indeed it has to be faced that any description of the scope and limits of this book – the obvious topic for this introductory section – immediately runs into complications. For not only is the 'subject' itself elusive, but the questions to be discussed are embattled between partly contrasting partly overlappling disciplines. Neither the central concepts nor what these fundamentally refer to are agreed.

This first chapter must therefore open with some consideration of these issues, including the problems in what at first sight seem innocent matters of terminology. This is followed, first, by a survey of some influential theoretical perspectives (chapter 2), then more detailed discussions of the once-typical stages of: preparing for the field (chapter 3), collecting and observing while there (4 and 5), useful questions and classifications (6 and 7), analysing and processing the data (8 and 9) and, finally, the ethical issues that social researchers – and particularly those involved in fieldwork – need to bear in mind (10). Not all research on oral traditions and verbal arts follows this traditional order, of course. Fieldwork may be neither fulltime nor in another culture; analysis may be of texts recorded by others; and collecting, observing and processing may be continuous rather than separated stages. But since *any* texts or reports relating to oral tradition or the verbal arts are shaped through some such processes as those discussed in chapters 3–9 (and affected by ethically-contentious decisions too) understanding these phases is as relevant for those dealing with collections made by others as for those engaged in firsthand recording or observing.

Both this opening chapter and the later presentation are influenced by a view of oral traditions and verbal arts not as neutral textual data – in the past often the dominant model – but as ultimately based in, perhaps constituted by, social processes. The procedures of recording, presenting or analysing them are, similarly, human and interactive processes which in turn play a part in structuring the objects of study. These themes will be familiar ones for anthropologists. They are consonant both with the continuing anthropological tradition of studying the conventions of human culture in their own meaningful context and with recent sensitivities to the processes, ambiguities and reflexivities of human action.

1.2 'LANGUAGE', 'SPEECH' AND 'TEXT': SOME INITIAL QUESTIONS

Obviously it is impossible for either this volume or the keenest researcher to follow up *everything* on language or on 'tradition', and the focus here is on the kinds of issues which concern anthropologists. These could be summed up provisionally as the more formalised and recurrent conventions relating to verbal expression, considered in their cultural context. However, to say that is immediately to come face to face with the problems. For there is nothing automatic about just how and what someone interested in the cultural aspects of formalised verbal expression (or similar phrases) should be studying, nor does the 'object of study' present itself as already defined and separated for the observer. Given the seamless texture of speech, ideas, action, performance that make up human living – or is it seamless? – the processes of isolating its elements for abstraction and analysis are themselves problematic. For example:

How far do human beings in particular situations express and clothe their ideas, emotions or actions in recurrent verbal forms and in what ways are these traditional?

In what sense *are* certain forms of verbal expression more 'formalised' or 'heightened', and what – if anything – is excluded?

How far is theorising or interpretation imposed by researchers, how far already there, and formulated in verbal expression?

Can we separate the 'verbal' from other aspects of communication and action?

Can oral texts be divorced from those in writing?

How can researchers go about settling such questions, developing a vocabulary, and carving out suitable phenomena for investigation?

These questions are not susceptible to once-and-for-all answers. Indeed researchers often bypass them and merely delimit their material in the light of their own interests and practicalities. Nevertheless, however the essential matter for investigation is selected, *some* decisions have been made, if often unconsciously, in response to such issues.

These decisions have both a theoretical and an empirical side (insofar as these aspects are distinguishable). So another theme throughout this book is the importance of being aware not just of comparative theory, but also of ethnographic specificities. Anthropologists sometimes forget that cultural relativity applies to verbal expression as much as to other cultural conventions, for here too categories we take as self-evident (even that basic western concept of 'text') may not be universally applicable. So responses to the questions above may also need to take account of culturally specific values and practices. In a given cultural context how far *are* different verbal genres recognised, and by whom and how and by what criteria? Apparent parallels from our own cultural experience, or even apparently unambiguous statements by (some) participants themselves, may need critical analysis. Is 'oral tradition' transmitted in crystallised narratives – controlled perhaps by a particular category of people – or is it undifferentiated 'common knowledge', elicited and formulated by the researcher? Do 'oral' and 'written' traditions operate in separate spheres or is there overlap or interaction between them – and does this vary at different periods and places? How far is there a concept of verbal 'text' divorced from, say, music or performance? Exploring these questions often needs to go beyond both prior generalisation and theoretical self-contemplation to detailed ethnographic investigation.

The issues examined in this volume do not add up to one clearly delimited subject. This is both because disciplinary coverage and key terms are not agreed, and also – more interestingly – because abstracting the elements for study is itself a controversial process. It needs to be constantly remembered that the units chosen for classification and analysis – whether genres of 'oral literature', texts of 'myths', syntheses of 'oral tradition', modes of verbal performance, or whatever – are seldom as self-evident as they seem in the published accounts. They have been partly formulated by particular groups of performers and adherents, partly constructed by researchers, in both cases in some sense abstracted from the flow of human action. Comparative terms can never be presumed in advance to fit exactly the ideas and practices they purport to describe, far less provide a definitive and unchallengeable account.

1.3 SOME CENTRAL TERMS – ACCEPTED AND DISPUTED

Dissecting key concepts will be nothing new to anthropologists, with their sensitivity to the danger of squeezing the rich variety of cultures into categories set by our own cultural assumptions. But the terms used in the study of oral arts and traditions seem to be particularly prone to such dangers. Certain technical-sounding terms may give the appearance of being established and universally accepted: unambiguously 'there' in the world. But most are at best elusive, either in principle or in their application to particular contexts, and often intensely disputed or value-laden – even, in some circumstances, offensive. As will quickly emerge too, the terms used in the title of this book are themselves contentious and ambiguous, not least that emotive word 'tradition'.

Some terms have to be used to start from, of course. As always, though, terminology can only be illuminating when used critically. Furthermore, it may affect not only how you construct your subject of study, but how those cooperating with you envisage it. Some consideration of the most commonly used terms and their implications is therefore needed at the outset.

1.3.1 Oral and orality

The much-used adjective 'oral' is often used as a prime criterion for marking out particular disciplines or research interests. Thus 'folklore' is commonly defined in terms of *orally* transmitted material, the term is basic to 'oral-formulaic' and 'oral literature' studies, and it also of course appears in the title of this book. It is also the subject of much current debate.

The dictionary definition gives a start: 'uttered in spoken words; transacted by word of mouth; spoken, verbal' (*OED*). This is frequently the primary meaning in much apparently technical terminology: 'oral tradition', 'oral literature', 'oral narrative', 'oral testimony' and so on. 'Oral' is often contrasted with 'written' (an apparently obvious but in practice somewhat slippery distinction), as in 'oral literature' opposed to – or a parallel of – written literature, or 'oral history' as a pointer to non-documentary sources. 'Oral' also qualifies general terms like 'texts', 'poetry' or 'narrative', either emphasising distinctions between written and oral forms or drawing them within the same comparative perspective.

'Oral' also contrasts with what is *not* verbal or *not* based on words – thus the second dictionary meaning of 'using speech only', as opposed, say, to sign language. Hence 'oral folklore' like stories, songs or proverbs is distinguished from material culture. Such contrasts need care for they sometimes reflect less local distinctions than unthinking western models of verbal 'text' as self-evidently differentiated from visual, auditory or bodily signs. One of the themes in recent studies of orally-delivered art forms is that, though in one sense they centre on words, in another they involve *more* than words (see chapter 5 and 1.4 below).

Because 'oral' is thus opposed – sometimes contentiously opposed – both to 'written/literate' and to 'non-verbal', its meaning is correspondingly ambiguous. 'Oral tradition' sometimes means any kind of unwritten tradition (including physical monuments, religious statues or church frescoes), sometimes only tradition(s) enunciated or transmitted through words (thus *ex*cluding and contrasting with the previous examples).

The more generalised term 'orality' has been increasingly in vogue in recent years. This usually implies a general contrast with 'literacy', sometimes associated with assumptions about the social and cognitive characteristics of oral communication or the significance of oral culture within broad stages of historical development. These questions are currently the subject of controversy. Some scholars are interested in establishing general features of 'orality' as opposed to literacy, as in Ong's *Orality and Literacy* (1982), partly inspired by the work of Parry and Lord (see 2.4.9) or by the more anthropologically-focused studies of Jack Goody (1968, 1977, also his more qualified analyses 1986, 1987). Others criticise this as technological determinism or as based on west-centred views of history; or even, in some cases, as evoking out-dated concepts of 'primitive mentality'. Such scholars would instead stress socially conditioned arrangements and usages (Street 1984, Scribner and Cole 1981, Finnegan 1988, 1989b, Goody et al. 1988, Schousboe and Larsen 1989; for further discussion or examples see also Stock 1983, Tannen 1982, Chafe and Tannen 1987, DeMaria and Kitzinger 1989, R. Thomas 1989; on the term 'oral' more generally see Henige 1988, Finnegan 1990, also Foley 1990a: chap. 1).

Ambiguities or controversy are not necessarily reasons for avoiding a term and 'oral' remains popular. But it is worth examining one's own and others' work for possible misreadings of whichever sense was meant or for overtones not intended.

1.3.2 Tradition(s)

'Tradition' is both common in everyday speech and a term much used by anthropologists, folklorists and oral historians, indeed sometimes regarded as at the heart of these disciplines (particularly folklore, see Bauman 1989c, Honko and Laaksonen 1983, Honko 1988: 9–10). It has many different meanings however. It is used, variously, of: 'culture' as a whole; any established way of doing things whether or not of any antiquity; the process of handing down practices, ideas or values; the products so handed down, sometimes with the connotation of being 'old' or having arisen in some 'natural' and non-polemical way. It has other overtones too. Something called a 'tradition' is often taken to somehow belong to the whole of the 'community' rather than to specific individuals or interest groups; to be unwritten; to be valuable or (less often) out-dated; or to mark out a group's identity. Recently there has been emerging interest in the processes through which 'traditions' are created or maintained in specific historical conditions to fit particular interests or values (as in Hobsbawm and Ranger's concept of 'the invention of tradition' (1983), and similar treatments in Cohen 1989, Finnegan 1988: esp. chap.6; on the concept of 'tradition' generally see also Shils 1984, Ben-Amos 1984, Finnegan 1991, and, on oral history, Vansina 1965, 1985, Henige 1982; also 6.1).

The phrase 'oral tradition' conceals similar ambiguities, with the apparently more specific 'oral' in fact complicating it even further. The addition of 'oral' often implies that the tradition in question is in some way 1) verbal or 2) non-written (not necessarily the same thing), sometimes also or alternatively 3) belonging to the 'people' or the 'folk', usually with the connotation of non-educated, non-élite, and/or 4) fundamental and valued, often supposedly transmitted over generations, perhaps by the community or 'folk' rather than conscious individual action. In the context of oral history Henige defines oral tradition as 'strictly speaking . . . those recollections of the past that are commonly or universally known in a given culture . . . [and] have been handed down for at least a few generations' (1982: 2). Not all follow this limitation, however, and even here there is room for disagreement: handed down in what form? how many generations?

These many implied (but differing) attributes are the source of many confusions. It is tempting to dub any verbalisation captured in research as 'oral tradition', and proceed to assume a series of consequential – but perhaps false – properties. For example, *belwo* love poems among the Somali could be called 'oral tradition' in the sense of an unwritten local form. But it does not follow, as that term might then imply, that they go far back in time, are purely 'verbal' or are produced communally (see Andrzejewski and Lewis 1964, J.W. Johnson 1974, Andrzejewski 1967). Equally it can be misleading to accept claims about tradition at face value, specially since the term is widely used 'to represent just about anything to which anyone wishes to give legitimacy or added luster' (Henige 1982:2). Statements about 'oral tradition' tend to be buttressed by a series of politically and personally entrenched values, often intertwined with questions of national or group identity, so it can be particularly difficult to examine these critically or investigate how far each meaning is really supported by ethnographic evidence.

The answer is not necessarily to give it up – though some researchers now find other terms more useful. But it is important to consider how far its various associations (perhaps assumed by your readers even if not by you) do or do not apply to the particular item or process under study. The following checklist can help to confront ambiguities explicitly.

1 Is the 'tradition' (or 'oral tradition') under discussion 'old'? if so, *how* old and in what sense?
2 Is it shared by everyone in the society or group, and, if not, who controls or uses it and in what situations?
3 Is the term 'tradition' (or a parallel vernacular equivalent) an evaluative one for a) all the people being studied; b) specific groups; c) specific spokesmen and/or outsiders; d) the researcher? If so, how, and are these values manifested in people's actions?
4 Is the 'tradition' process or product?
5 If the 'tradition' is passed on, whether 'through the generations' or for a shorter period, how is this done and by whom? Was it 'invented' in any sense, and if so, by whom, and why?
6 How far is 'tradition' crystallised or explicit in the perceptions and practice of (some or all) the people being studied, how far a construct of the researcher?
7 Is 'tradition' differentiated into different media, versions, or genres? Might 'traditions' be a better term than the generalised 'tradition'?

1.3.3 Oral literature

This is another widely employed term, sometimes overlapping with 'oral tradition', but usually with somewhat different coverage and connotations. Often assumed to date from recent scholarship, in fact the idea of unwritten literature already occurred in nineteenth-century writing (Koelle 1854, Macdonald 1882, Burton 1865, Chatelain 1894). The concept was further propagated by H.M. and N.K. Chadwick's massive opus on the 'growth of literature', where, they explain, 'the connection between literature and writing is accidental, and belongs to a secondary phase in the history of literature' (vol. 3, 1940: xi). They thus drew examples not just from European and Eastern classical civilisations, but also from non-literate or semi-literate cultures and included lengthy accounts of the 'oral literature' of the Tatars, Polynesia, and Africa. Many recent studies employ the term (Jacobs 1959, 1966, Finnegan 1970, Görög-Karady 1982, Burns 1983, the journal *Cahiers de Littérature Orale*; on oral-formulaic writing see 2.4.9), and it is widely used among anthropologists and others for what are deemed unwritten but somehow 'literary' forms.

The term is not universally approved however. Some argue that it is self-contradictory (how can 'literature', etymologically implying writing, be *un*written?) or that it imposes written and ethnocentric models on activities which may have other elements than the purely verbal and/or aesthetic, highlighting textual rather than performance aspects. Opposing arguments are that it is short-sighted to be constrained by etymologies, particularly culture-bound ones based on the English language, and that avoiding the terms 'literature'/'literary' for non-written forms evokes west-centred or élitist preconceptions dividing 'them' and 'us' – drawing the further retort that terms should be used to bring out, rather than blur over, cultural distinctions. (For further elaboration see: broadly in favour of the term: Finnegan 1970: 15ff, 1988: 61ff, Andrzejewski 1985, Bauman 1986: 1f; against: Ong 1982: 10–15, Huntsman 1981: 214, Finnegan 1982: 2ff, Sweeney 1987: 9ff, Herzfeld 1985: 202ff).

Whether and how far 'oral literature' is useful depends on both the material being studied and your research questions. The following summary of its implications can help to assess its appropriateness.

1 It emphasises the 'literary' or 'artistic' aspects.
2 It allows for the creative action of individuals and for new as well as old forms.

3 It points to the possibility of differing forms and genres both within and between cultures rather than the undifferentiated whole sometimes implied by 'oral tradition'.

4 It can draw on illuminating parallels through interacting with theoretical and comparative work on literature and written forms (with the corresponding dangers of over-reliance on western literary canons).

5 It provides a comparative term recognised by scholars working on other cultures and historical periods – with the parallel danger of ignoring local meanings or interactions.

6 It shares the same definitional problems as with 'literature' anywhere, about what 'literature' essentially is and how it can be differentiated from other verbal formulation, with oral forms perhaps particularly tricky. There is also the position that, rather than trying to delimit the 'literary', there are merits in bringing together *all* forms of heightened verbalisation (see Howell 1986, Sherzer 1974, 1990, Sweeney 1987: 12).

7 The term 'oral' carries its own insights and problems (see 1.3.1).

There is no need for an 'all or nothing' approach. Some avoid 'oral literature' as a general term (hence by-passing its controversies) but exploit its advantages by using the adjective 'literary', or the less contentious 'oral narrative', 'oral poetry' etc.

1.3.4 Verbal art

'Verbal art' was introduced in Bascom's classic article as 'a convenient and appropriate term for folktales, myths, legends, proverbs, riddles, and other "literary forms" ' (1955: 245). A great deal of work has been carried out under this label, particularly by American folklorists and anthropologists. It now usually also covers songs and poems, together with verbal processes like naming, rhetoric or tongue twisters.

The term is somewhat less contentious than many of the others here. It tends to highlight aesthetic aspects while avoiding the implicit constraints of 'oral literature' in not being confined to longer textually articulated forms. It thus facilitates verbal artistry of all kinds being treated together, while avoiding the emotive overtones sometimes associated with the term 'oral' (see 1.3.1). The cost is the loss of parallels with literary forms and analysis, and some researchers prefer 'oral literature' for 'literary' genres like heroic poetry or lengthy narratives. Taken literally it implies a limitation to *words*, excluding plastic, musical or gestural facets, but most scholars using this term are sensitive to non-verbal aspects, and interpret it as referring to performance rather than purely verbal text.

The term inevitably raises the question of how, or by whose criteria, 'art' or 'play' can be delimited – the answers cannot just be assumed. It therefore links with wider theoretical debates about the nature of 'art'(see 7.2.4), as well as needing further empirical investigation about its appropriateness within the particular culture or genre under study.

1.3.5 Folklore, folk art etc.

The term 'folklore' is often used to encompass many of the topics considered in this volume. It sometimes has the broad sense of *all* forms of 'orally transmitted tradition', including material culture, but its most common referent is to verbal forms such as stories, songs or proverbs, with special emphasis on the collection or analysis of texts. (Because 'folklore' refers to a discipline as well as its subject matter, there is a large scholarly literature on its scope, methodology, and history, see Bauman 1989c, Brunvand 1976, 1986, Dorson 1983, Dundes n.d., Paredes 1969, 1977, Toelken 1979, also 2.4.1–2.)

This heading, and associated terms like 'folk stories', 'folktales', or 'folk narratives', has long inspired the study of forms that might otherwise have remained hidden to scholarship, resulting in colossal efforts in collecting and analysing narratives, poetry, song, riddles, and proverbs. Much of the earlier work in the name of 'folklore' was in the antiquarian tradition, amassing extensive archives with little analysis. Some however was of the highest scholarship, closely akin to anthropological approaches. This is particularly true of recent research among contemporary American or Scandinavian folklorists (a fact of which British anthropologists often seem unaware). Using – or, at the least, recognising – the term is thus a link into sophisticated international scholarship.

It has notorious problems too. It was first coined in 1846 to replace 'popular antiquities' and 'popular literature' by 'a good Saxon compound, Folklore, – *the Lore of the People*', referring then to what were regarded as survivals from the long past: 'the few ears which are remaining, scattered over that field from which our forefathers might have gathered a goodly crop' (Thoms 1846: 862). A more recent definition runs:

Folklore (or traditional and popular culture) is the totality of tradition-based creations of a cultural community, expressed by a group or individuals and recognized as reflecting the expectations of a community in so far as they reflect its cultural and social identity; its standards and values are transmitted orally, by imitation or by other means. Its forms include, among others, language, literature, music, dance, games, mythology, rituals, customs, handicrafts, architecture and other arts.

(UNESCO, cited in Honko 1989a: 8)

In common parlance the term still sometimes keeps the original evolutionist connotations of a survival from ancient and communal tradition, of anonymity, and of belonging to the rural and unlettered 'folk'. For this reason the term 'folklore', and the items which it supposedly studies, is avoided by many British anthropologists. But these older associations are now challenged by leading professional folklorists who stress the significance of individual creativity, of modern forms, and of urban as well as rural contexts. Some widen it, as in recent Russian folklore, to 'everything connected with the contemporary poetic life of the people' (Oinas 1984: 170). The modern discipline of 'folklore' is thus now established in many countries as a highly reputable and often innovative academic subject. The earlier connotations are still powerful, however, so if you use the term 'folklore' it is important to discuss these explicitly, if only to make clear to yourself, your readers *and* those cooperating in your study (who may react against the term) where you stand on these questions.

1 Who defines 'folk' and for what purpose?
2 Are the 'folk' in question really rural, 'traditional', non-literate or somehow close-to-nature, as often implied? Are they, alternatively, any group bound together by some bond or sharing a common factor (as in Dundes 1977: 22, see also A.L. Lloyd 1952) and, if so, in what ways if at all do their artefacts or activities differ from those of other social groupings?
3 What about the old suggestion that 'folklore' is created by 'the folk' rather than the individual, or that modern urban peoples have no verbal arts worth studying? (Despite new developments, urban and industrial forms are arguably still under-emphasised by folklorists).
4 If 'folklore' is transmitted through *oral* tradition, are literate subjects or interactions between oral and written elements outside its scope?

5 Does the term mean that only old or 'traditional' forms are being studied, excluding newly composed items and those that have not yet 'sunk into tradition' (Dorson 1972b:17, cf. 9ff)?

1.3.6 Performance and performance events

These terms have been emerging as major organising concepts for the recording and analysing of oral forms. They are particularly developed among 'performance-oriented' American anthropologists/ folklorists who urge that oral expression and verbal art is realised in performance rather than as verbal or writable text.

In one sense such terms are nothing new. Most anthropologists presumably take for granted that, with oral forms in particular, performance is part of the context that should receive attention. But recent 'performance' terminologies open up distinctive interests both in the rhetorical and aesthetic techniques of delivery and in the specifics of performances and audiences, with the idea too that performance is not mere 'context' but of the essence.

This terminology has sometimes been taken as implying a rejection of the apparently counter-term of 'text'. Recently however performance-based terms have also been used as complementary rather than contrasting approaches to analysis (Blackburn 1988, Sherzer and Woodbury 1987, Okpewho 1990) and as providing new ways into looking at textual features (see Bauman and Briggs 1990, Hanks 1989; for further discussion see 1.4 (on texts), 2.4.10, and 5.1).

1.3.7 Narrative and narration

These terms are sometimes used in a wide sense, referring to *all* verbal forms where temporal sequence is implied, indeed to other media too, including visual and plastic art forms, or to life itself. Perhaps more often they have the sense of fiction, novels, myths, tales and legends, broadly contrasted with non-narrative forms like conversations, proverbs or riddles, and often in practice excluding poetry. The terms have been the focus of a great deal of interest both among narratological scholars and in some recent ethnographically or historically based work on oral forms (for references see 2.4.8, 8.3.4).

They do not correspond precisely to the areas of interest discussed in this volume, being either too broad (covering much else besides verbal media), or, when used in a more limited sense, excluding non-narrative forms. However, for certain purposes they are well worth considering:

1 They cut across older written/oral, traditional/modern and verbal/ non-verbal divides in ways that may be more illuminating than terms building in such divisions whether or not they are appropriate.
2 Being broader than specific genre terms they can be specially helpful for comparative and cross-cultural analysis.
3 Narratologists' work on differing voices, metanarration, or narrative structure adds a new dimension to older analyses.
4 The concept of 'narration' (the act of telling) highlights the process, not just the product.

1.3.8 Discourse

'Discourse' is often used as an umbrella term to cover *all* forms of verbal communication in society. A great deal of both detailed ethnographic work and theoretical analysis is now conducted under this heading, particularly by sociolinguists and American linguistic anthropologists.

Some react against the term because of its associations with specialist linguistic and literary theories or its usage as a metaphor for the hegemonic, disputed and ideological nature of society. It can be amorphous too, as in some linguists' negative definition as 'anything beyond the sentence'. However in the sense in which the term is often used in the study of verbal art and expression, it is applied more positively and directly to all kinds of active verbal communication: 'the broadest and most comprehensive level of linguistic form, content, and use . . . large and small, written and oral, permanent and fleeting' (Sherzer 1987a: 305, 297): or, more briefly, 'language in context across all forms and modes' (Tannen 1982b: x). Such studies centre on verbal forms in the context of actual use – on 'language event or linguistic usage', as Ricoeur has it (1971: 530) – and often question the traditional distinction in much Anglo-Saxon social science between meaning and action. Modern 'discourse' scholars are also usually sensitive to paralinguistic, musical or kinesic aspects (the more so since their focus is often playful and artistic uses of language), to meaning, and, in some cases, to related political and ideological issues.

The term has thus provided an occasion for ethnographically-based investigation of *all* the linguistic usages in a culture, challenging others' limitations to only 'literary' forms. It gets away both from the old oral/written or traditional/modern divisions and from ethnocentric pre-selection via such terms as 'folklore' or 'oral literature' (well argued in Sweeney 1987: 12), and directs attention to the *processes* of linguistic interaction rather than just to the products (for further discussion and references see specially Sherzer 1987a, also Tannen 1982b, Parkin 1984, Hanks 1989, and 2.4.10).

1.3.9 Popular arts/popular culture

Some scholars who reject the proposition that only 'traditional' or 'folk' expression should delimit their field are now exploring combinations using the term 'popular'. This turns attention to the contemporary world: the many forms of popular, local or amateur verbal expression which can be studied now that, as Hannerz puts it, 'cultural interrelatedness increasingly reaches across the world' (1989: 66). Historians too have been uncovering non-élite 'popular culture' forms that do not easily fall under 'folk' or 'traditional' headings (Burke 1978, Gurevitch 1988, Vincent 1989). So 'popular culture' and its associated terms is now more and more entering into academic analysis and discussion. It is frequently used to direct attention to 'ordinary' as opposed to professional practitioners or activities, and to take account of 'mixed' or 'creolised' forms, as well as providing a way to explore the sectional, changing or political elements in these practices.

The term has problems too. For a time it was taken to refer just to *certain* forms like television, football or the mass press, or associated with an arguably limited class-based definition. The implication of something homogeneous can also be misleading, and 'oral' and 'popular' do not necessarily coincide. Further, the traditional threefold division between: 1) traditional or folk; 2) élite or high culture; and 3) popular, commercial or mass is still powerful and can cause confusions. Such distinctions are not universally observed however. In some languages there is no clear differentiation between terms for 'folk' and 'popular' (as in Russian studies according to Oinas 1984: 165), while in other areas – particularly Latin America – popular culture often means the practices of resistance by subordinate classes against imposed mass culture.

As often precise definition poses problems: 'popular' in the sense of being produced and/or consumed by 'the people' (and if so which people); of being approved by large numbers; of 'working class' production or consumption; 'amateur' rather than 'specialist' or 'professional' production; 'unofficial' rather than 'official' culture; any form opposed to 'high' or 'élite' culture; or outside the 'commercial' sphere? The answers are not simple – but for some one merit of the term is precisely that such questions are raised explicitly (for recent discussion see Barber, Cosentino and others 1987 (an important discussion), Hannerz 1987, 1989, Coplan 1986, Waterman 1988; also, on 'popular culture' more generally Bigsby 1976, Fabian 1978, Kaplan 1984, Burke 1978, S. Hall 1964, 1981, Hall and Whannel 1964, Middleton and Horn 1981, Pickering and Green 1987, Waites et al. 1982; the term 'vernacular' has occasionally been used with similar meanings).

1.3.10 Other terms

The following, though less common than those above, do have some currency and are worth noting briefly:

Aural: an alternative to 'oral', but stressing particularly the quality of being 'shaped by the ear and intended to be followed by ear' (Russo 1976: 49).

Ethnopoetics: a term implying particular focus on the voices of non-western peoples – 'a redefinition of poetry in terms of cultural specifics, with an emphasis on those alternative traditions to which the West gave names like "pagan", "gentile", "tribal", "oral", and "ethnic" ' (Rothenberg 1983: xi, see Hymes 1981, Tedlock 1977, 1983, 1989, and the journal *Alcheringa–Ethnopoetics*: also 2.4.10).

Expressive arts: a concept of broader application than just to the oral or verbal but sometimes helpful in avoiding a split between verbal and non-verbal.

Oracy: an alternative to 'orality', but usually with less generalising connotations (see Tonkin 1974); often used of the complex of spoken skills in an educational context.

Oral testimony: particularly used by oral historians (see 2.4.12) to stress the evidential role of oral sources. Researchers interested in aesthetic and contextual aspects avoid the term on the grounds that directing attention just to 'testimony' may misunderstand the speaker's intentions or the utterance's other role(s).

Orature: an alternative to 'oral literature'. It avoids the etymological problems of 'oral literature' and is also a positive term in its own right (the parallel to *écriture*) in the context of 'decolonising the mind' (see Ngugi 1986: 94 also Chinweizu and Madubuiko 1983: 32ff, Cancel 1989: 17).

Poetics, rhetoric: sometimes used of ordered language in general, sometimes of just one special aspect of language (see Jakobson 1960).
Spoken art (Berry 1961) or *oral art* (Herskovits 1961): alternatives to 'verbal art'.

There are also more specific genre and similar terms (see chapter 7). These are too numerous to list individually, but it is worth noting that *epos*, *epic*, *myth*, and *saga* while used mostly as limited genre words, are also occasionally used – confusingly – to sum up the whole field of oral traditions and the verbal arts (see 7.4).

1.4 'TEXT(S)': A SPECIAL CASE

Another common practice in this general field is to speak of 'oral texts'. However, the notion of 'text' presents particular problems. It has in the past usually been taken as a neutral concept – seldom explicitly discussed – encompassing both the units for research and the medium for representing and crystallising the findings. Thus it has commonly been assumed that a central research aim is to collect and study texts, that there is agreement about what texts are, and that they are somehow out there waiting to be picked up and analysed. 'The raw materials of oral folklore research are texts' (Brunvand 1986: 19) has been a recurrent theme in more disciplines than just folklore.

This fits the preconception in the writing-dominated intellectual traditions of western culture over the last centuries that words, communication and art forms are most naturally mediated – and should thus be represented and analysed – through verbal texts. When humanistic scholarship was extended to include oral forms, these too were naturally seen as essentially a type of verbal texts, on the same model. Texts in writing have thus been the focus for linguistic or literary study, have been taken as one form of 'objective data' in anthropological fieldwork (Ellen 1984: 73ff), and make up the main body of material in folklore and other archives. Indeed the voluminous collections and analyses of verbal texts seem clear evidence both of their importance in the world and the interest of studying them, the more so that we have all been trained in the procedures for working with word-based texts, whether these take the form of works composed in writing or of written transcriptions in some way elicited from oral sources.

Much of the study of oral traditions, oral narrative and the verbal arts has thus been based on collections and analyses taking the notion of 'text' as the point of departure. This focus will of course continue. Quite apart from institutional and ideological arrangements fostering it, the study of verbal texts has brought many insights in the past and will no doubt do so in the future too; hence this – and any similar – book has to be preoccupied with the mechanics of collecting texts and approaches to their analysis.

But there is now no longer the same universal confidence that texts in this, or any, sense form the natural focus for research into oral arts and traditions, and earlier assumptions are challenged in current work within social, literary and anthropological studies. This section indicates controversies that need to be confronted if in any way the concept of text underlies your research (as it almost certainly will, if only indirectly and implicitly). It does not try to cover the extended meaning of 'text' as shorthand for the rhetorical conventions shaping ethnographic and other presentations (as in Clifford and Marcus 1986, Atkinson 1990) nor the broader sense of 'text' as 'any coherent complex of signs' (Bakhtin 1986: 103) – though these meanings are not unrelated to current critiques. Rather it concentrates on issues arising from traditional approaches to written transcriptions – once taken as 'the' obvious units for the study of oral forms – and the now-controversial model of 'text' often underlying these.

The rethinking comes from three separate, if related, perspectives.

The first results from challenging certain ethnocentric assumptions apparently current in western culture, both academic and 'folk'. Among these is the picture of 'text' as having some kind of continuance in its own right, outside of temporal constraints, existing almost in a spatial way over and above the specific conditions in which it from time to time is read or delivered. Thus the works of Homer or of Shakespeare are pictured coming down through the ages as somehow self-existing entities, and when we speak of a novel or poem, what we mean is the verbal text – the absolute mode in which it is envisaged as existing irrespective of its contingent readings or printings. So deep does this go that even with music the score, rather than the performance, is often taken to be what defines the work (for further discussion see Finnegan 1982: 2ff, 1988: 123ff; Lord 1960: esp. chapters 5 and 6).

Unpacking unstated cultural assumptions is of course a constant preoccupation of anthropologists. It is true that uncovering them in our *own* society is hardly uncontentious. But that some such cultural preconception about the role and nature of text is at work comes through in manifold instances of research where the western observer has begun from the model of a fixed verbal 'text' existing out there, ready made and waiting for collection and analysis.

Questioning this (folk) model of 'text' has implications for research on oral traditions and arts. Much past research started from the common western experience, based on many years of dealing with published written texts, that not only are texts the appropriate object of study, but that they are indeed 'objects', and – almost by definition – finalised products existing in their own right, with their own correct and enduring essence. But in the case of many oral forms (and perhaps of some written ones?) this model is an uncomfortable one. Detailed field studies, among them Parry and Lord's famous analyses of South Slavic epic performances (see Lord 1960, also 2.4.9 and 6.1.3), have documented how what from one viewpoint might seem the 'same' text may differ among different performances with each version being equally authentic. In many such cases, it turns out, it is misleading to impose the notion of a fixed, correct and self-existing text.

The dominant scholarly model of word-based written text seems in any case particularly inappropriate for oral formulations. Any orally delivered 'text' is likely to rest on performance and that in turn means that more than just 'verbal' elements are involved. The art and meaning of West African Limba stories, say, or modern tall tales by Texan dog traders (Finnegan 1967, Bauman 1986) are realised not just in words but also in the teller's delivery skills, the occasion, or the actions and reception of the audience. Merely looking at words and assuming, in keeping with the textual model, that *they* constitute the essence can miss the reality. One reaction against the traditional approach is to attend to the whole speech act or performance event and take contextual, paralinguistic, gestural, musical and even visual elements as constituent of, not mere extras to, the verbal text and its meaning. Not everyone would wish to go the whole way with the performance theorists (see 2.4.10), but there is now widespread appreciation of the relevance of such challenges to a purely verbal model, above all in the analysis of oral performance genres.

Once one starts querying the traditional concept of text, further questions emerge. Do all art forms (even verbal art forms) necessarily come in the form of essentially word-based texts – or of sustained, fixed or bounded textual units? Is text (and 'textness') a relative or polysemous rather than absolute phenomenon, needing subtle empirical investigation rather than just recording? Or if there is, in some sense, a more or less settled text, is verbal textness the most significant element and for whom? What if anything is the relation between verbal text and visual image? Some of the consequential questions, it seems, are ethnographic and factual ones. It begins to emerge that referring to something as a 'text' needs to be the start of detailed investigation rather than the end of the matter.

A second influence is the general move within anthropology – among other disciplines – away from studying neutral fixed 'objects' or supposedly homogeneous institutions, towards greater emphasis on process and practice. It is now clearer that some of what in the past were presented as 'the' texts (stories, myths, songs etc.) of a particular culture were sometimes just one performance by one individual on one particular occcasion, or produced or privileged by only one among several sections of the population. Along with this goes increasing interest not in texts as just objects for collection, but in the processes of composition, performance, reception, circulation or manipulation of verbal formulations.

There is similarly now a sharper awareness of the researcher's role in the research process, including the process of creating text – that apparently hard 'object' of study. What settings are chosen for collecting, and from whom; how texts are recorded; what decisions are made about transcription, written representation, translation and publication – all these affect the final product and hence the interpretation and assessment of that text. At the same time anthropologists and others have become more sensitive to multiple voices and to the distortions resulting from outsiders' reductions of these to single-line written texts. This awareness of the constructed nature of what used to look like neutral texts has been one of the most powerful ideas in the recent study of oral forms.

Thirdly, recent moves in critical theory bring these ideas into conjunction with current questioning of the once-taken-for-granted primacy, independence or homogeneity of the verbal text (see 2.4.7 below on 'post-structuralism', also Barthes 1977, Fish 1980, Davis 1986 esp. Part 8, Rice and Waugh 1989 esp. Part 2, and, for recent work by anthropologists and others questioning traditional models of texts even in more literate contexts, Basso 1974, S. Stewart 1979, Szwed 1981, and the overview in Hanks 1989). The stress on instability, plurality and lack of closure thus links with questions already being considered in the study of oral arts and traditions.

A number of related terms have developed out of these more critical recent approaches to 'text'. Chief among these are 'textuality' ('the quality of coherence or connectivity that characterizes text' is Hanks' definition, 1989: 96) and 'intertextuality' (the relation of one literary text to another, particularly as experienced by the reader/audience – a single text cannot be fully understood as an independent self-standing entity). Other more detailed terms include the concept of 'anti-textual' elements within a text, while, to quote from Hanks' recent overview,

> 'Co-text' designates the accompanying discourse in a single text . . . . 'Meta-text' is any discourse that refers to, describes, or frames the intepretation of text. 'Con-text' is the broader environment (linguistic, social, psychological) to which text responds and on which it operates . . . . 'Pre-text' encompasses whatever prepares the ground for or justifies the production or interpretation of text. 'Sub-text' focuses on whatever understanding or themes form the background or tacit dimensions of a text, inferable but not explicitly stated. The constellation of consequences and outcomes of producing, distributing, or receiving a text, whether intended and foreseen or not, might be thought of as an 'after-text'. The precise semantic shading and extension of the term 'text' changes, depending upon which portions of this range of concepts one choses to include.
>
> (Hanks 1989: 96)

Whether or not these more specialised terms prove useful in detail, they exemplify the need to break down the once-unquestioned and over-arching concept of text, and consider complementing it by a series of more specific questions. In any given investigation these might include, for example:

1 In what *sense(s)* if at all can the particular verbal formulations in question be regarded as texts, and how is this related to local concepts and/or practice?
2 How 'stable' is what is being presented as text? is it as fixed and final in local practice as it looks when recorded on the page?
3 What is its function in relation to actual performance: a one-for-one match in every respect; a score prescribing, or summarising, or shadowing some but not all elements of performance? an aide-memoire for selected elements? some kind of ideal standard, whether in a book or in the mind?

4 Was it frequently (or ever) delivered or recognised as a crystallised or coherent text prior to the researcher's request?
5 Are some genres more textually fixed than others?
6 How far are the words (rather than, say, musical performance
   or visual display) regarded as 'central'?
7 Is there any sense in which, whether or not explicitly recognised
   in the culture, we can sensibly speak of some kind of permanent
   text existing over and beyond specific performances or variants?
8 How is it best to deal with presentation and publication? Since
   written texts are the commonly accepted currency in our culture
   final reports are likely to be primarily made up of the words,
   which will then probably be understood by readers as *the* definitive and comprehensive reality. How limited a view will this be?

1.5 THE INTEREST OF THE PROBLEMS

The lack of 'standard terms' or agreed delimitations is sometimes
regarded as a glaring defect. But it is hardly surprising that different
scholars have taken different terms to encapsulate their insights
within this complex and elusive area of human culture. The proliferation of terms may be healthier than one closed system, for their
mutual struggles contribute not just to self-regarding academic dispute, but towards what terms are surely ultimately for: to enhance
understanding of the world and open up new insights into areas
which, we have to recognise, are *not* already pre-defined for us.
Further, precisely because the terms are often loaded or ethnocentric, clarifying your own usage, and how it resembles and differs
from that of others, can direct attention to important points of
research.

The varied terms have provided an essential framework and inspiration for research. In the past the most influential ones have been
'oral tradition', 'oral literature', 'verbal art' and, most notably,
'folklore' (a term which, whatever its connotations, has led to a
vast amount of research) together with the underlying concept of
verbal text. Each could be criticised from one viewpoint or another.
But between them they have been used by generations of
researchers in the past and present, both professional scholars and
amateur enthusiasts, to collect and analyse material which illumi-
nates our understanding of human arts and traditions and the varied
ways in which they are expressed – from explorations of English
school childrens' rhymes, or songs in southern Africa, to the great
Finnish traditions in the *Kalevala* and other poetry, oral tradition

in the composition and transmission of the Bible, Homeric epic and its possible parallels, performance in Tamil bow songs, American women's pentecostalist sermons, party political songs in Africa, the transmission and creation of 'myth' in the Pacific islands, the long oral retention of English ballads in the Appalachian mountains, the tradition of the Fenian hero over centuries of Irish narrative, the clothing of mourning in beautiful and poetic words, or currently circulating stories about computers (Opie 1961 etc., Blacking 1967, Almqvist et al. 1987, Whybray 1987, Lord 1960, Blackburn 1988, Lawless 1987, 1988, Finnegan 1970, 1988, Sharp 1932, Nagy 1985, Feld 1990, Dundes 1977). Without the stimulus of these terms, however controversial, much of this work might never have been undertaken, nor would scholars initially attending to only certain limited aspects have been challenged to consider a wider range of human cultural activity.

It is interesting to notice the general move away from terms associated with earlier evolutionist or 'Great Divide' theories towards, in one direction, more specific genre words and, in the other, wider terms like 'discourse', 'popular culture' or 'narrative'. No doubt these reassessments of terminology will continue, shedding new light on human communication and culture. But both the older and the newer terms discussed here, despite their problems and their related territorial disputes between disciplines, can open and not just close doors to our appreciation of elements of human culture which might otherwise have been ignored. They also present opportunities for the kind of interdisciplinary and critically imaginative perspective that, while certainly not confined to anthropologists, is one they are particularly well qualified to apply.

What lies at the heart of this area of research, therefore, is not so much a common terminology or a clearly delimited subject, as a set of questions and issues which are now more and more attracting the interest of scholars from many backgrounds: questions about the nature of 'texts', of framed linguistic expression, or of 'narrative'; the significance of context or performance and their relevance for the understanding of verbal formulation; the interactions of verbal and non-verbal in expressive art, or of writing and orality; the conventions of style and of artistry emergent in performance; the processes by which 'texts' and 'traditions' are created, enacted and maintained; the politics and ethics of the researcher's role in the processing of oral traditions, texts and verbal art forms; and, most significantly, questions about how people *in practice* behave and communicate in the sphere of oral tradition and verbal arts, and how the researcher can understand, record and analyse this process and its products.

These at any rate are the kinds of questions and issues – surely central to anthropological concerns – around which the following chapters are principally focused.

2 Theoretical perspectives

2.1 THE ROLE OF THEORY

Anthropologists' interest in oral tradition and verbal art is, no doubt, to understand people's cultural activities and artistries, rather than to build theory. But some knowledge of the existing theoretical and comparative literature opens up greater appreciation of problems and possibilities, whether in developing the most appropriate research strategy, raising previously unconsidered questions, or assessing the work of others. And although anthropologists rightly stress the importance of being open to cultural specifics rather than sticking rigidly to some general 'theory', the conduct of research inevitably depends on *some* theoretical assumptions – so these are best recognised explicitly.

In this general area, the theoretical controversies extend not only to terminology but also to what the forms or processes under study essentially *are*, and to how or why they can be investigated. The responses to such questions link anthropological research to other disciplines too, from literary criticism to history, philology, and social or linguistic theory. They also tend to cluster round a series of relatively distinctive viewpoints, summarily outlined in this chapter. There is space only for an extremely simplified run-through here, so since any approach(es) taken up for serious development would eventually have to be pursued in greater depth, there are also brief guides to some relevant literature.

2.2 CONTINUING METHODOLOGICAL TENSIONS

Certain recurrent debates cut across the more specific theories. Some relate to general controversies within social research – already familiar ground for anthropologists – others link more directly to oral traditions and verbal arts. They include:

1 The role of *comparison and generalisation* as against investigating *uniqueness and specificity*. Complementing the long tradition of classification and generalisation there is now a counter-trend towards exploring people's own views and artistry rather than analysing through outsiders' categories, but the debate continues about how far researchers can or should look for underlying generalities, how far for culture-specific conventions or individual events/personalities.

2 The *collection and analysis of texts* as against *intensive fieldwork* on social processes. In some circles there has been a marked shift towards the latter, but the former is still important, particularly in countries with large archive collections.

3 The *nature of the essential subject matter*: verbal texts? contexts? performance(s)? the dynamics of a particular occasion? There are disagreements too about how far one can isolate any one of these elements, and in particular about the nature and status of texts (see 1.4).

4 *Who researches* and *on whom*? These questions often turn on a contrast between researchers as outsiders and/or superiors as opposed to local scholars and native speakers. Similar questions also arise in 'own culture' research: this too is sometimes under-taken in a spirit of looking down on (sometimes romanticising) certain groups or activities. There is also the question of whether a foreign culture or one's own should be the object of study. Those labelling themselves folklorists in the past mainly concentrated on the second, anthropologists on the first, but such distinctions are becoming more blurred.

Whatever your specific methodology these more general debates will continue to arise. In critiquing both your own analyses and those of others it can be illuminating to complement your own views by sometimes looking again at the *other* side of these ultimately unresolvable tensions.

2.3 BACKGROUND TO STUDIES OF ORAL TRADITION AND VERBAL ART

It is a commonplace that the study of oral traditions and verbal art has moved from earlier preoccupations with origins and the 'old', to more recent emphases on meaning, structure and contemporary dynamics. This is a fair summary as far as it goes, although the one-line development it suggests obscures the many complexities and downplays the intellectual and political contexts of earlier studies. Earlier scholars too interacted with changing historical experiences and philosophies and were at least implicitly concerned with understanding themselves and their contemporary culture through comparative insights into the human condition, not just in a mechanical search for origins.

The sequence of intellectual fashions is ultimately no different in the study of oral arts and traditions from that in any other sphere of anthropological study. There are however some particular emphases and applications worth noting. As for other fields, one formative strand in earlier studies was the evolutionist model of one-way progress – particularly powerful in the nineteenth century, but still extant in such notions as 'development' and 'modernisation'. This for long directly affected the analysis of anything interpretable as 'early' or belonging to 'oral tradition', particularly 'myths' collected from overseas peoples or 'folklore' from European traditions. The related interest in origins also meant that historical preoccupations – often extremely speculative and generalised – focused interest away from current forms or meanings towards the search for the 'pure', 'original' or 'traditional' stages, 'uncontaminated' by 'outside' influences. Thus stories or songs, provided they could be described as 'traditional', 'folk', or 'tribal', could be analysed as survivals from – and thus 'really' belonging with – some earlier stage of society. The further assumption that oral forms collected from or belonging to the 'old', the colonised or the nonwestern could be analysed as basically other than those found in European contexts, and as somehow closer to 'nature', also fitted with nineteenth-century (and to some extent still-current) preconceptions: the binary 'us/them' opposition developed in both social theory and popular understanding as one rationale for the modern experience of industrialisation and the expansion of Europe.

The influential nationalist movements and the intellectuals associated with them formed another influential strand. This was often closely related to preoccupations with traditions and roots, with a theoretical basis in German romanticism and the concept of the 'folk'. In both nineteenth and early twentieth-century Europe and in more recent ex-colonial nations, the search for national and 'folk' identity has fostered the collection and creation of texts expressing national culture or providing a focus for nation-building and local education – one basis for the often-emotive status of texts classified as 'oral tradition' or 'folklore'. This nationalist theme was central to the development of the discipline of 'folklore' and the many collections and studies associated with it.

A further influence came from philology. Research on the development and divergences of languages laid the basis for work drawing on explanations in terms of Indo-European origins and linkages. Philological scholarship also validated the study of texts within a framework of such concepts as a chain of manuscript sources and the analysis of detailed stylistic, grammatical and syntactical patterns – a scholarly tradition based on writing and on the idea of *words* as the essential constituent units.

The result of these various influences was extensive collection and publication of texts. Some countries amassed huge archive collections of texts taken down from dictation, written by local scholars, or welded together by collectors or scholars from a mixture of sources.

Later developments both built on and changed the earlier approaches. Social and political reassessments consequent on experience in and, later, disengagement from empire, and on more recent cultural interactions in a global framework, both reinforced and questioned the binary and evolutionary models. Wider scholarly developments also played a part, among them the general moves in the social sciences (and perhaps in intellectual approaches generally) towards a greater interest in societal conditions, social dynamics, and specific historical processes rather than generalised origins. Also important was the anthropological emphasis on fieldwork and detailed ethnography, turning away from a preoccupation with origins and evolution to understanding contemporary forms in their own setting.

Mastering the details of these historical developments – a subject of study in its own right – may not be essential for contemporary research, but this background does help to put recent views into greater perspective. As always, the theoretical approaches were intertwined with social and political processes as well as with wider intellectual movements, so that now, as earlier, assessing existing or emerging theories demands sensitivity to social and ethical – not just to technical – issues.

(For further discussion and references see Cocchiara 1981, Burke 1978, Wilgus 1959, Kaplan 1984, Finnegan 1970: 27ff, 1977: 30ff, also W.A. Wilson 1973 (folklore and nationalism), Holbek 1983: 145ff (changing approaches to prose narratives), and Dundes n.d (international aspects). Since the subject is bound in with the development of anthropology (and of social science more generally), as well as of philology and the humanities, histories of these subjects are also relevant. Treatments of folklore as a discipline often include particularly relevant historical overviews, e.g., Dundes 1965, Dorson 1968, Brunvand 1976, 1986, Zumwalt 1988, Bauman 1989c.)

2.4 INFLUENTIAL METHODOLOGIES AND THEORIES

This section provides a summary checklist of some leading perspectives – inevitably selective and personal, though I have tried to be even-handed. The emphasis is on their specific implications for the study of oral arts and traditions (rather than more general accounts), with particular stress on the kinds of *questions* they focus on, together with some guidance to further sources. Theoretical viewpoints can be divided up in different ways: the following provides merely one point of departure.

2.4.1 Some nineteenth- and early twentieth-century theories

Earlier approaches were mostly designed to elucidate the history of particular forms (principally narrative) in terms of origins, diffusion or evolution. Amidst the many variants around this theme the following are worth listing briefly, for though widely regarded as out-dated in their original form, they still sometimes surface or are disinterred for re-analysis into more up-to-date theories.

1 Development and deterioration theories: fairy tales are broken-down myths, sunk down from higher levels to that of children and/or of lower classes; epics developed from composite folk-songs; and similar theories (see Dundes 1969, Holbek 1987: chaps 1–2).
2 Andrew Lang's 'anthropological view': forms like wonder tales originated in a period when what now looks irrational would have seemed, at that primitive stage of savagery, to have been intelligible; they were then passed down through the generations.
3 Nature mythology: stories were essentially about – and derived from – the forces of nature, specially the sun (this also linked with Max Müller's 'disease of language' theory and Indo-European mythology).
4 Contending theories of origin: monogenesis as against polygenesis of tales (the former often taking India as the diffusion centre);

or the 'communal' and, as it were, unconscious creation of ballads and other 'folklore', as against creation by single great individuals (see Holbek 1987: 29ff).

5 Developmental theories of genres, linking them to particular stages of society, as in the idea that epic comes first in national development or is associated with a 'heroic' stage (see Chadwick 1932–40, Finnegan 1977: 266ff); also in some Eastern European analyses with roots in Marxist-evolutionist theory.

6 Myth-ritual theories: myths (and forms like hero narratives) originate in and from rituals. This was in the past often linked to concepts of 'survivals' and Frazerian anthropology, but has also been extended into more modern forms (see discussion in Okpewho 1983: 45ff).

(For discussion and references on the above see Bausinger 1968, Brunvand 1976: chap. 1, Cocchiara 1981, Dorson 1968, S.Thompson 1946, Toelken 1979: 12ff, Finnegan 1969a, Dundes 1965, Bauman 1989c.)

2.4.2 'Finnish' historical-geographical method

Partly a reaction against the kind of generalised speculations listed above, this attempted instead to use scientific and empirical methods to classify and analyse the vast body of material that had been collected. Since any given tale was assumed to have originated in the distant past, then travelled outward through a series of variants, the aim was to discover the origin and *Urform*, then track its diffusion. The method consisted in

> assembling as complete a list of versions as possible, in dividing the story into a series of episodes, in minutely comparing each episode's variations as found in the whole body of texts to establish a prototypic original, and in deducing from this comparison the story's wanderings.
>
> (Taylor 1928: 481–2)

The main emphases and questions were:

1 A search for the archetypal form of a given tale, defined in terms of its content or plot (pictured as *the* 'basic' tale, over and above its particular tellings).

2 Questions about a tale's origin and its later travels in space and time, the aim being to create its 'life history' (the history being

that of the *tale* itself rather than its relations to specific historical contexts).

3 As a corollary, little or no interest in questions of performance, local meaning, artistry, social conditions, or stylistic details.

4 A stress on classification and typology (part of the 'scientific' approach); this mostly assumed stable and 'pure' tale-types and genres, ultimately resulting in the tale-type and motif-indexes.

5 A focus on narrative texts, usually under the title of 'tales' (and related sub-categories), very occasionally extended to other genres.

6 Initially mainly about Indo-European forms (still the main focus); later more interest in tales from elsewhere.

7 A dominant (though not exclusive) interest in library and archive-based research rather than intensive fieldwork.

Though many scholars (including Finnish folklorists) are now less interested in such questions, there has recently been some resurgence of interest in these methods through narratological and other questions about the relation between 'text' and 'narration' or the status of 'story'. Overall this long-dominant approach has resulted in massive compilations and collections of texts.

(For further discussions or references see Azzolina 1987, Brunvand 1976: 14ff, Finnegan 1970: 320ff, Georges 1983, 1986, Goldberg 1984, Holbek 1987: 31ff, 242ff, Honko 1985, Jason 1970, Krohn 1971, Rosenberg and Smith 1974, Utley 1978, Zumwalt 1988: 107ff, also B.H. Smith 1981 and 8.2 below.)

2.4.3 Comparative philology and mythology

There is a long-established interest in Indo-European origins and connections, based in the comparative work of such scholars as William Jones or Max Müller. Indo-European roots have been seen as the basis not only for the classical civilizations of Greece and Rome but for Western culture as a whole, an approach still popular in recent writings. Dumézil's works on Indo-European mythology stand out particularly:

A series of studies devoted to a comparative exploration of the religion of Indo-European peoples, to the ideas those peoples had formed of human and divine society, and to [their] social and cosmic hierarchy

(Dumézil 1988: 9)

Dumézil's writings – a huge series of volumes – have been immensely influential among certain scholars: 'a landmark fusion of philological, literary, and anthropological methods in the study of belief systems and traditional narrative' (Nagy 1986: 38). The main interests are:

1 The exploration of basic Indo-European patterns of social organ-isation and symbolism, together with their associated rituals.
2 The way these are related to – and arguably underly and shape – mythology across the Indo-European areas, including myths which on the surface have become elaborated in different ways.
3 (Perhaps) the extension of similar methods outside the Indo-European area.

(For further discussion and exemplification see Dumézil 1970, 1973, 1983, 1986, 1988 (only a small selection of Dumézil's vast output), also Belmont 1983, Oosten 1985, Puhvel 1987, Rivière 1979.)

2.4.4 Psychological analyses

Psychological approaches of various kinds are well recognised in the study of literature and art (see Kiell 1982, Eagleton 1983: chap. 5), and have also been taken up in recent work within anthropology. It is not therefore surprising to find them also applied to oral forms. There is a vast range, from earlier (and sometimes still influential) evolutionist versions, and Freudian or Jungian interpretations by both scholars and therapists, to more culturally specific analyses by anthropologists or oral historians. The concepts of 'myth' and 'mythic' are usually prominent, as are dreams and fantasies, some-times now combined with structuralist, Marxist or feminist approaches. Particular points include:

1 Theories linking psychic and human/social development, often expressed in myths.
2 Interest in such questions as the psychological significance of fantasy and of symbolic representations (male–female relations or parent–child antagonisms in fairy tales, for example), the social psychological roles of story-telling, or the psychic power of myth in shaping action or imagination.
3 Interpretations of the content of folktales and myths in terms of sexual symbolism (psychoanalytic) or universal archetypes (Jungian).

4 The interpretation of fairy tales and other narrratives as a potential schema for an individual's life course.

5 The relation between dreams and narratives as expressions of unconscious feelings and/or symbolic structures.

6 The significance of myth for universal archetypes, for the course of human development, and/or for individual or group identity.

7 The development and significance of the emotions, a subject in which anthropologists have recently started to take more interest.

(For further examples or discussion, see Holbek 1987: 259–322, Brunvand 1986: 28, 34 (and references there), Dundes 1965: 88ff, 1982: 200ff, 1980, 1987, Limón and Young 1986: 448–9; also for further examples: Campbell 1959–68, Hobbs 1987, von Franz 1972a, b, Jung and Kerenyi 1963, Grolnick 1986, Schwartz 1956, Lüthi 1982: esp. 116ff, Edmunds and Dundes 1983, Bettelheim 1976, Dieckmann 1986, Fischer 1963, Weigle 1982, 1989; on emotions, Lutz and White 1986, Lutz and Abu-Lughod 1990; on dreams Tedlock 1987, Descola 1989; on recent approaches in oral history Samuel and Thompson 1990.)

2.4.5 Functionalist and 'reflection' approaches

A cluster of more sociological approaches focus round differing assumptions about how art forms, oral traditions, etc., are related to society. These reject explanations in terms of either individual personality or of origins, in favour of more synchronic and socially-oriented questions. In addition to explicitly Marxist approaches (see 2.4.6) the main forms are:

1) *'Reflection' theories*

There is something initially attractive about the model of a one-to-one relation between art/literature/oral tradition on the one hand and 'society' (however defined) on the other. The resultant 'reflection view of art' is sometimes classed as one distinctive theoretical approach (Albrecht 1954, Watt 1964, Finnegan 1977: 262ff). Detailed analysis of specifics however tends to disabuse researchers of simplistic and literal reflection ideas (compare Poyatos 1988: xiiff with 327ff on 'literary anthropology', moving from 'reflection' to complexity). Such views, however, still sometimes appeal to researchers who assume that unwritten 'tales' or 'folksongs' are somehow more closely reflective of the 'community' than western 'individually inspired' literature.

2) *'Functionalism'*

The functionalist approach dominant in British anthropology in the mid-twentieth century, particularly the 'structural-functional' form emphasising stability and homogeneity, had direct implications for the study of oral arts and traditions in that period. These included:

1 A focus on the function of 'myth' (the favoured term) in upholding the status quo. The concept of a 'mythical charter' was particularly prominent, usually as an origin myth sanctioning the current ruler's position (a concept derived from Malinowski 1948 – where in fact he takes a wider view of narrative and its artistry).
2 Little interest in other forms of verbal art as 'only' of artistic significance, hence marginal for social structure, with the possible exception of moral tales for educating children or reinforcing socially sanctioned norms.
3 A playing down of local meanings, artistry, individual creativity, or conflicting interpretations in favour of the generalised function of upholding the overall social order.
4 Usually an emphasis on the 'traditional' order with little interest in diachronic analysis or 'new' forms. (On specific implications for the study of oral art/tradition see Finnegan 1969a, 1970: 330ff, Okpewho 1983: 20ff).

3) *Functions and functional inter-relationships more generally*

A more common view now is that verbal arts and traditions both mould and are moulded by the culture (as well as by interested groups or individuals within it) and that the functions fulfilled by art in society are likely to be multiplex rather than single. To that extent perhaps all social scientific approaches are functionalist in the sense of relating art and tradition to the wider social arrangements of the society in which they are practised. But in recent work a wider set of possible functions and roles are emphasised (see 6.3) than the limited ones developed in the specific structural-functional phase of anthropology. (On sociological approaches to art more generally see also Wilson 1964, Wolff 1983, Zolberg 1990.)

2.4.6 Marxist perspectives

The multiplicity of approaches influenced or deemed to be influenced by insights ultimately drawing their inspiration from Marx and his followers are too extensive to present or even summarise here. It should be said however that despite their relative absence in traditional 'folklore' studies they are as applicable to the subject matter of this volume as any other theoretical approach. This body of writing is yet another resource to draw on, and – the other way round – there is a set of topics here to which Marxist writers could pay greater attention.

The following list gives a simplified impression of a developing and complex set of approaches but can illustrate the kinds of themes round which Marxist writings have focused:

1 The relevance of prevailing social conditions (interpreted largely in economic and political-power terms, often but not always using the terminology of the class struggle). The nature of the relationship between cultural productions and social conditions is a matter for debate: approaches range from cruder theories prevalent in the 30's – art as reflection of social conditions – or the view of 'folklore' as 'a weapon of class conflict' (Sokolov 1971: 15), to the Frankfurt School's concern with the dominant class's incorporation of popular culture through the culture industry, interest in the processes of hegemony and consent by Gramsci and his followers, or interpretations of the way the dominant class imposes meanings while concealing the power on which these are based. Unlike the a-social framework of many historical-geographical or psychological approaches, the processes of social and cultural reproduction are seen as essentially bound in with current social conditions.

All the other aspects follow from this, but some points are worth drawing out further:

2 An interest in questions of power and of conflicting (or at any rate differing) interest groups and interpretations: a contrast to the homogeneity pictured in functionalist or romantic analyses. A sensitivity to multiplicities of meanings or the contested nature of certain interpretations follows on here. This is particularly important among Latin American Marxist writers, who dispute the 'meanings' put onto their popular forms by ruling powers or by researchers from outside dominant cultures.

3 Interpretations of 'meaning' as not in the 'text' itself or in 'free' and independent individual authors, but as related to current social conditions. There are disagreements too: over how far popular songs, 'folktales', etc., should be regarded as merely reflecting class interests, the class struggle, or the incorporation

and domination by those in power, how far as expressions of 'counter-cultural' resistance by oppressed or marginal groups, and how far as an area of relative freedom for individual expression outside the power struggle. There are debates between 'optimistic' or 'pessimistic' prognoses for emergent popular expression in the face of western capitalism, state domination or mass culture.

4 Debates over the nature and significance of items defined as 'folklore', 'oral', or 'traditional'. The evolutionary influences within Marxism have sometimes found expression in theories about 'stages' of society as related to particular genres; for example a pre-industrial origin was sometimes posited for fairy tales which thus remain as survivals outside the conditioning of modern industrial society and hence of only marginal interest. Much recent writing however takes all items in current circulation as part of the processes of social and cultural reproduction.

5 The production and consumption of art forms are proper objects of study (not just their style, meaning or earlier history), leading to such questions as how particular forms are composed and circulated, in what conditions, by and to whom, and in whose interests. Similarly questions arise about the artistic division of labour or the construction of symbols.

Since almost everyone is now at least up to a point interested in social behaviour and contexts, and relatively sensitised to the possibility of opposing interests, many of the questions above might no longer be seen as distinctively Marxist but to have become absorbed into the social scientific repertoire in general or woven into other approaches. It is only when such approaches are articulated explicitly (using, perhaps, particular terminologies or citations) that they tend to be labelled 'Marxist' as such.

(For discussion or examples see Williams 1973, 1977, Eagleton 1976, and other works on Marxist approaches to literature (sometimes overlapping with feminist, structuralist and post-structuralist approaches), also specific examples or references in Bottomore 1984, Gramsci 1971, S. Hall 1973, 1981, 1985, Hall et al. 1978, Bourdieu 1984, Mattelart 1989; for lively discussion using or extending the 'folklore' terminology see Holbek 1987: 391ff, Limón 1983, 1984, Limón and Young 1986: 449, W.S. Fox 1980, P. Thompson 1978, also the controversial 'radical' interpretations in Zipes 1979, 1983, 1984; for Soviet work under the label 'folklore'; see Sokolov 1971, Oinas 1984, also the interdisciplinary influence of writers such as Propp 1968, Bakhtin 1968, 1981, 1986.)

2.4.7 Structuralism and post-structuralism

1) *Structuralism*

Structuralist approaches have been extremely influential in the study of oral tradition and the verbal arts. Drawing on both Saussurean linguistics and literary theory, they focus, obviously, on the structure of the item being studied, elucidating the laws which underlie it and in a sense constitute its essence. The rules and relationships of human behaviour may, like grammar and syntax in linguistic communication, lie below the level of the actors' consciousness, but in structuralist analysis they form the foundation and the conditions for specific actions and meanings: thus the key topic for study.

Of the different strands within structuralism, the relevant ones here are those derived 1) from Propp and the Russian Formalists, primarily on similarities in form – plot, narrative moves, recurrent types of actors; and 2) from Lévi-Strauss, on the logical relationships and binary oppositions within 'myth', these in turn being interpreted as representing universal logical processes of the human mind, mediated through local symbolic interrelationships. Despite the differences, certain broad similarities mark out these approaches:

1 The aim of uncovering the underlying mechanisms/logic/codes/ rules: the 'real' structure beneath and behind the contingent surface phenomena (although just *which* underlying principles are sought may vary: Jason and Segal for example distinguish the four levels of: wording; poetic texture; narrative; and meaning or symbolic component, 1977: 3ff).
2 An interest in abiding structural rules – usually cross-cultural and universal – rather than the specifics of, say, context, local meanings, history, specific literary works, or individual human actors.
3 The constituent units seen as meaningful in relation to each other and within an overall system or code, rather than independently or through correspondence with outside 'reality'.
4 Focus on reaching conclusions about 'form' or 'grammar' rather than 'content', particularly in the Proppian versions (though again what is 'form' and what 'content' may not be agreed).
5 Interest in a-temporal and scientifically generalisable patterns irrespective of particular dates or versions, and little concern with changing contexts, social interactions or ideologies through time.
6 A prime emphasis on narrative (though any form is in principle susceptible to structural analysis).

Structuralism has been criticised for de-emphasising local meaning, performance, context, or human interaction, but this has not prevented it from being extremely influential not just in anthropology and folklore but throughout the arts and social sciences. It also sometimes combines with other approaches (specially Marxist, feminist and narratological) as well as providing the foundation and the foil for post-structuralist work.

(This is a large and controversial subject on which there has been a great deal of writing. See, for general collections, references or discussion: Maranda and Maranda 1971, Lane 1970, Culler 1975, Dundes 1976, 1982: 245f, Holbek 1977b, 1987 (esp. 323ff), Pace 1982, Davis 1986 esp. Parts 2, 6, Todorov 1986, Eagleton 1983: 94ff, 1989; for mainly morphological and formalist analyses: Dundes 1964a, 1965, Propp 1968, Ben-Amos 1989: 184, Jason and Segal 1977, Pentikäinen and Juurikka 1976, Todorov 1975, 1977, 1986; for Lévi-Strauss and structuralism: Lévi-Strauss 1963, 1967 and the 4–volume *Mythologiques* 1969–81, Leach 1970a, b. See also 8.3 and references there.)

2) *Post-structuralism*

This diverse and argued-over complex of approaches, drawing inspiration from such writers as Derrida and Foucault, both developed from and reacted against structuralist approaches in literature and the social sciences. Relevant points here are their focus on:

1 Challenging the laws supposedly detected by structuralists as *not* after all agreed, fixed or value-free.
2 Querying the possibility of discovering neutral principles or meanings through scientific investigation; among other reasons 'meaning' is indeterminate and open-ended, shaped by particularistic and fleeting factors, without objective underpinning.
3 Arguing that texts are less hard, bounded and self-consistent than had been assumed in other analyses; the process of 'deconstruction' reveals dissonant and unresolved contradictions within texts, undermining their meanings.
4 Challenging the assumption that a single text has a clear status in its own right, far less is explicable in terms of its author's individual originality; it can only be understood in the context of other related texts through which the readers/audience make sense of it: 'intertextuality'.

'Post-structuralism' is even more elusive than other schools of thought, means different things to different writers, and has been much criticised. Some see it as leading to anarchy, or, as Margolis put it of similar moves within aesthetics, 'a drift toward extreme relativism on the one hand or the opportunistic imposition of meanings by fiat on the other' (1989: 30). However even those unpersuaded by this school are sometimes indirectly influenced by its critical approach. Thus, while few studies of oral tradition and arts may directly label themselves 'post-structuralist', recent work has quite often made use of post-structuralist themes such as those of intertextuality, of multiple rather than single meanings, of rejecting a search for objectively-fixed laws, and generally questioning fixed models of text and meaning.

(For discussion and references see Harari 1979, Culler 1981, 1982, Eagleton 1983: esp. chap. 4 and 227–8, Attridge et al. 1987, Davis 1986: Part 8, Krupat 1987.)

2.4.8 Narratology

The narratology school partly developed out of structuralism, with special focus on narrative. This term can be used in a wide sense, eloquently summed up in Barthes' 'Introduction to the structural analysis of narrative':

> There are countless forms of narrative in the world. First of all, there is a prodigious variety of genres, each of which branches out into a variety of media, as if all substances could be relied upon to accommodate man's stories. Among the vehicles of narrative are articulated language, whether oral or written, pictures, still or moving, gestures, and an ordered mixture of all those substances; narrative is present in myth, legend, fables, tales, short stories, epics, history, tragedy, *drame* [suspense drama], comedy, pantomime, paintings (in Santa Ursula by Carpaccio, for instance), stained-glass windows, movies, local news, conversation. Moreover, in this infinite variety of forms, it is present at all times, in all places, in all societies; indeed narrative starts with the very history of mankind; there is not, there has never been anywhere, any people without narrative; all classes, all human groups, have their stories, and very often those stories are enjoyed by men of different and even opposite cultural backgrounds: narrative remains largely unconcerned with good or bad literature. Like life itself, it is there, international, transhistorical, transcultural.
>
> (1975: 37)

Despite this breadth, the central focus is usually on verbally-realised narrative. Narratologists seek to uncover the general patterns irrespective of specific medium or content, and there is now an extensive body of work on written literature. Since narratives form a high proportion of most oral collections, and classic writings in narratology include both Propp's work on fairy tales (1968) and, to a lesser extent, Lévi-Strauss on myth (1963, 1969–81), some interest in oral texts has also always played some part (though arguably not enough, see Parks 1987: 527). In one sense narratologists are only saying some of the same old things about narrative. But they are doing so with new vigour, more focused questions and terminology, and within a wider comparative framework.

It is interesting to locate this approach in the wider study of verbal art forms. Much of the nineteenth- and early twentieth-century work was on stories, with poetic forms only becoming a major focus of interest later (no doubt helped by developments in recording techniques) and conversational genres more recently still. Thus self-consciously innovative work often focused on performance and event, or on the oral-formulaic analysis of mainly poetic texts, avoiding the study of tales as supposedly the domain of the older historical-geographical approach. But narratological work has revived interest in story, sometimes in conjunction with other approaches (as in Abrahams 1985b, Bauman 1986), and has directly or indirectly influenced much recent work on oral narratives (such as Bauman 1986, Calame-Griaule et al. 1980, Cancel 1989, Feld 1989, Shuman 1986, LeRoy 1985, Jason and Segal 1977, see also Paulme 1976, Cosentino 1982, M. Jackson 1982). Since narrative across all media is brought within the same framework, forms once separately classified as being 'oral' or 'African' or 'folk', can take their full part in comparative analysis.

The kinds of topics investigated and analysed include:

1 Recurrent patterns in the roles of narrative characters like the villain, hero, trickster.
2 The recurrent moves in, and hence structure of, plots (overlapping with structuralist-morphological analyses, see 2.4.7).
3 The ordering and sequences within narrative, how it is 'framed', and the degree of 'narrativity'.
4 The varying 'voices' and viewpoints in the narration.
5 The interaction of 'fiction' and 'event'.
6 The interactive or 'dialogic' relationship with the critic, reader or audience.

Many of the earlier analyses focused on textual and formal questions but recently there has been more stress on social context, performance or audience, as well as on the roles of narrative, narrator and reader(s)/audience. Some writers approach narration as a performance or speech act, thus linking with discourse and performance theorists (B.H. Smith 1978, 1981; see also 2.4.10 below). Indeed 'narratology' can perhaps now be regarded as encompassing almost any kind of analysis of narrative, developing in a way typical of many approaches in the social sciences from formalist studies to social-context, interpretive, or post-structuralist questions.

(See also general accounts and references in Scholes and Kellogg 1966, Chatman 1978, Culler 1981: chap. 9, Genette 1980, Mosher 1981, Mitchell 1981, Prince 1982, 1987 (a guide to the burgeoning technical terms), 1989, Jameson 1981; examples or discussions in Bakhtin 1981, Bauman 1986: esp. 5ff, Shuman 1986, Parks 1987; also 8.3.4.)

2.4.9 The 'oral theory'

The so-called 'oral theory' first started from controversies about the nature and composition of the Homeric epics, inspiring Milman Parry's studies of Homeric formulae, followed by fieldwork on South Slavic oral heroic poetry in the 1930's. The results appeared in Albert Lord's enormously influential *The Singer of Tales* (1960). This demonstrated how songs many thousands of lines long could be composed without writing, by the singer's drawing on a store of formulae and formulaic expressions with no need to prepare a text beforehand: composition and performance were not separate stages but facets of the same act. Some formulae were short phrases fitting a given metrical position, but longer formulaic expressions included runs of several lines, themes, topics and narrative plots. There was no fixed or 'correct' text, as in written literature, for each performance was different and equally authentic: ' "an" original, if not "the" original' (Lord 1960: 101).

The discovery of this 'special technique' (Lord 1960: 17) elucidated one widely-spread pattern for oral delivery, as well as illuminating text as process rather than fixed product. It also laid a comparative framework for the analysis or re-analysis of oral (or arguably oral) texts from a whole range of disciplines and areas, and for the idea of 'oral composition' as a process lying behind texts previously assumed to originate in writing. As such it was interpreted by many scholars as a general theory about composition in oral literature, extending not just to Yugoslav and Homeric epic poetry but also to traditional heroic poetry generally, and in some views to other forms of oral poetry and even to prose. For some time this 'oral-formulaic' model swept the field almost unquestioned and has inspired an immense and increasingly sophisticated literature. Some recent developments and applications in oral-formulaic scholarship are described later (see 6.1.3), but from the point of view of comparing it with other theories and methodologies, its distinctive features have been:

1 Particular emphasis on historical texts, specially but not exclusively in European languages, and (till recently) less interest in field studies of 'living' traditions or performance other than the classic South Slavic singers.
2 Special focus on formulaic analysis of texts, often with the aim of distinguishing originally 'oral' from 'literary' texts, in terms of the oral-formulaic composition-in-performance held to underlie all truly oral texts.
3 Interest in the processes of textual formation (the mode of composition, use of traditional forms/formulae, individual shaping by the singer, and influence of situation and audience on the performance; less interest in the effects of wider social conditions or interest groups). This view of text as process, though often not explicitly elaborated in the textual analyses which till recently made up the bulk of oral-formulaic scholarship, has also been taken up in other approaches.
4 Elucidation of the oral-formulaic 'composition-in-performance' mode characteristic (in this view) of many forms of oral literature and of the oral precursors of written texts.

(The classic work is Lord 1960; for general discussion and history see A. Parry 1971, Foley 1985, 1987b, 1988a, 1990b, Renoir 1988: esp. chap. 4 and Foreword by Lord, Finnegan 1976, 1977 chap. 3, and the journal *Oral Tradition*; also 6.1.3, 8.6.2.)

2.4.10 The 'ethnography of speaking': discourse analysis, performance theory and ethnopoetics

This is a complex of approaches with a base in the 'ethnography of speaking' approach pioneered by Dell Hymes and specially associated with a group of American linguistic anthropologists and folklorists. They focus on an action-centred and expressive view of language, on performance, and on detailed ethnographic observation of how people actually *use* language. Despite emerging diversities some common threads run through:

1 A view of language – or, rather, communication – as best studied through its enactment in actual social settings rather than as an essentially cognitive phenomenon or set of linguistic laws. This links with speech act theory but it is more than a narrow 'linguistic' approach, due to its view of communication as shaped by – and in turn shaping – cultural symbols and social interaction.
2 A focus on studying process and practice, and the specificities of time and place, rather than generalised functionalist or structuralist questions.
3 Emphasis on human artistry – in conversational performance as much as in 'major' art forms like the epic.
4 Interaction with students of literature and of popular culture by bridging the once-assumed oral/written divide and the 'high'/ 'low' art hierarchy.
5 Interest in studying *all* forms of verbal communication and performance in a culture, and sensitivity to the ways dominant cultural ideologies can blind us to less visible forms.
6 Particular interest in artistic or playful uses of language.

(For influential statements or discussions see Abrahams 1970c, Bauman and Sherzer 1974 (also Introduction to 2nd edition 1989), Ben-Amos and Goldstein 1975, Fine 1984, Hymes 1974, 1975a, b, 1981, Paredes and Bauman 1972, Sherzer 1983, Sherzer and Woodbury 1987, Tedlock 1977, also appreciation and critique in Briggs 1988: chap. 1, Okpewho 1990: chap. 1; on speech act theory, Searle 1969.)

A number of more specific developments have also grown out of this general complex of approaches.

1) *A 'performance-centred view' of human communication and artistry*

This is currently influential among American anthropologists and folklorists (also to some extent elsewhere) and specially highlights:

1 The significance of the *performance* of any text or item of verbal art/tradition: delivery arts and audience participation are an essential constituent, not a mere extra.
2 A focus on specific communicative *events* rather than on the supposedly enduring and a-social text or script.

3 The 'emergent' nature of cultural forms and genres in performance.

(For some key texts (in addition to those cited above) see Abrahams 1968a, 1985a, Bauman 1977a, 1989a, b, Feld 1987, 1989, Kapferer 1986, Mannheim and Tedlock 1990, Schieffelin 1985, also chapter 5 below.)

2) *Discourse-centred analyses*

'Discourse' can mean many things (see 1.3.8), but in the extensive work developing directly from the 'ethnography of speaking' and the action approach to language the focus is on:

1 The dynamic interplay within a given culture across *all* uses of language in context (oral and written, permanent and fleeting, and across all groups), bypassing the implicit divisions in earlier analyses.
2 The way cultural symbols and the particular resources of the language are *used*.
3 'Discourse' viewed as 'the concrete expression of language-culture relationships [that] creates, recreates, focuses, modifies, and transmits both culture and language and their intersection' (Sherzer 1987a: 295).
4 Although centred on linguistic usage, also attention to paralinguistic, visual, musical and other performance elements.
5 (Sometimes) an interest in the relation to wider political and cultural structures or ideologies.

(See general account and references in Sherzer 1987a, also examples or developments (often overlapping with the 'performance' and 'ethnopoetics' terminologies) in Basso 1985, Bauman 1986, Feld 1982, Gossen 1974, Sherzer 1990, Sherzer and Urban 1986, Sherzer and Woodbury 1987, Sweeney 1987, Tannen 1982b, 1984, Urban 1986.)

3) *Ethnopoetics*

The distinctive focus here is on stylistics and poetic artistry, including paralinguistic features detectable in actual delivery or through re-analyses of earlier transcriptions. The style and structure of the 'line' in American Indian narrative has attracted particular attention, with many scholars now arguing that earlier prose transcriptions should be re-interpreted as poetry (see Hymes 1977, 1987). The general aim of raising consciousness of the *poetic* status of verbal art is expressed in the 'Statement of Intent' in the influential journal *Alcheringa–Ethnopoetics:*

> As the first magazine of the world's tribal poetries, ALCHER-INGA will not be a scholarly 'journal of ethnopoetics' so much as a place where tribal poetry can appear in English translation & can act (in the oldest & newest of poetic traditions) to change men's minds & lives. We hope by exploring the full range of man's poetries, to enlarge our understanding of what a poem may be . . . and to assist the free development of ethnic self-awareness among young Indians & others so concerned, by encouraging a knowledgeable, loving respect among them & all people for the world's tribal past and present.
>
> (*Alcheringa* 1, 1, 1970)

(For other examples or discussions see Hymes 1981, Rothenberg 1983, Tedlock 1972, 1983, 1989, Briggs 1988: 10 and later issues of *Alcheringa*.)

This group of approaches is highly valued in some circles, and many (including myself) consider that much of the most illuminating current work is being conducted under its auspices. However there has also been some reaction – or development? – away from what could be regarded as an over-emphasis on performance and its processes. Cancel expresses this well in his analysis of Tabwa oral narratives from Zambia. After praising these approaches as remedying the older concentration on 'the literate side of the equation, without taking into account the frames of living performance and contextual relationships linking a narrative tradition with its active participant listeners', he goes on, however:

> To treat oral narrative as spoken discourse alone is too simple a solution. It is a form of discourse and it is spoken, but it is also a storytelling activity. We must treat the narrative dimension of performance. We run a risk in applying a model from sociolinguist-ics to the material, wherein we say interesting things about language and human interaction to the exclusion of story, plot, character, and theme, all part of the storytelling process.
>
> (Cancel 1989: 6)

2.4.11 Feminist approaches

In this field it is only quite recently that a distinctively feminist stance has developed, perhaps because the products of women were already taken more seriously in studies of oral arts and tradition than in other branches of the social sciences; 'personal narratives' analysis by oral historians and others had also raised the visibility of women's viewpoints. It has also long been realised that gender is one factor in the division of labour structuring the composition, performance or consumption of many verbal genres (as in Sherzer 1987b).

Explicitly feminist critiques are now emerging however. Their characteristics are well summed up by Kay Stone:

> Three differing assumptions have underlain the development of feminist writing in general, and in their approaches to *Märchen* and myth. The earliest feminists saw women as artificially separated from and wrongly considered unequal to men; the next generation of writers insisted that women were naturally separate from men and rightly superior; and many recent writers consider both women and men as naturally separate but potentially equal – if men shape up. The *Märchen* has been examined from all three approaches, and feminist reactions have ranged from sharp criticism to firm support of the images of women presented in them. Early writers, unhappy with the images they perceived as reflected in the *Märchen* insisted that the mirror was at fault, while later writers pointed out that other images could be perceived in the same mirror. If we care to look again at both *Märchen* and myth we might see that they offer flexible paradigms for positive transformations – female *and* male.
>
> (Stone 1986: 233–4)

Feminist writers have also made use of insights from other approaches, especially psychology and Marxism.

The kinds of studies pursued include:

1   Exploration of gender biases in the collection, classification or presentation of verbal forms, such as shaping by (male) editors and transcribers, or the connection of 'folklore' with the patriarchal view of the 'Fatherland' in some nationalistic movements.
2   Drawing attention to the effects on women of role models in fairy tales, etc., thus codifying or reinforcing current – but questionable – gender values.
3   Questioning the downplaying of women's mythology in androcentric definitions, and replacing or complementing this by female-centred presentations and analyses.
4   Emphasising the need for sensitivity to the role of gender in

verbal art and the importance of paying attention to 'counter-narratives', to women's identity and voices, and to the relevance of women's social position and actions.

(For discussion or examples see Abu-Lughod 1986, American Folklore Society 1987, Bennett 1989, Bottigheimer 1986a, Fox 1987, Kligman 1984, Jordan and Kalčik 1985, Lawless 1987, Lundell 1986, Nenola-Kallio 1985, Nenola and Timonen 1990, Personal Narratives Group 1989, Rowe 1986, Stoeltje 1988, Stone 1986, Tual 1986, Vander 1988, Von Franz 1972a, and Weigle 1982, 1989.)

2.4.12 The rise of oral history

The study of the past through oral sources has no doubt been going on as long as history itself (see Thompson 1978 esp. chap. 2, Dunaway and Baum 1984 Part 1), but since the 1940's and, more explicitly, from the 1960's and 70's 'oral history' has come to be recognised as an approach, even a discipline, in its own right. Although it is more a methodology for exploiting certain sets of sources than a theory as such, nonetheless the values and emphases associated with the term have wider theoretical implications.

The impetus to take non-written sources seriously arose from two main directions. First, there was the aspiration to find out more about those societies and peoples which, according to the earlier stereotype, 'had no history': no history, that is, in the 'normal' sense of documentary records. Oral historians' counter-claims were that oral sources – 'oral tradition' as Vansina termed it in his pioneering work on Africa (1965) – could be used in a way parallel to those in writing to discover the history of non- or partially-literate cultures. Some of the earlier work was arguably romanticising or speculative, but in time laid the basis for the rigorous use of oral sources in studying the histories of colonial or ex-colonial peoples, by now often alongside the use of documentary sources where available. The second strand was an interest in experiences of 'underneath' peoples in literate societies, from the earlier American attempts to record former slaves' reminiscences in the 1930's, to the more articulated approaches of recent scholars (like those associated with *History Workshop Journal*) to the history of the 'voiceless', whether rural dwellers, women, or members of non-élite organisations. This often meant relying on personal recollections and using oral as well as written sources: 'history from below'.

By now the subject is well-established, particularly in social history, with its own specialist journals and organisations. Audio-recording is much used – indeed most oral history is directly linked to this developing technology – with consequent debates about the best way of conducting and transcribing tape-recorded interviews (see Ives 1980). Oral historians rebut traditional historians' scepticism about oral sources by the positive point that oral recordings can be *more* rather than less 'objective' than written documents. A face-to-face situation allows for direct questioning and probing in a way not open with documentary sources; and the personal frame of oral expression is explicit, so, unlike the arguably equal subjectivity of written records, can be directly taken into account.

The discipline of history is, of course, rent by controversies about aims, methodology and scope so it is not surprising to find similar debates under the 'oral history' head. There are the familiar disagreements between a search for 'the facts' and an interest in eliciting otherwise hidden voices; between greater and lesser confidence in oral sources (or particular forms of oral sources); and in the assessment of the role of 'amateur' as against 'professional' historians (those associated with oral history usually more sympathetic to the former than are historians in the traditional mould).

One set of disagreements has clustered round viewpoints taken up by those who primarily regarded themselves as historians on the one side and anthropologists or folklorists on the other. The historians' prime interest has often been in *evidence* – oral forms as 'witness' or 'testimony' from which researchers should eliminate 'bias', distortion or faulty recollection to build up a picture of the past. The opposed perspective sees these forms not essentially as *sources*, but as worthy of study in their own right. Many argue further that even for their use as evidence, it is essential to remember that oral forms are not always primarily intended for information or historical record (as implied by the term 'oral testimony'). In any given situation they may have quite other implications which it can be thoroughly misleading to ignore; and taking serious account of *performance* in oral forms may mean having to radically alter what previously seemed the 'obvious' interpretation of some recorded text. Oral expression after all takes many different forms and functions – myth as well as historical record, aesthetic expressiveness for its own sake rather than for empirical description, fantasy as well as fact. Personal narratives for example – often a central source for oral historians – can have the role of validating and expressing someone's life, making sense of the various experiences lived through and, in a sense, created through the narrative, and are of interest as structured aesthetic and personal creations in the present as well as (or even instead of) just a witness to the past.

The arguments continue, but by now oral historians themselves are putting forward such viewpoints (see Grele 1985, Samuel 1988, Samuel and Thompson 1990). Indeed most of the questions treated in this volume are increasingly being appreciated as of direct relevance to oral history: for *any* text, but perhaps particularly those said to come from 'oral sources', has to be seen not as a neutral and a-social datum, but as inevitably related to its context of telling and subject to shaping and selecting by performer, audience, collector, transcriber and presenter.

(See also, besides references above, Henige 1982, Tonkin 1974, 1982 and 1991, Vansina 1985, Tedlock 1985, also on personal narratives and autobiographies Meyerhoff 1980, Oring 1987, Personal Narratives Group 1989, Stahl 1977, Zeitlin et al. 1982, Abrahams 1985b.)

2.4.13 Pluralism

These perspectives have been presented as if separate. This indeed is how they are sometimes used, and the contrasts come out vividly in volumes bringing together contrasting treatments of one subject or problem (for example the 'Garland Casebooks in Folklore', or such surveys or collections as Okpewho 1983: chap. 1, Dundes 1965, Andrzejewski and Innes 1975). But they are seldom totally divided in practice and some of the best studies draw on a mixture. In the last analysis the approaches are only as good – and as separate – as the uses made of them.

The list here, furthermore, is certainly not closed. As new approaches are developed elsewhere there are opportunities to find fresh viewpoints or look again at the old. Developments in literary theory, drama, rhetoric, or media studies can all be drawn on for further approaches and questions (on literary theory see references in 2.4.6–8 and chapter 8, esp. 8.5; on drama and rhetoric: 7.4.5 and 7.5.1; on media studies: Collins et al. 1986). The possibility of these mutual cross-links are a sign both of the move to de-ghettoise oral forms and the increasing openness of anthropology to interdisciplinary work and to exploring a range of differing rather than unitary paradigms. The knowledgeable use of insights from a number of different schools – the more so if also based in both ethnographic specifics and comparative perspective – may increasingly become a mark of the scholarly analysis of oral traditions and the verbal arts.

2.5   CURRENT TRENDS

Developments for the future are always hard to predict, and in any case depend on your present intellectual perspective and resources. However, the following can perhaps sum up some of the currently emerging lines, all of them, interestingly, also consonant with more general trends both within anthropology and in the wider interdisciplinary arena of which anthropology has increasingly to take account.

One set of developments concerns what it is we think we are studying, and its place in the contemporary world. Culture used to be defined in terms of Greek, Latin, or Hebrew models – or, at the least, as comprising the high art written forms. But wider approaches are now taking over, not just in anthropology and folklore but also in philosophy, literature and history. These work at several levels: a more global and cross-cultural framework; studying spoken not just written forms; and widening education and research to supplement normative prescription by ethnographic description. In face of changing values and power-shifts, and of the expanding cultural links in a world-wide perspective, it is no longer easy to maintain old boundaries (primitive/civilised, industrial/non-industrial, traditional/modern), or to regard oral or 'traditional' forms as separate items or less worthy of academic attention than those of 'classical' culture. There is also deepening understanding of the interaction of oral and written forms – or, rather, not of the 'interaction' of, as it were, two separate 'things' as of the whole communication process in which there may at any one time be a number of different media and processes (see 8.5). The older search for 'pure' forms, furthermore, is being replaced by work on changing, emergent, or 'creole' forms – valid and analysable in their own right – while such terms as 'discourse', 'narrative', 'performance' and 'popular culture' which bridge or bypass the divisions implied by 'folk' or 'traditional' are becoming more widespread as scholars turn from generalised divides to more focused comparative questions (as in narratology) or historically and culturally specific approaches to local communication processes.

Equally striking is the growing awareness of the 'political' nature both of the material to be studied and of the research process itself. This is increasingly appreciated within anthropology, but also runs across many disciplines, from emphasis on the politics of language or of literary theory, to the socially constructed nature of artistic forms or the many-layered nature of human expression. Similarly there is now more sensitivity to the ethical and political issues of researching, above all when this involves interaction between those of more, and of less, dominant groups. Research on oral forms can no longer be presented as mere 'academic' exercises or theorising about the far away and long ago, but as bringing the researcher into complex involvements with the other – equal – inhabitants of the planet.

Linked with this is the modern interest in the detailed study of practices on the ground rather than formalistic analyses or high theory, and in processes as well as just the final products – a feature of anthropology over recent years, meeting with comparable interdisciplinary trends within the social sciences more widely. These have their equivalences in the study of oral forms too. They are particularly evident in the 'performance' and 'discourse' approaches, supported by detailed ethnographic study of specific human activities, but also run through recent work of varying theoretical backgrounds, sometimes also linking with such other writings as Howard Becker's on 'art as collective action' (Becker 1984), or the older – but still relevant – symbolic interactionist approaches.

A parallel shift is away from a focus on generalising about such characteristics as comparative content, functions or broad historical sweeps to more interpretive and ethnographically specific approaches. One theme is a greater concern with individual voices, repertoire and creativity, part of the move within anthropology and other disciplines from 'structure' to 'agency'. Another is an emerging interest in work on the emotions and in aesthetic and expressive facets of human activity. A more explicit focus on 'meaning' comes in too, both meanings to be gleaned from the 'text' and those expressed through a multiplicity of voices. What is involved, further, is more than just the voice of the composer/poet (in the past pictured as *the* central figure), but also the other participants who help to form the work and mediate its meaning and the dynamics through which this occurs.

A number of disciplines have also seen a move away from the older views of text as hard-edged, spatial, fully comprised by its verbal components, existent independent of its performance, analysable separately from other texts or other aesthetic media, or, finally, as *the* form in which artistic expression quintessentially exists and should be analysed. This in turn raises new questions, among them the complex relation between 'texts' and 'textuality' on the one hand and specific performances or events on the other (if indeed this is a proper distinction) and of how to treat these relationships. How can we conceptualise or study what lies 'behind' or 'between' separate performances of what in *some* (elusive) sense is the 'same' work? Should we widen the sense of 'text' to include *non*-linguistic elements which may give it its full import as communicative and aesthetic form, or do we need to consider a different term (hence perhaps the popularity of the concept of 'discourse')? How can these wider facets be recorded and represented, or treated seriously as 'real' formulations for appreciation or analysis?

Such questions are partly a matter of ethnographic investigation (and in 'literate' as well as in 'oral' frameworks), partly of developing new theoretical and analytic tools for getting a handle on them. These will need to build on some of the still-relevant older work on oral tradition and verbal arts and – very important – on anthropology's strong ethnographic tradition, but also to be conducted within an interdisciplinary framework which takes account of current rethinking across several related disciplines.

One result has been somewhat uncomfortable reassessments of the concepts of 'tradition' and of 'oral'. Since the 'verbal' can no longer be assumed to be separate and self-standing, simple generalised concepts of 'oral' (and of 'literate') need to be replaced by more ethnographically-based and complex studies. Similarly older ideas about 'tradition' are affected by recent discussion about the socially constructed formulation of traditions, so that what is called 'tradition' has also to be viewed critically as a process to be located in historically specific situations rather than a 'natural' 'thing'. These reassessments go along with the trends noted earlier: emphasis on processes and multiplicity; actor-oriented and interpretive approaches; questioning of binary divides; move away from 'pure' and from narrowly 'verbal' forms; and an interest in the potentially political, contested, or contingent nature of much that had in the past been regarded as fixed and essentially definable as verbally-transcribed texts.

These concurrent emphases once again imply the need for culturally-specific research, whether from documentary or from field evidence. But at the same time it seems likely – judging from recent studies – that the most illuminating analyses will also be increasingly informed by a comparative and interdisciplinary perspective based in the wider theoretical literature and the various debates this raises.

3 Some prior issues and practicalities

Whatever kind of research is being undertaken, certain strategic and practical issues will need to be faced at some point. This phase often comes before fieldwork, so the discussion here is expressed in these terms, and in relation to studies of oral tradition and verbal arts (more general treatments of pre-field preparation can be found in standard guides like Burgess 1982, Ellen 1984, B. Jackson 1987). A separated field trip abroad is nowadays not the only possibility, however, and the points here are also worth considering whatever the research conditions, and for archive-based as well as field study.

Too much pre-planning may be inappropriate for some kinds of research, perhaps particularly in the spheres considered in this volume, and the capacity to respond to specifics as they are encountered may be as important as a tight prior 'research design'. But without some preparation it is easy to jump to conclusions about the objects of study, waste time reinventing the wheel, and maybe lose potential opportunities or cooperation. At the very least it is a mark of responsibility to acquire the relevant tools, skills and knowledge and reflect on the chosen strategies in wider perspective. It is also often helpful to try to anticipate possible ethical dilemmas: it may be too late once committed to particular lines of action.

3.1 SOME STRATEGIC QUESTIONS

The many decisions and possibilities that need consideration include the following:

3.1.1 Who?

The team expedition is one accepted method (popular in Eastern Europe for example). The advantage is that large amounts of data (usually in the form of texts) can be collected simultaneously from a given area, not just from the single genre, medium or interest group that is often all one researcher has time for. There is the corresponding problem that, at least unless the teamwork is over a lengthy period, this may miss the deeper understanding gained through intensive personal participation.

Anthropologists have traditionally taken a more individual approach, stressing personal immersion in the field, and this is still one option. But practices (and practicalities) may be changing and in any case cooperative work between scholars with different but overlapping interests is always worth considering. Collaboration between visiting and local scholars is becoming more common, often reinforced by governmental insistence that local scholars or institutes of learning should be involved in research by foreigners.

Whatever the degree of collaboration – and there is almost certain to be some – questions about the division of labour and its practical implications are worth asking. The older distinctions between researcher and 'subjects', or between researcher and 'assistants', are now under challenge, in favour of a more cooperative model of collaboration between colleagues and equals. This is particularly relevant for the topics under study here: in verbal art and tradition the participants are *already* in some sense reflective analysers through the very fact of their verbal formulations and performances, and there is a sense in which, in this field above all, research is always a cooperative rather than single-person endeavour.

3.1.2 Where: own or other culture?

The traditional anthropological strategy of intensive fieldwork abroad remains a valuable one, in this as in other topics. Much of the anthropological literature on methods (such as Ellen 1984, Fetterman 1989) is devoted to this style, usually stressing the value of a detached, comparative outsider's eye, while pointing out the limitations of not possessing the insider's familiarity with local perceptions, experience and language.

Research at home is, however, now increasingly an accepted alternative even among anthropologists, and folklorists have of course for long studied and collected verbal arts/traditions in their own cultures. Further, scholars in the countries which used to be reserved, as it were, for the incursions of outside anthropologists, now commonly carry out their own local research, often on a part-time basis. Other researchers are drawn to research through personal involvement or enthusiasm for local forms, and then wish to go on to present this within a scholarly framework, either at home, or, perhaps, in an overseas university context. Similarly studies of modern urban life with its verbal and other traditions are everywhere becoming more common. Any consideration of research strategies thus now needs to recognise own-culture research as one viable option among others rather than a second-rate approximation to the 'primary' overseas context. These own-culture studies bring an insider's understanding but also problems, in particular the difficulty of seeing the findings from a comparative and detached viewpoint and of being aware of the perhaps privileged or interested nature of one's own experience (despite some useful discussions (A. Jackson 1987, Messerschmidt 1981), the methodological literature in anthropology has not really caught up with this).

Whatever strategy is adopted the choice of locality (as of historical period) also needs some thought. Practicality may be as important as intellectual or methodological rationale, but either way we can no longer take for granted – as was often done in the past – that whatever area is chosen is necessarily 'representative' or neutral.

3.1.3 How?

Participant observation is widely regarded as the central anthropological method, and in this field as in others is one to consider seriously. The various questions about how it should be applied, how far it should be supplemented or replaced by such other methods as questionnaires, interviews, experiments, non-participant observation or the use of documentary and/or recorded sources, or how to cope with the simultaneous pulls of participant and observer are well treated in the standard books at a general level (see for example Ellen 1984, Agar 1980, Spradley 1980, Van Maanen 1988, Clifford and Marcus 1986, Georges and Jones 1980, Bernard 1988, Fetterman 1989, and the annotated bibliography in Gravel and Ridinger 1988). These need not be repeated except to say that for the most part they apply here as to any other topic. Some special points however are worth noting for the study of oral forms.

Among these is the question of your role, whether as participant-observer, interviewer or collector. Should you be – or present yourself as – a performer yourself; a student (and of whom); a tourist; a non-performing but informed fan or audience member; a recording engineer; an entrepreneur taking back local recordings for commercial use elsewhere? One factor must be how you *are* regarded locally, but some thought about possibilities beforehand can minimise potential difficulties (see also 4.1). Again, how much weight will you put on collecting or recording, how much on observing, and in what situations: aiming at 'naturalistic' occasions, hoping appropriate and accessible ones will occur during your stay, or deliberately eliciting performances or recording situations (see 4.2)? Also, since there will almost certainly be *differing* interpretations, interest groups and performers, will you try to gain some idea of all or concentrate on only a selection? It is easy to be sucked into just one (often value-laden) viewpoint without appreciating the existence of others.

If lengthy and full-time fieldwork is not practicable, there may be alternatives. Part-time participant observation of oral forms is now common, specially within one's own culture or group. This too can raise problems about differing viewpoints, sometimes even harder to appreciate in own-culture study where you already 'know' the truth. Short-term participation can have its value too – like taking part in one particular sequence of performances – but for a serious study may need supplementing by other methods or a series of such visits.

There are other strategies too, both complementary and alternative to participant observation and other standard social research methods. Their relevance depends on your aims and resources. Chief among these is the collection and recording of texts. In the past this often took place with little reliance on participation or even observation, and the consequent publications thus gave little information about context or performance. These collections do arguably encapture *one* aspect of reality, and recording verbal texts is still certainly one viable strategy. It is the more valuable however if modern standards of scholarship are observed in the sense of also obtaining relevant personal and contextual detail and giving some explicit account of the rationale for the selection, settings or overall scope of the collecting.

There are also alternatives to either collecting a large corpus of texts or intensive 'naturalistic' observation – often assumed as the two opposite methodological poles. You may choose, for example, to blend the participant observation characteristic of traditional anthropological fieldwork with the collecting techniques once more typical of folklorists, or to follow up life history or repertoire analysis where the analysis of texts may be accompanied by repeated visits and recordings over many years. Again there is the possibility of a case study analysis of a particular event or process in depth (as in Glassie et al. 1970). (For other accounts of field methods specially related to collecting or observing oral forms see specially Goldstein 1964 (still useful despite its date), Ives 1980, B. Jackson 1987, and some of the ethnomusicology and oral history guides such as Herndon and McLeod 1983, Henige 1982, Baum 1977, P. Thompson 1978/88.)

The analysis or re-analysis of texts collected by others, whether in published works or archive collections, is another strategy, the more feasible because of the huge numbers of texts collected not just in recent years but in the last century (for textual analysis see chapter 8). There are sometimes more clues in the texts than have been recognised in the past, so this too is an area in which anthropologists and others sensitive both to recent theoretical thinking and to the relevant historical or ethnographic background may have much to contribute. Experience of field research or personal collecting can add new insights to archive work – and vice versa.

3.1.4 What?

There is an almost infinite range of questions and topics for investigation (see specially chapter 2 – also all the later chapters). But certain specific issues often surface.

First, is the aim to observe/understand performances and practices, or to collect and analyse texts? That such a contrast is too simple will by now be obvious (see 1.4), but some such question is still worth pondering if only because the latter – the products – are so often taken for granted as constituting the reality of what has to be studied. The answer will have direct implications for your research strategies. Researchers are now more aware than in the past of the problematic nature of textual transcriptions from oral forms, likely to be shaped not only by the researcher's assumptions and practices but also by the specific interests of the performers or other participants so that choices and assumptions made in the early stages may pre-empt options for later analysis.

You may, second, have already decided to study local verbal art or performance. If so, will you concentrate on just one or two specific genres or events, or try to reach some conspectus of the whole range? The answer may need to depend as much on access and practical constraints as on theory.

Finally which formulations are you going to select for collection, observation or analysis? Will you take the best performers (however 'best' is defined)? Or – as is now increasingly common in folklore and sociolinguistics – should you include a range of 'good' and 'bad'? Will you look to what is – or appears to be – 'old', 'traditional' or 'pure', or also or instead at current practices? And where there are different groups or ideologies, which will you focus on?

3.1.5 Some ethical questions

Ethical issues are elaborated later (chapter 10), but some initial questions need consideration near the start.

For example: Who 'owns' the material to be collected or analysed? How far will local voices be recognised? Where will texts, recordings or films ultimately be deposited and for whom? How and when will you seek local permissions for recording or filming? Should you prepare 'release forms' in advance (see 4.3.3)? Are there local sensibilities, political disputes, or censorship to complicate both the investigation and your own moral and political position? If there are opposing views about the nature or meaning of particular forms, how will you align yourself? Even when there is no ideal solution it is responsible to think about such possibilities before being confronted by them.

Ethical problems may also arise in relation to gatekeepers, colleagues, or sponsors, as well as to funders. It is important – though not easy – to avoid giving a false idea of what will be achieved or entering into undertakings which you cannot practically or morally fulfil.

3.1.6 Flexibility

No one strategy will suit every person or every situation. And a whole host of factors – your aims, resources, access, nature of the material, personal relations, unexpected events, or changing participants or politics – may affect your plans over time. Hence one final point about planning ahead is also to allow for flexibility to respond positively to unforeseen problems or opportunities.

Whatever the final outcome *some* decisions on the kinds of questions discussed above will inevitably lie behind your research whether you recognise this or not. In each case, the decisions could have been otherwise and have had different consequences – worth remembering not only in your own research, but also when assessing collections or analyses by others.

3.2 BACKGROUND PREPARATION

The necessary theoretical, ethnographic or linguistic preparation is commonly undertaken prior to fieldwork, but often continues throughout the research or, in cases where there is no clear 'start' to the research, has to be fitted in later. The different aspects converge, but it is convenient to distinguish the following:

1) *Theoretical issues*

Without some awareness of comparative work or current theoretical debates, it is easy to fall into naive preconceptions, miss opportunities or laboriously re-discover what is known. Thus, whether planning field- or archive-based research, it is worth having some acquaintance with the main contending viewpoints (such as those in chapter 2), perhaps also consulting some recent monographs or collections (e.g., Feld 1982/90, Bauman 1986, Holbek 1987, Honko 1988, Briggs 1988, Okpewho 1990, Foley 1990a) or samples of the leading journals. Glancing through later chapters here can also give some idea of the range of possible questions – and controversies.

This applies to work in both foreign and home cultures, but is perhaps particularly important for the latter. In own-culture researching it is especially tempting to take institutions as 'natural' and miss facets to which comparative and theoretical studies can alert you.

2) *The ethnographic area*

It is now taken for granted that researchers should consult the literature on the specific cultural area or historical period before plunging into fieldwork. Some of the following may provide helpful background or starting points: Smith and Damien 1981 (guide to anthropological bibliographies), and the reference works listed in 4) below and in 8.2.2 (also on Africa: Finnegan 1970, Dorson 1972b, Lindfors 1977, Scheub 1977b, Görög 1981, Okpewho 1979, 1983, Andrzejewski 1985; on South Asia: Kirkland 1966; on India: Gupta 1967; on Japan: Algarin 1982; on South Pacific: Orbell 1974, Finnegan and Orbell 1990; on Arabic: Boullata 1989; on American Indian/Native American: Niles 1981, Sherzer and Woodbury 1987, Sherzer and Urban 1986; on North America: Haywood 1961; on Afro-American: Szwed and Abrahams 1978; on Russia: Sokolov 1971; on work on specific genres, 7.4.). But the above list merely consists of scattered and unsystematic references and there is ultimately no alternative to pursuing the usual bibliographical strategies and getting specialist advice.

It may also be worth exploring all or any of the following:

1 Unpublished archives.
2 Vernacular published examples e.g. from local newspapers – a rich but relatively untapped source – and other locally published sources and ephemera (see Opland 1984, Ben-Amos 1978, Bloch 1989).
3 Audio and video recordings: these may be in archives (sometimes traceable through such reference works as Weerasinghe 1989), in private hands, or made and distributed commercially as films or recordings, sometimes in conjunction with local or national broadcasting organisations or tourist promotions.
4 School textbooks and syllabuses, including materials from local literacy campaigns.
5 Manuscript handbooks and aide memoires: in some cultures an important feature of tradition and performance.
6 Other researchers and collectors, including those at institutes of higher education, churches, local administration, schools, as well as local amateur researchers and antiquarians.

All these sources have limitations as well as advantages and need to be seen in context and in the light of your questions. But in almost all cases they are likely to be more extensive than the older images of untouched 'folk' or 'primitive' forms imply, and to have affected local practices and perceptions. There is no longer much excuse for plunging in assuming that nothing has ever been done in the area before.

3) *Language*

Linguistic competence, important for any study in a foreign language, presents special difficulties in the case of verbal expression where linguistic form or artistry, far from being tangential, is part of the very subject under study. As Paredes points out (1977) it is only too easy for a non-native researcher, even if in general 'fluent', to be unaware of local subtleties in the deployment of language.

Some therefore argue that research on language usage, above all on verbal art, should only be conducted by native speakers or those with many years immersion in the language – certainly not a visit of a year or less. The counter-view is that this ideal is plainly not attainable in every case, and that many influential scholars do *not* have native or near-native command of the language and, though open to criticism on this score, have still added to comparative understanding. It is also arguable that foreign scholars have their own insights to bring, the more so because of needing a conscious effort to learn the culture. Native speakers do not necessarily possess full mastery of all registers and vocabulary either – though it is easy to assume that they somehow must, the more so because of earlier models of homogeneous and 'primitive' culture. But if the ideal of 'full' fluency is not always achieveable, nevertheless modern standards of professionalism assume a serious approach to linguistic competence, in justice not only to scholarship but also to the abilities and sophistication of those being studied. At the very least it is worth considering:

1 How far your insights will outweigh possible deficiencies. Since lack of linguistic mastery is probably more disastrous in some spheres than others, this might be one factor in your choice of approach and subject matter.
2 Some conscious strategy to maximise linguistic competence both beforehand and in the field, and to become sensitised to artistic and riddling (not just denotative) aspects of language.
3 Potential problems for native speakers too. It is easy to take knowledge for granted or forget the often political, differentiated and loaded nature of language. However, provided these potential dangers are borne in mind, the native speaker has an enormous advantage, worth exploiting wherever possible.

4) *Reference books*

It may be helpful to include here a brief list of reference works particularly relevant to this general field but not as widely known as they deserve. These, depending on your specific interests, may be worth consulting before or during your research: Barnouw 1989 (authoritative and comprehensive: possibly the most useful single reference work; includes brief up-to-date bibliographies); Preminger 1974 (discusses both general concepts and specific poetic traditions, including oral as well as written poetry/poetics); Crystal 1987 (an informative and comprehensive source for recent discussion and references on language); M. Leach 1949 (dated but still with some useful entries: recently reprinted); S. Thompson 1955–8 (useful bibliographic sources for certain purposes even for those not interested in motif analysis as such: see 8.2.2); Ranke 1977– (several volumes, in process: an authoritative and continuing production of European scholarship); Bødker 1965 (detailed list of technical terms, together with further references, which, while focusing on 'Germanic folk literature', is also of wider comparative interest); *Garland Folklore Bibliographies* 1981– (general editor Alan Dundes – a series of thorough bibliographical volumes on various topics and/or geographical areas).

3.3 RECORDING EQUIPMENT

The choice of recording equipment needs level-headed consideration since inappropriate decisions can be costly. This section points to factors to consider – not in the sense of describing equipment in general nor listing the latest technical details, but highlighting issues to bear in mind when assessing specialist advice. (On general questions about equipment – widely treated in the standard texts – see specially Blacking in Ellen 1984: 199–206, B. Jackson 1987 (excellent accounts, much relied on here), Herndon and McLeod 1983: esp. chap. 3, Fetterman 1989: chap. 4, Dorson 1983: Part 3.)

3.3.1   What equipment – if any?

Making and keeping a record can be valuable in research on oral forms, and nowadays visual, audio, and (within limits) video media supplement the traditional, but still relevant, recording devices of pen and paper. New opportunities are opening up because recording equipment is now increasingly smaller, cheaper, more reliable, more automatic, easier to manage, more powerful and of a higher technical quality than before (the likelihood that this trend will continue is one reason for the absence of specialist technical points here: it will always be essential to consult the latest information for up-to-date details).

There are various reasons to consider recording:

1 Oral forms are, almost by definition, ephemeral. If you want to preserve, disseminate or analyse them it is near-essential to employ some means to make them more lasting.
2 Recordings arguably give direct access to 'primary' voices and sources.
3 Certain aspects of oral performance, such as sound effects or

gestures, can only be captured (and later analysed) through particular forms of recording.

4 Mechanical recording can be a convenient, quick and sometimes unobtrusive way of gathering information.

5 Developments in the technology of recording sometimes have wider theoretical implications. Parry and Lord's use of the phonograph, for example, led from the older model of fixed verbal texts to an understanding of variability and unique performance (see Lord 1960), while recent audio and video technologies highlight performance elements previously less visible to scholars.

But if technological devices can be illuminating – and by now most serious field researchers would consider taking at least a portable tape or cassette recorder – it is equally important to beware of taking equipment without careful thought. 'The-more-the-better' mentality means not only unnecessary expense and bother, but also the risk of the machinery getting in the way or even providing a seductive rationale for bypassing your original aims. There are many pressures selling the view that without state-of-the-art technology you cannot be a professional fieldworker. The opposite view is equally worth considering. Technology can be a barrier, and each item needs to be weighed against the specific needs of the research, and the intellectual and personal (not just financial) costs.

Here are some commonly mentioned problems:

1 Equipment management takes time, attention and organisation from other things and imposes constraints on where and when and with whom you carry out your research. The more complex and expensive the equipment, the more it can distract through what Bruce Jackson neatly terms 'the law of inverse attention' (1987: 110ff).

2 Which machine(s) you use – and how – will influence your questions and definitions. It is tempting to think you've got 'it' (*the* 'primary' source) when you've made a recording, and you may forget after a while to ask what 'it' is, in whose terms, and what is left out. The technology encourages a focus on certain aspects of reality rather than others: at worst the machine defines the situation.

3 Reliance on mechanical recording can seem to absolve you from other forms of observation and documentation: the 'machine is doing the recording'. But a) machines break down; b) machine management can distract from observing the human interactions; c) there is always *more* going on than the machine captures.

4 With the sophisticated photographic, audio and video technology

now available, high technical quality can become an end in itself. This has implications not just for finance, but also for selection and analysis. Will the choice of performers be influenced by whether they look good on film, or of venue by the 'better quality' available in the studio, where the research aims might be equally or better met through 'ordinary' performers or on location recordings? Bruce Jackson's advice would be echoed by many researchers: 'Every machine limits your mobility and defines your options. Know what your needs really are and never use more technology than you need' (1987: 109).

The crux is thus to consider research scope and purpose before getting committed to particular types of equipment rather than the other way round (though the resources offered by the latter *may* then encourage you to adapt or develop initial ideas further). The aim is surely to further the research rather than prove technological brilliance. The following questions provide a useful checklist:

1 What is the general focus of the research: people's *ideas* about oral art; public performance (and if so the arts of the 'primary' performer(s) and/or of the audience and/or of other participants?); the social role of myths; the plot structure of stories; or what? The answers have implications for what – if any – machine(s) might be needed.

2 How important is it for the research aims to have a *record* (audio, visual, written) of certain actions – and of which aspects of what actions?

3 *What* will need recording: a group: individual; public festival; informal conversation; a one-voice or multi-voice situation?

4 What will be the settings for recording? Studio conditions where you can, more or less, set up the microphones, lighting, etc. as you want them and have the performer come to *you*? Or will you go to the performers taking your equipment with you? Or something between the two? Will you be one of the main participants and controllers, or one in a mass audience?

5 What are the other constraints in terms of cost, time, assistance, transport, mobility?

6 What will be done with the recordings once made (in terms of analysis; distribution; deposit)?

A final point is that there is no need to record everything. Despite the comments in this volume about all the things that can be recorded, these are merely possibilities and the choice among them has to be yours. And a further corollary is that while you should no doubt be open to new ideas and media as you go along, in the last instance you may need to be firm in not dissipating your energies. Bruce Jackson's summary cannot be bettered:

> Trying to document in too many media at once is like going on a hike with 200 pounds of supplies and equipment in your backpack: you may have everything you might need, but you won't last long in the company of the rational travelers. In fieldwork, less is sometimes more. Far better to decide in advance the form of documentation most appropriate to your needs and skills and limit yourself to that and do it well than come home with inadequate notes, inadequate recordings, and inadequate photographs. You'll never get everything anyway.
>
> (1987: 108–9)

3.3.2 Some issues to consider

If you do use recording equipment – and very likely you will want *something* – detailed advice on particular models needs to be sought both from up-to-date technical sources and from those familiar with your intended ethnographic area. There are few generally applicable rules, since the 'right' option has to be worked out (and perhaps later modified) to suit particular circumstances and resources. Some key issues keep cropping up however. So when you are offered specialist advice on particular media and models here are some questions to ask:

1 *Cost*: relevant not just for initial capital outlay but also for maintenance, running, and replacements; consumables like tapes, cassettes or film are another expense (something it may not be sensible to economise on). Questions of reliability, durability, compatibility with other equipment, training needs, and likely obsolescence can have cost implications too.
2 *Usability and convenience*: often the most important of all but difficult to assess in general terms. Glaring *in*conveniences, like machines that need three hands, constant adjustment, or a 'record' button not secured against accidental use (and erasure), may be relatively easy to spot. Others are more subjective. How easy is the equipment to set up and in what circumstances? How much attention does it need? How convenient will *all* the intended stages of processing be (not just recording, but also transcribing, copying, playing back)?
3 *Portability and mobility*: important if you are intending to work

not in a pre-planned venue but in differing situations, specially if you wish to record events as they happen, and if such events cannot be predicted or controlled in advance. This in turn raises questions about weight, durability, resistance to heat, light or damp, manoevrability, and dependence or otherwise on mains electricity (and what kind).

4 *Training*. If you are inexperienced with the particular medium or machine, how much training will be needed for you and/or appropriate assistants? This is not a minor matter, for whoever is operating the recording needs to do so effectively and without fuss. It is true that much technology is now more user-friendly than in the past, but if despite this you feel you and others will not be able to master the necessary skills, it might be best to resist that machine – however wonderful – and think of alternatives.

5 *Flexibility and control*: again depends on your needs. For some purposes the more automatic the better; for others you may want to set things up to your own – perhaps changing – specifications.

6 *Security and permanence*. Being able to keep records secret may not be relevant, but if there are issues of confidentiality, copyright or ownership, you may need to prevent unauthorised access or copying. There is also the question of the ultimate destination of your typescripts, photos, tapes or whatever, leading to the need to consider specific materials or precautions in advance (some forms of paper, tape, or film are more durable than others).

7 *Compatibility*. With certain kinds of technology there are problems in collaborating with other equipment (and hence with other scholars). Interchange between different technological systems is becoming easier but you still need to discover what link-ups are and are not possible (*really* possible in practice, that is) and what are the alternative systems. This may apply to systems in your field locations as well as at home, if only for such things as the local availability of spare parts, replacements, or consumables like tapes. And as newer devices are developed there is the danger of being stuck with an obsolescent design or being forced to find enhancements even for recent purchases to make them work with the latest 'improvement' which has now flooded the market. All you can do is to be aware of this, perhaps avoid going for way-out models however brilliant or cheap they sound, and consult several experts not just one.

8 *Reliability*. How important this is will partly depend on finances, aims, and circumstances but it is worth remembering that some

machines and media are less reliable than others (or less reliable in certain respects).

9 *Capacity and quality*. It may be worth considering equipment just a bit bigger or better than you think you need but it is best to keep your head in the face of persuasions that specific models are exceptionally powerful or fast or able to produce recordings, photos, etc., of stunning quality. Do you actually need extra power for what you want to do? Is it suited to your likely recording contexts? What would be the costs not just in capital outlay but in distraction, maintenance, time? There is no point in taking on the highest quality machine if you can't learn to use it or can only do so by sacrificing other things you want to do.

10 *Acceptability*. It is also worth thinking about local norms and practices in regard to particular types of equipment. In some contexts tape recording or photographing – even making notes – are perceived as intrusive or threatening; in others cassettes or cameras are a regular part of life and *not* using them may seem an insult. Since the likely effects on local relationships, contacts, and performances will influence the research, time spent on exploring local expectations before deciding on equipment may be well spent.

Considering these different factors will seldom result in clear 'winners', rather a need for balancing varying strengths and weaknesses, and maybe reassessing them at later stages. Here again your own priorities, resources and capabilities are what matter, whatever the 'experts' say. (For further helpful discussion on these and similar issues, see specially B. Jackson 1987, Herndon and McLeod 1983: 30ff, 92ff.)

3.3.3 Specific forms of recording devices

As well as the general questions above there are some specific issues connected with the commonly-used – but differing – forms of recording.

A couple of preliminary points need emphasising. First, *all* recording (including writing) involves personal interaction and some shaping of what is recorded. What may look like merely limpid documenting raises both theoretical and ethical issues: the elements you are focusing on, for example, or questions of ownership and permission. This is the essential background to any assessment of how the characteristics of different media and devices are likely to affect your own research and its conditions.

Second, some technical decisions run across several media – for example choices about mono/stereo, tape/cassette, colour/black-and-white, film/video, digital or other, more or less automatic and/or computerised, specific linkages of audio and video. Here again these decisions need to be made in accordance with both what is currently available and your own research needs.

1 *Writing.* Writing has been the dominant technology of recording in the study of oral forms in the past and is still worth considering. It remains a convenient method for some purposes, particularly commentary on the general situation, descriptions of action, and, within limits, for documenting and capturing textual content. It also has fewer constraints on mobility and (sometimes) attention than more mechanical means, and may be more reliable. On the other hand writing texts from dictation or – as in the past – relying on specially written versions by assistants or 'informants' has problems for performance-oriented art forms where not only the flow of live delivery but also visual and auditory elements and the combination of several voices may be important.

Writing can come in at various levels and need not be confined to collecting texts or to pen and paper means, for typing and word-processing may be convenient at some stages. Writing can also be useful for documenting observations of performance events and participants, while written transcriptions of recordings constitute further representations of the original events (on transcription see 4.4, 9.2).

2 *Photography.* This can capture elements of which scholars are now more aware than in the past, such as a) the settings and visual properties of oral performances; b) the personality of individual participants; c) details of performance like gestures, facial expression, audience participation. Photographs record different aspects from writing and have the advantage over film/video of generally being cheaper, less intrusive, and easier to distribute. Athough not directly representing movement as such, they can document sequential actions and represent a valuable recording technique for many aspects of oral performance (as in the sequences of photographs to illustrate a story-teller's art, etc., in Cancel 1989, Scheub 1977a, Calame-Griaule 1977, 1982; on photographs generally see Collier 1986, Becker 1974, 1981, Riley 1990).

3 *Audio recording*. There are many reasons why modern researchers routinely consider some form of audio recording, among them speed and convenience, the range of information which can be represented, and the ability to record chronological sequences as they happen. The availablity of mechanical recording to capture live sound including music has profoundly affected our understanding of oral forms (has in a sense become the basis for defining them), bringing in a dimension missed by pen-and-paper recording. In some contexts audio recordings can also be *less* intrusive than written documenting as well as freeing the researcher's eyes and hands from the page. Their wider communication is now becoming cheaper and easier though still not very welcome to publishers of printed books. There is a huge range of audio recording devices in terms of cost, capacity, portability, quality, or complexity as well as choices between tape and cassette, mono and stereo.

A couple of conseqential points should be noted. First, audio recordings often (though not always) need transcribing. In comparison to the speedy and easy business of recording, this is a large task (see 4.4 and 9.2). Second, a high-quality microphone is often as important as the basic machine and equally, if not more, worth spending money on. It is now possible to choose between unidirectional, bidirectional and omnidirectional microphones: the first help to cut out unwanted sound (often a real problem in field as against studio settings, or if one is aiming for the common commercial ideal of eliminating 'extraneous noise'), while omnidirectional microphones are valued by researchers interested in ambience or the interplay of several participants.

4 *Video and film*. These can capture yet further elements of performance, including kinesic, proxemic and choreographic aspects to supplement acoustic elements (on whose linkage with the visual sequences you will have to make some decisions). They do so, furthermore, in dynamic sequence. Because of this some argue that film/video are *the* way to record live oral performance. Certainly they can bring a sense of immediacy and personality, but there are potential problems too, among them questions about selection (video/film are limiting media in focusing on just one scene), intrusiveness, cost and constraints on the fieldworkers' time, mobility and attention. The tasks of later processing and editing may also be burdensome. And as Bruce Jackson reminds us:

Film and video are wonderful tools for the fieldworker, permitting us to preserve kinds and quantities of information we could never before preserve, but they also make us more distant from what we're watching than any other kind of instrument we've ever had at our disposal.

(1987: 243)

(Film and visual anthropology are now a specialised subject within anthropology; for further references and ideas see Blakely 1989, Henley 1985, Rollwagen 1988, and the journal *Studies in Visual Communication*. Since the focus is on recording oral forms, computers are not discussed here, but see 8.6.3. For further comments on recording generally in the context of performance see 5.3.3, and of presentation/publication 9.3.3.)

3.3.4 Summary: fool's guide to do's and don'ts

Experts know when to break the rules but for those less confident, the following advice is usually given by experienced fieldworkers:

1 Think beforehand about likely problems and issues so as to stay in control of your own decisions (even if your philosophy is to be flexible).

2 Try to anticipate the *practical* circumstances in which you will be recording and relate these to your choices of equipment and media.

3 Don't take more or higher-quality equipment than you need for the purposes of your research.

4 Take advice from those experienced in the relevant technology, in your particular ethnographic area, and in the kind of research you are interested in; but don't swallow everything they tell you uncritically. What is right for them may not suit you and your research.

5 Get to know your equipment beforehand – 'obvious', but not always done. This applies both to its general operation and to its detailed use, for example in the placement of microphones or lighting, life of batteries, how to change over cassettes, speeds, recording levels, accessibility and security of switches, different kinds of tape, etc. Also get some experience of what your recordings sound like (it is amazing what the human ear – unlike a microphone – includes or screens out). Obviously detailed problems can only be solved when you meet them but in general nothing is more unprofessional – or more insulting to those being

recorded – than fieldworkers not in command of the technology they themselves have chosen to use.

3.4 RELEVANCE FOR ARCHIVE RESEARCH

The points above may seem tangential if you are not intending to use field methods. But even if all your research material is in archives, libraries or published sources, it is still important to bear in mind that, insofar as it is in any sense oral, it has at some time been collected, written or transcribed using one or more of the methods and approaches discussed above. One important stage in understanding your sources therefore, is to consider their genesis: that is, the decisions which the original collector or compiler took on these prior issues and their implications for the nature and form of what was recorded.

4 Collecting, recording and creating texts: preliminaries and mechanics

All studies of oral traditions and the verbal arts are directly or indirectly implicated in the complexities of collecting and recording texts. This chapter largely takes the notion of text as given, concentrating on such practical questions as how to start collecting, the implications of different settings for recording, the mechanics of logging and keeping records, and preliminary transcribing. But collecting also links with the views of text as process. What you collect and record is affected by a whole series of prior decisions: theoretical preconceptions, aims, equipment, settings, and decisions about who or what is to be recorded. The points here therefore ultimately need supplementing by wider theoretical considerations (see specially 1.4) and by the particular aspects discussed later: performance (chapter 5), social context (chapter 6), textual analysis (chapter 8) and the detailed processing of texts and transcriptions (chapter 9).

Although the discussion below takes active collecting and recording as the main framework, the issues are also relevant for those engaged in analysing texts recorded by others.

4.1 SOME INITIAL TECHNIQUES AND PROVISOS

Experiences differ, as does the field situation, research aims and human relationships, so there is no one right way to go about collecting and recording. However, some of the methods commonly used by other researchers – specially at the start of their research – may be worth thinking about.

The general strategies for starting off in unfamiliar field situations are already well discussed in anthropological textbooks (such as Ellen 1984: 194ff, Fetterman 1989: 43ff), but one point to remember in explaining research on oral forms is the overtones of terms like 'folklore', 'traditional' or even 'vernacular'. These may convey unintended meanings or raise questions of definition, ownership or control which might start the research off on the wrong footing. Such connotations may never be totally avoidable but it is important to be sensitive to them from the outset.

There are a variety of techniques for getting going on recording – many of them useful later on too. One is just a direct request for stories or songs (or whatever). Despite potential problems of prior definition by researcher rather than performer, this straightforward means may be perfectly satisfactory for your purposes (how fast or slowly to go in making such requests will need to be judged by local conventions as well as your own circumstances). Another possibility is to follow up contacts at local festivals or attend public performances and perhaps make some recordings on the spot (even on 'public' occasions permissions may still need to be sought), at the same time giving some thought to how 'representative' these occasions and their participants are. Some researchers enquire about locally admired performers, then try to meet them or hear them perform, or ask indirect questions which could lead to the kinds of activities or forms being investigated (e.g., about the beginnings of things, past history, local celebrations). Other techniques include a notice in local newspapers or broadcast on radio to invite replies and submission of material; arranging a competition for the 'best' essay, song or story, preferably in cooperation with some local institution; encouraging letters and written submissions; or providing open access to a tape-recorder where people can make recordings when it suits them. Performing yourself can be a useful stimulus, provided you don't steal the show or convey misleading or intimidating models for others, as can playing back your own recordings to the original performers (or to others), hearing or discussing commercial recordings, or listening to live or recorded broadcasts. It can also sometimes be productive to introduce some new or foreign element into a performance and consider current reactions or what happens to this over time (as in Bohannan 1966, Finnegan 1967: 99) or to engage in joint composition yourself (as in Messenger's Irish 'ballad-mongering' 1983). Another approach is to go quietly at first, unobtrusively observing and making notes as and when feasible. For certain topics, particularly the conversational genres, this may need to be a major method throughout. (For further discussions of the initial phases see Toelken 1979: 292ff, Ives 1980: 33ff, Jackson 1987: 42ff, Brunvand 1986: 19ff.)

Researching in a familiar culture (either your own or one known from an earlier visit) has the advantage that you will already be sensitive to which routes are best pursued or avoided. There are disadvantages too however. You will be less able to play the uncommitted or ignorant outsider, and may have to reassess what you think you already know *as if* a stranger, testing it out in relation to the points made here. Another difficulty can be getting people to treat you and your research seriously: why would anyone want to study such already-known forms? You may even feel this yourself. One tactic for dealing with this has been the traditional stress on the unusual or the 'old', which somehow validates this as 'research'. Another is to exploit the formality of recording devices: though in some circumstances a nuisance this can help through giving a special frame to the procedures and findings.

A problem in both familiar and unfamiliar cultures can be not so much finding occasions to record as, once started, of how to refuse an inundation of offers. Since people's individual feelings and pride may be involved it is worth thinking in advance about how to handle this tactfully, preferably in the light of local conventions.

There are also such questions as whose versions you are drawing on and how fixed the texts are. There may be different interpretations, wordings or performances depending on who is asked and how, or on where a recording is made (these disputes are sometimes in themselves illuminating). It is easy, but sometimes misleading, to assume that there is only one correct form and that once that has been captured you have 'got it'. Repeated recordings of the 'same' text and continued observations of differing audiences and interpretations may be essential to the questions you are exploring.

Whatever your techniques or overall situation, you need to be cautious about engaging in recording, photographing, etc., without due permission (see 4.3.3 below, also 10.3).

Finally, collecting and recording texts involves not just mechanics but people and situations. It is therefore important to think about the personal and cultural relationships involved, and the ways in which you and the other participants can act together in a jointly acceptable manner. Among the questions will be your own perceived or intended role in the context of performance and text collection: an expert, a learner, a fan, a technician, an outside visitor, a competent practitioner in particular audience roles, a chorus member – or whatever. These may vary according to the situation, your own competence, whether or not you are a foreigner, or the stage in the research, and may not always turn out just how you expect (for further discussion and examples see Koning 1980, Titon 1985).

It is easy for the enthusiasm for recording and its end result – surely a 'good thing' for everyone! – to obliterate the fact that some occasions are more acceptable than others for the participants, some forms normally delivered only within culturally defined constraints (and thus uncomfortable, even if physically possible, outside these bounds), and your convenience and expectations not necessarily universally shared. Important as it is to get the technology right, the human relationships involved may be equally, if not more, central for the final result. The texts that are finally recorded are the joint creation of all the participants in the research – and that means the performers and their audiences, not just the researcher, each with their own rights, assumptions and relationships.

4.2 THE SETTINGS FOR COLLECTING AND RECORDING

The settings for collecting and recording depend, naturally, on your overall strategy: the particular mix of, say, unobtrusive participant observation, formal interviews, explicit field collecting, short or long-term visits. The general advantages or limitations of these differing strategies are widely discussed (see references in 3.1.3) but there are also some specific points relating to the actual settings for collecting and recording.

Some of these are really just down-to-earth and practical questions. The time and place for recording or observing can probably be any occasion which the opportunist researcher can exploit: storytelling in a crowded railway carriage, oratory or singing in the street, a tramping song during a long trek along bush paths – not just the more explicitly structured contexts of a verandah or inside room in the evening. Each of these settings will have its own conventions and influences. The song on the remote path may be in a fine 'natural' setting, but may also be disjointed and hard to record, as against a fuller, more 'finished' and more recordable version performed to request later. It is not however a forgone conclusion that the second is more 'correct', or indeed the first more 'authentic'. Each is affected by its particular conditions, and these too should be part of the record.

But though *any* time or place can be grist to the researcher's mill, some conditions are particularly common or acceptable. Some genres, it is true, can be performed at any time, while certain work songs and ceremonies often take place in the day. One of the commonest settings however is during rest times – most often the evening, holidays or lax times in the yearly cycle. This is when most adults have leisure to engage in formulated oral performance, whether of their own accord or in some sense induced by the researcher. This means you too have to be prepared to practise at such times (sometimes in darkness – not a trivial matter), and cannot assume that people will be free or willing to produce performances at other times just to suit research convenience. Sometimes there are explicit sanctions concerning when or where a particular genre can or cannot be performed, or to whom. Even if such conventions on occasion can be broken, you need to be aware of them.

There are also more general and theoretical debates about settings. These are important to consider explicitly. It has in the past seemed acceptable to collect texts of oral forms in many different contexts, and in this field – in contrast to their usual insistence on the significance of context – anthropologists have often paid relatively little attention to the implications of the collecting and recording situation itself (those working under the label of folklore seem to have been more conscious of the problems). As Wilgus pertinently points out, even the usual charge of recording texts 'out of context' is itself too simple: 'in truth, material is always collected "in context" – it is just that . . . the context is usually that of an interview' (Wilgus 1983: 373, see also Jackson 1987: 63ff). This warning about the effects of the *actual* settings for recording – whether interview or whatever – is of central importance.

In this connection, the most commonly cited classification is Kenneth Goldstein's categories of 'natural', 'artificial', and 'induced natural' contexts (1964: 80ff). These can be criticised and extended, but are still extremely illuminating distinctions to start from.

4.2.1 'Natural' settings

The concept of a 'natural' setting for recording may not be altogether clear, but is what most researchers implicitly claim. And because this is often tacitly assumed, researchers – and their readers – seem to be absolved from the need to discuss consequential questions about the nature or implications of their recording contexts.

A little thought makes it evident that few recorded examples of oral tradition and verbal art have been collected in 'natural' settings in any literal sense, particularly if this is defined (as in Goldstein) as meaning that the participants are unaware that a researcher is present. Possible exceptions are covert or unobtrusive observation of conversational genres or of relatively uncrystallised forms of oral tradition where it is often not feasible to keep reminding participants that they are being observed or that the tape-recorder is still running; or public artistic displays where observing or recording as a member of a mass audience is possible without in any way engaging in subterfuge. 'Natural' settings in Goldstein's sense however are relatively unusual for the making of deliberate recordings. Not only are people's activities likely to be affected to some extent or another by the presence of a fieldworker but this presence may be specially intrusive if the researcher is, as often, trying to get a systematic recording of some event (though it must be said that a small tape-recorder is sometimes surprisingly ignored once things get going).

Although it is hard to draw a line between 'natural' and other contexts (*all* events are in a sense socially contrived), there clearly are degrees of 'artificiality'. It is only fair to those cooperating in the collecting not to take it for granted nor imply to others that any recordings are further towards the 'natural' end of the continuum than is justified by the circumstances.

4.2.2 'Artificial' settings

Goldstein's second category is a form of 'simulation': the re-enactment of a no longer current practice or the performance of 'an activity out of context for the purpose of an ethnographic description' (Ellen 1984: 72). Much collecting of oral forms broadly falls under this head – little though the final publications or recordings usually convey this.

Some of the background to this lies in earlier collecting traditions. In the past specially set up sessions had a rationale within the antiquarian tradition by which items of oral tradition were collected and filed rather like physical elements in the natural world: just as pebbles could be amassed irrespective of their habitat, so texts could be collected equally well anywhere, whether 'in situ' or using an overseas informant in one's study at home. Similarly earlier emphases on salvaging 'old' or 'traditional' forms justified setting up collecting sessions with any informants that could be found – an emergency operation before everything got 'lost', applying equally to the recording of linguistic phenomena generally and to items of verbal art in particular. Anthropological fieldworkers too sometimes followed the same model, for collecting vernacular texts used to be standard procedure, viewed as providing 'the most accurate and objective picture of the minds and preoccupations of the people studied' (Ellen 1984: 73), with the implication that the texts so collected represented an unmediated vehicle of local expression. Such rationales look more questionable today.

Specially set up occasions for observation or recording obviously have advantages. They make available events which it might otherwise be impossible to see or record at all, and can be organised to suit the researcher's convenience, in conditions which allow recording, observing or questioning. For short forms like stories or proverbs, this method can facilitate recording a large corpus of material (quicker than waiting for scattered occasions), while longer or more specialised genres may only be accessible within a researcher's timespan if using this method. Participants may also give of their 'best' when an outside researcher is known to be present, and performances may seem more complete and serious.

But these very advantages of convenience and accessibility can of course also lead to distortion or misunderstanding. Specially set up performances may look neutral, but they always take place in a specific setting – that arranged by the researcher. This in turn has its own characteristics: bringing certain expectations about what is wanted, encouraging shorter – or longer – performances, or resulting in more – or less – contrived delivery (these are only examples: the specific features vary according to culture and genre and always need exploring). Recording in artificial settings also risks wrong assumptions about the usual conventions. In the absence of observed evidence, it is easy to substitute personal but unconscious presuppositions – for instance assuming that the usual setting 'must have been' that appropriate for, say, a coherent and lengthy 'myth' or an 'epic' and classifying accordingly (for examples see Finnegan 1988: 169ff). Such consequences do not make recordings from such settings valueless – but do provide a warning to interpret the results with care and supplement them by investigation of other types of occasions.

Some of the implications partly depend on what method of recording is being used. Most collections of 'traditional narratives', 'myths', 'folktales' and so on were collected from dictation or from a version specially written for the collector, and such methods are still used. Their worth depends on your purpose and on the nature of the texts under study (some seem to be more independent than others of their specific conditions of performance, for example).

Writing down verbal texts away from the occasion of performance may be an accepted local convention; in this case such a setting becomes in that respect no longer an 'artificial' one (it may be in others). In most cases, however, conscious recording through dictation will almost certainly affect such features as content, length and meaning as compared to the usual performances, with far-reaching implications for later analysis. Quite apart from the absence of audience and ambience, artificial situations make many performance arts difficult or impossible to deploy. It is sometimes argued that written documenting in specially set up sessions is sometimes the only available method and so 'better than nothing'. For certain kinds of research this is no doubt so. But there is also the counter-argument that if this is the only option and there are no complementary methods to supplement it, maybe the aims and viability of the research should be reconsidered (perhaps instead focusing on local practices or concepts relating to writing and dictating).

Audio recording sessions at least avoid the barriers of writing or dictation. But this arrangement too may affect some accustomed patterns. The performer(s) may find it strange or uncomfortable to address just one person (rather than the usual audience), or to perform in an unusual venue, at an abnormal time of day, in unfamiliar clothes, or divorced from the usual warm-up procedures or ritual framing. These features may be exacerbated when – as in one common pattern – 'informants' are recorded right away from their own cultural setting, such as on a university campus, in a broadcasting studio or in another country altogether, or where the extra pressures of video recording are added.

How important these problems are depends not only on the purpose of the recording but also on local conventions. Settings which at first sight look 'artificial' can sometimes be the natural ones. In a study of how oral forms are used in radio, for example, or performances put on for visiting fieldworkers, the studio setting, the front parlour or the hotel lounge might indeed be the right and proper setting to use. For some purposes and in some cultures, so-called artificial settings can certainly be useful, particularly if they involve audio recording, are complemented by other methods, or relate only to certain phases of the research (an initial stimulus, perhaps, for more substantial efforts by other methods). For most types of research in verbal art and tradition, however, many would now hold that reliance on artificial contexts should be a second rather than first choice as the primary method. At the least it is essential to recognise the features of this kind of setting and be open about its possible effects.

4.2.3 'Induced natural' settings and similar contexts

Kenneth Goldstein's third category 'induced natural' (1964: 87ff) has been particularly useful in both setting the terms of debate and describing common practice. As he explains it, the researcher first discovers the 'natural context or contexts' for the performance of a specific genre, then recruits one of the potential participants to bring about the context in which he and others will perform.

> This he achieves by calling together a group of his cronies or friends for an evening of story-telling, singing, riddling, or any other lore normally performed in such a context . . . without informing the participants that the purpose of the session is to allow a collector to observe them in action. When the participants arrive at the place selected for the session (usually the home of one of them), the collector is introduced casually as if he had dropped in unexpectedly (or it may be planned for him to actually arrive after the others have gathered). Preferably there should be no recording equipment present to inhibit the context.
>   Once the session starts, the collector can either observe as a participant or simply drop into the background, sitting on the fringe of the group where he may take notes on the situation. If a tape recorder is not being used for recording the materials of the session, the collector should indicate the pieces performed by means of a code system or some mnemonic device. He can later call on each of the participants individually to obtain the actual materials themselves in an artificial context or interview session.
>
> (Goldstein 1964: 88–9)

The researcher too, if already known as a participant, can perform this role. In a riddle session which Goldstein started off

> By playing the role of the instigator, I was able to hide the real purpose of the evening from every one of the other participants, thereby assuring a more natural context
>
> (Goldstein 1964: 89)

Goldstein's analysis assumes covert observation. But there is also a variety of 'natural induced' contexts in which the performers know their performances are being recorded but do not find performing in this kind of situation strange. Thus researchers sometimes exploit local conventions by inviting a praise singer to perform at a party, contributing towards the cost of putting on a memorial ceremony, or acting as host for a regular session of riddling and story-telling, whilst not concealing the presence of a tape-recorder in the background (often ignored). Since, after all, performances regularly depend on the instigation of groups and individuals it may not seem unnatural for the researcher to take an overt role.

Such settings clearly have some advantages over fully 'natural' contexts. Merely waiting around hopefully may mean never having access to certain genres or events. The practice of induced settings may even be a locally recognised one, as in putting on displays for a visitor or for special occasions. Compared to 'artificial' settings, 'induced' performances may be closer to the normal interactions, particularly if involving an audience – often important for performance (though again the regular conventions of audience composition and behaviour need investigation). There may also be fewer problems about payment or other recompense than in artificial settings.

There are potential problems too. As with artificial contexts it can be tempting to put your own expectations and interpretations onto the event, and the dangers of over-emphasising textual crystallisation may be more tempting to ignore when recording in contexts which can be presented as at least partly 'natural'. The 'inducing' may alter the setting more than had been assumed: still an interesting event, but not necessarily of the kind intended.

As with all methods, the balance between advantages and disadvantages has to be drawn in the light of circumstances and aims. There may be ways to minimise the disadvantages, not least by considering the various components in performance situations (see 5.3) and how each of these might or might not be affected by the 'inducing'.

4.2.4 Critique

Despite the usefulness of Goldstein's categories for illuminating often-neglected aspects of the collecting process, they can also be criticised as themselves resting on questionable assumptions (hence the 'scare quotes' around them above). Is there really any such thing as a truly 'natural' or truly 'artificial' situation? Surely *all* settings are in some way socially constructed? Is a misleading model of the research process being implied, as if the items are already there if we can just get the right setting for recording them, even perhaps some romantic search for 'natural' or 'folk' ways uncontaminated by researchers from outside? It is true that some settings may indeed be more contrived than others, or devised more by 'outsiders' than 'insiders' (insofar as this distinction applies) – but understanding this might be better accomplished not by constructing generalised definitions of settings but by taking account of specifics in the setting: not just the various performance elements and the background social framework and expectations (the kinds of points discussed in chapters 5 and 6), but also the actors in the situation, who took what role in setting it up, what powers they exerted, and the constraints and inducements they are acting under. The researcher then becomes one – but only one – of these many different participants whose actions and viewpoints all need attention.

Any performance, finally, is a complex process rather than an entity to be picked up in this or that 'setting'. Similarly 'context' is more than a fixed and static backdrop separate from the 'text' or detachable from the relationships involved. In this kind of critique, it is still important to emphasise contextualisation and be sensitive to the relationships involved in any performance and its recording. But these are more complicated and more dynamic than can be fully covered by the generalised – if still useful – typologies of 'natural', 'artificial', and 'induced natural'. (For further comments on the interactions of text, context and setting see Ben-Amos 1972, Briggs 1988, Georges 1980, Zan 1982, Bauman and Briggs 1990.)

4.2.5 Implications for archive materials

Questions about settings might seem irrelevant for texts already published or archived: the problematic process of recording is by now over and gone. But of course those texts too were collected in *some* setting, so exactly the same questions arose at one point and affect the outcome.

In many cases it is a fair presumption that (to use the categories above) the collection was towards the 'artificial' end of the continuum. Even so it is worth trying to check if that is correct and if so, in what sense, where and when. With recently collected texts or audio recordings, the possibilities of more 'natural' or of 'induced natural' settings is worth exploring, and may lead to further insights into certain features of the texts. Such questions and the critiques to which they lead may well be central rather than, as previously assumed, merely marginal to an informed understanding of the material.

4.3 MAKING AND KEEPING RECORDS

Whatever your specific interest in texts, you are likely to want some records of their verbal content, performance or contexts. The various recording devices (writing as well as machines) were discussed earlier (see 3.3.3), together with comments on problems and opportunities arising from specific technical forms and their properties. These same issues are still relevant for actual usage in the field, but the practicalities of equipment management and organisation raise some additional points.

However carefully you plan, you are almost bound to encounter some problems in recording. Sometimes these can be capitalised on, showing you as human not just a technical wizard, or anyway built on in an upward learning curve. Recurrent problems can even illuminate interesting differential expectations between researcher and other participants. But stupid mistakes are best avoided and many fieldworkers advise roughly the following guidelines (common sense, but sometimes forgotten):

1 Be familiar with your equipment and what it can do in what conditions and for how long (this applies not only to yourself but to anyone expected to use it).
2 Keep a checklist of what needs to be taken on each occasion (like spare batteries and cassettes).
3 Consider questions of secure storage and back-up copying for your recordings (using copies not originals for replaying, presenting, transcribing).
4 Both in choice of settings and items for recording, and in your management of the specifics of the setting (e.g., placement of microphones and lighting) remember local susceptibilities as well as your own research aims. Recording can be threatening or glamorising (or both) and your own reactions as well as those of the participants whom you are recording may make the occasion more emotive and selective than you had intended.
5 Remember that collectors don't own the events they record (and probably not the recording either: see 4.3.3 on permissions).
6 Learn from mistakes and don't let the equipment either dictate your priorities (or anyway not too often) or make you forget that ultimately you are interacting with people rather than machinery.

4.3.1 Different forms of recording

The differing media were discussed earlier, but is worth reviewing the main possibilities:

1 Written or taped summaries from memory (usually though not always by the researcher).
2 Dictation and semi-dictation (i.e., more, or less, full).
3 Writing by informants or assistants (this may or may not overlap with 1 and 2 above).

The above three, common in the past, are now often frowned on, specially given the current stress on performance. Certainly the idea that these represent primary documents, with no intervention from the medium of recording or the individuals involved in the process, is less often accepted nowadays. But provided this is remembered, these forms can be useful for certain purposes – and might in fact be the subject of research in their own right.

4 Audio: many forms now available and routinely used by field-workers for recording texts.
5 Video: great for some purposes, like documenting performance, usually not primarily used for verbal texts as such.
6 Existing sources (manuscript, print, recordings, radio, television): not always to be despised.

Finally, there may be other local institutions or activities which might be seen as forms of recording, even if very different from your own usage: for example a tradition of local manuscripts, plastic forms, dance, separately memorised verbal texts of songs, broadcasts, or local film or audio cassette industries. Whether or not you exploit these, being aware of them will put your own recordings in context by pointing up your processes of selection as comparable to or contrasting with local practices, and perhaps raising consequential questions about *which* textual aspects are regarded as the most significant and why.

4.3.2 Documenting specific recordings

Every researcher has probably had the experience of wishing later that the details so apparently unforgettable at the time had been recorded in some permanent and accessible form. Although this applies in all branches of research, keeping track of field-recorded items in the form of dictated texts and audio or video recordings raises some specific problems.

Missing a crucial detail at the time can never be fully avoided but a partial safeguard is to follow standard procedures developed by earlier researchers, modified, no doubt, to suit your own interests. These provide basic information for yourself and others, sharpen your awareness of features which might otherwise get omitted, and ensure that your records will be reasonably systematic for later analysis or deposit.

1) *Labelling*.   Tapes, film rolls, cassettes, texts, etc., need to be physically labelled in a systematic and permanent form. This normally includes some kind of serial number to enable easy cross-reference to related notes. Chronologically-based systems are popular; alternatively or additionally by place or person, provided these are systematic. There is also usually a brief title indicating subject, performer and (if relevant) person recording. It is amazing how easy it is to forget all this – and how infuriating and time-consuming when you do.

Some fieldworkers record some or all of this onto the tape itself before starting the recording proper. Although the circumstances of recording have to be considered (it may not be feasible or courteous), this can be effective, and on audio tape at least can be quicker and less obtrusive than a written note. Where conditions preclude this at the time, a brief description can be recorded later if a short section of tape is left blank.

2) *Logging*.   Many fieldworkers also keep a more detailed log with further information about the recordings, keyed to the serial numbers on the labels. This normally includes at least the first five of the following

1 Serial number (plus room for cross-reference to related commentary, transcription, translation, etc.).
2 Person doing the recording.
3 Date and time.
4 Summary description of contents (making clear whether any title is the performers' or the researcher's).
5 Name of performer(s) and/or group.
6 Nature of performance and (if applicable) instrumentation.
7 Number and nature of audience.
8 Equipment used.
9 Comments (a brief note on any special circumstances).

A pre-prepared proforma can be useful, specially if, as often, you need several copies of each entry; however, there are sometimes dangers in fixing this too soon if you are not yet sure what kind of recordings you will be making. Some such checklist as the above will probably cover the main information needed if you deposit your recordings in an archive, but if you know you will be doing this, checking on their format in advance might save time later.

This form of record is only a summary and loses its convenience if too much is inserted.

3) *Related commentary.* Background notes are also needed on the circumstances of the recording, the interaction between the participants and so on (keyed to the log). What goes into these depends on your interests and situation. Some fieldworkers recommend very full coverage, others just a basic minimum. However where recording is a serious part of the research, all or most of the following would be worth considering seriously:

Name and relevant details of the speaker(s)/participant(s).

When the recording was made, where and by whom (and perhaps with what equipment).

Who else was there and what was their role.

The occasion and purpose (from the participants' viewpoint).

The setting and the researcher's role.

Comments on any special circumstances during recording (explanation of background noises, problems with tape, demeanour of participants, etc.).

Comment on performance qualities, specially those not reproduced on the recording (e.g. gestures or dress for audio recordings, non-verbal elements for dictated texts).

Bruce Jackson's basic principle is worth thinking about:

What would [a complete stranger] need to know in order to be able to utilize fully the whole and the parts of your collection? Memory being what it is, and time going as fast as it does, that stranger may very well turn out to be you, coming back to the material several years from now for reasons you never expected or thought of back then when you were getting sore feet from all that walking.

(Jackson 1987: 245)

4.3.3 Permissions and releases

Informal personal interaction is often pictured as typical of anthropological fieldwork, so it may seem a betrayal to consider paperwork or official permissions. However, obtaining written releases from the participants for photographic, audio (and, later, video) recordings has been common practice among many folklorists researching in their own cultures. It could be asked whether this care should not be extended to material collected from people elsewhere too, and to written as well as audiovisual media. Further, the older model by which anthropologists 'left the field' and circulated their findings elsewhere with little responsibility to their original 'subjects' is now under challenge. Commercial exploitation of performances that, it could be argued, belong to the originators rather than the recorders has raised questions about intellectual property rights, and fieldworkers are now more conscious of the ethical dimensions of their research.

Obtaining formal releases at the time of recording is one strategy. Another view is that, as Paul Thompson argues, 'An insistence on a formal transfer of legal rights through explicit, written consent may not only worry an informant, but will actually reduce quite proper protection against exploitation' (1978/88: 225). Whatever

---

RELEASE
to (*ethnomusicologist's name*)

I hereby consent to your use, or the use of anyone you authorize, of my name and/or picture, or photograph of me, for the purpose of illustration and publication.

I hereby consent to the use of my picture or photograph for purposes of illustration and publication, but require that:

    _____ my name not be used

    _____ my facial features be disguised

        _____
        Date/Place

        _____
        Signature

Figure 4.1 Example of a release form (*source*: Herndon and McLeod 1983: 102)

your own position and that of your informants/colleagues, this question deserves some thought, if only because it is important to consider the wishes and expectations of the participants and not to make implicit or explicit promises that you will not be in a position to keep. (Figs 4.1 and 4.2 illustrate some of the factors that may need considering; for further discussion on permissions see Henige 1982: 114, Ives 1980: 43, 84–5, Jackson 1987: 269ff, Thompson 1988: 224ff; also 10.4).

4.4 PRELIMINARY PROCESSING

One common piece of advice, particularly if working in an unfamiliar language, is to make at least a rough translation and/or transcription of every text *before* leaving the field. This gives the opportunity to check with local participants and make a record while the material is fresh in your memory; the discipline of making even rough versions can also lead to questions which themselves stimulate further enquiries. There are also the contrary arguments that not every recording is worth transcribing or translating, and that it can be misleading to fix definitions onto your material too early. The processes of transcribing, translating and presenting texts from recordings in fact raise complex issues which will ultimately have to be faced in some detail (see chapter 9, also 10.4). However if you do decide to make preliminary versions for your own use – as is very likely – there are some practical points worth noting.

Even initial drafts are time-consuming and taxing activities. An audio recording may be quick to make, but transcribing one hour of tape can take anything from 6 or 8 hours to 15 or more depending on the material and your purposes in transcribing. You also need to devote some preliminary thought to the aims of your transcriptions or translations as these will affect which elements you emphasise, and in how much detail. Some practicalities will need organising too like using copies rather than originals for such processing, or writing on durable paper, with double spacing, good margins, and on one side only (saves a lot of trouble later). It is also easy to forget such things as keying the transcription or translation to the tape and related notes, making it clear when you are uncertain (e.g. by question marks, or pencil rather than pen), and leaving enough room for other commentary, translation, etc., to follow. It can also be helpful to include basic 'stage directions' and explanatory comments where relevant (clearly distinguished, e.g. by square brackets) to indicate gestures, voices off, differing speakers,

In consideration of the work the Northeast Archives of Folklore and Oral History is doing to collect and preserve material of value for the study of ways of life past and present in the New England-Maritimes area, I would like to deposit with them for their use the items represented by the accession number given below.

This tape or tapes and the accompanying transcripts are the result of one or more recorded voluntary interviews with me. Any reader of the transcript should bear in mind that he is reading a transcript of my spoken, not my written, word, and that the tape, not the transcript, is the primary document.

I desire to place the following restrictions on this material.

That no use of any kind whatsoever is to be made of this material until _____

After that time it is understood that the Northeast Archives of Folklore and Oral History will, at the discretion of the Director, allow qualified scholars to listen to the tapes and read the transcripts in connection with their research or for other educational purposes of a university. It is further understood that, after that time, no copies of any kind will be made of the tape or transcript, nor will anything be used from them in any published form without the written permission of the Director.

Signed: _____

Date: _____

Understood and agreed to:

Interviewer: _____ Date: _____

Director: _____ Date: _____

Accession number: _____

In consideration of the work the Northeast Archives of Folklore and Oral History is doing to collect and preserve material of value for the study of ways of life past and present in the New England-Maritimes area, I would like to deposit with them for their use the items represented by the accession number given below.

This tape or tapes and the accompanying transcripts are the result of one or more recorded voluntary interviews with me. Any reader should bear in mind that he is reading a transcript of my spoken, not written, word and that the tape, not the transcript, is the primary document.

It is understood that the Northeast Archives of Folklore and Oral History will, at the discretion of the Director, allow qualified scholars to listen to the tapes and read the transcript and use them in connection with their research or for other educational purposes of the university. It is further understood that no copies of the tapes or transcript will be made and nothing may be used from them in any published form without my written permission until _____ after which time the Director's written permission will be required.

Signed: _____

Date: _____

Understood and agreed to:

Interviewer: _____ Date: _____

Director: _____ Date: _____

Accession number: _____

Figure 4.2 Examples of release forms (*source:* Ives 1980: 113–14; reprinted by permission of the University of Tennessee Press): release form A is used when the informant wishes to 'close' the accession for some specific length of time – until the given date, no one may either listen to the tapes or examine the catalogs or transcripts thereof; release form B gives the Archives permission to let people listen to the tapes and examine the catalogs or transcripts, but it leaves control over publication and the making of copies with the informant.

inexplicable sounds or gaps, and so on – these may need noting at the time of recording.

Even in the initial stages it is worth taking some account of the problematic and decision-laden nature of text processing. This will affect all those working on the texts, so, though you will often want to get expert help on some points, the choice of assistants also needs to be undertaken carefully: local participants as much as others will have assumptions about the equivalences between languages or between spoken and written words, as well as about what *should* be on the tape. Interpretations by native speakers as by anyone else are not necessarily unloaded, and implicit definitions can have more influence than you at first realise. Similarly treat your own assumptions critically too, if only because it is easy to hear what isn't there, and vice versa.

This should not prevent you undertaking preliminary processing and making working copies for your own purposes. It does, however, mean you should regard these, or comparable efforts by other researchers, as provisional versions rather than final and definitive texts.

5 Observing and analysing performance

Performance is in a sense perhaps an element in every action, and certainly a concept of general interest within anthropology and elsewhere. While it is not possible to follow up all these aspects here, the idea and practice of performance does clearly have a particular import for oral expression, and is nowadays one major focus of research in verbal arts and traditions. The problems and opportunities this raises form the subject of this chapter.

5.1 CONCEPTS OF 'PERFORMANCE' AND THEIR SIGNIFICANCE

There are a number of overlapping ideas and theories here which are particularly relevant for work on verbal art and expression (see also 1.3.6, 2.4.10).

One influential approach is to take the idea of 'performance' as a fundamental key to human action and to culture, often centred round the concept of 'drama' (Turner 1982, Burke 1966, see also Hare and Blumberg 1988 and references below). This particular social theory – or metaphor – is not essential for the direct observation and analysis of specific performances, but sometimes forms the background to it.

Another viewpoint picks out performance as one *specific* (rather than general) mode of human communication and action, distinguishing this from 'merely' describing in a 'normal or everyday' manner. Thus particular acts of communication are somehow marked out as 'performance' by a heightened and framed quality. It is performance(s) in this – admittedly elusive – sense that many students of verbal arts take as their focus (see 5.3.1).

Some scholars further point to the relative rather than absolute nature of this mode. Performing can range from full-scale orchestrated programmes before an audience at some scheduled place and time, right through to the more or less impromptu telling of an anecdote during informal conversation or 'a fleeting breakthrough into performance, as when a child employs a new and esoteric word with peers as a gesture of linguistic virtuosity' (Bauman 1989a: 264).

> Thus conceived, performance is a mode of language use, a way of speaking. The implication of such a concept for a theory of verbal art is this: it is no longer necessary to begin with artful texts, identified on independent formal grounds and then reinjected into situations of use, in order to conceptualize verbal art in communicative terms. Rather . . . performance becomes *constitutive* of the domain of verbal art as spoken communication.
>
> (Bauman 1977a: 11)

This approach, like that of other performance-centred scholars, highlights interaction between individual artistry and cultural expectations. It also encourages researchers to explore the (relative) processes of performing in particular situations, and local ideas and practices relating to this.

'Performance' is also used to refer to a concrete event in time: another sphere for investigation, which in recent years has extended beyond just a general look at performance attributes and settings to focus more directly on the communicative event itself. Questions for investigation thus include how or where performances take place as actual events; how they are organised and prepared for; who is there, how they behave and what their expectations are; how the performers deliver the specific genre and the audience react to it; how it is framed within and/or separate from the flow of everyday life.

'Performance' is, furthermore, often used to refer to the *actual* execution or practice of communication (as distinct from its potential, or its abstract formulation in knowledge or grammar) – a usage which fits with current interests among anthropologists, folklorists, sociolinguists and others in 'practice' and 'processes', or in 'speech acts'. While this distinction is in principle applicable to all forms of verbal communication it has a particular relevance – and set of problematics – in the study of oral forms. Performance seems essential for oral forms to be actualised at all – a significant contrast, on the face of it anyway, with the permanent and autonomous existence of a written text independent of its (merely contingent) performances.

This has consequences for the study of oral arts and tradition.

Performance in this sense has to be taken seriously as an intrinsic constituent of oral expression. It is a small step to seeing the mode, characteristics and circumstances of performance as needing to lie at the heart of any analysis. Questions then open up about whether or in what sense oral forms can be regarded as 'existing' apart from their actual utterance. If western models of the independently-existing text are inappropriate what, if any, model *can* we turn to? Is there *no* sense in which oral texts continue independent of performance?

There is also the related concept of performance as something complementary to, and opposed to, the script (or score or text): a familiar concept for the performing arts as perhaps for rituals more generally. With written scripts this relationship looks relatively clear, but raises different questions when the score, not just the performance, is unwritten. In what sense does it exist independently and what are its links with performance? How is the text of a particular story (to some extent known and shared – or is it?) related to its specific performances? What are the local concepts of this relationship – if any? Which if either is believed to have priority, and how far do such beliefs correspond to actual behaviour?

These various senses and theories differ as well as overlap, but between them have created much more serious attention than before to questions of performance, however exactly that is to be defined. This has had its effect in several areas of humanistic study, and is particularly developed in the study of oral arts and traditions. The following can serve as a summary checklist of the general research implications to which this bundle of 'performance' approaches more, or less, tends to lead:

1 Meaning and artistry emerge in performance: this means attention not just to words but also to how they are delivered: such elements as intonation, speed, rhythm, tone, dramatisation, rhetorical devices, and performance techniques generally.
2 Part of the reality lies in the interaction with, or behaviour of, *all* the participants, including the audience and its expectations, perhaps the researcher too: all important factors to explore.
3 The definition and meaning of particular oral genres may depend not just on verbal stylistics but also on *non*-verbal features such as music, gesture, dance or visual attributes like costume: these features too need investigation.
4 Oral forms are realised through performances carried out and

mediated by people (rather than existing 'independently'): thus the interaction of individual artistry and cultural conventions is another matter for investigation.

5 The context of the performance (including the organisation of the event and the participants within it) may be central rather than peripheral to its meaning.

The observation and analysis of these and similar topics – delivery arts, audience participation, communicative styles and registers, social organisation, local perceptions of performance – lead to different, if complementary, insights from the traditional textual analyses pursued by scholars who by choice or necessity are dealing with written texts. Following up performance opens up new questions for investigation which, though obvious once raised, have often been ignored in the past under the influence of the model of human communication which assumes some super-existent status for verbal texts independent of performance.

While clearly of prime interest for those particularly interested in the analysis of oral performance(s) as such, these questions are also relevant for those concerned with content, meaning or textual style. Knowing the characteristics or occasion(s) of delivery or of audience perception gives a new dimension to the explication of texts. Even for archive texts, where live observation is no longer possible, certain properties of their original performance can sometimes be deduced. At the least such questions draw attention to a gap in knowledge that may stimulate critical reassessment of hitherto dogmatic conclusions.

(For further discussion of performance generally see Abrahams 1968a, 1981b, Bauman 1977a, 1989a,b (particularly drawn on here) Béhague 1989, Bauman and Briggs 1990; also discussion or examples in Schechner 1988, Schechner and Appel 1990, Hymes 1975b, Ben-Amos and Goldstein 1975, Kapferer 1986, R.M. Stone 1982, Finnegan 1989a: chap. 12, Toelken 1979: chap. 3, Turner 1982. For the relevance of performance for written literature see Iser 1975, B.H. Smith 1978.)

5.2 AUDIENCES, PERFORMERS, PARTICIPANTS

Chief among the components of any performance are the human participants. These must therefore be among the prime targets of the enquirer's attention. Though often starting with performers (the familiar western focus), the investigation must also embrace those other participants whose roles supplement or overlap with those of the apparent leaders.

5.2.1 Performers

There are several straightforward questions to investigate. One concerns the performers' actions within the performance. They may be acting singly; in pairs; in a small or a large group; interacting or exchanging with other single or collective performers as leader, follower, or equal; overlapping or interchanging with more audience-like roles. (Such a list may seem too obvious to mention – except that such information is often lacking in published reports.) There are also questions about how performers carry out their role(s): relying mainly on words and gestures, or also exploiting music or dance; purporting to deliver works by others (human or supernatural); creative or otherwise in the sense of composing during or before performance; and so on.

Performers are also of certain ages, gender, social position, training, reputation, and competence – all needing investigation. There is also the simple but important fact (in the past often ignored) that they have names, individual personalities and life histories. Some are highly-acclaimed experts, set apart from others by their profession and esoteric knowledge; others in no striking way different from members of their audiences; others again anywhere between these two. And not only these outward facts but also their local significance needs to be noted: in some cultures or genres a performer's age or name may be of little moment, in others crucial. The relationship of the performers to the general artistic division of labour, their economic position, or their place in the social hierarchy too may be significant for the performance and its local meaning in the large sense of the term. At the very least they form the background to any full understanding of the performance and its expected conventions (see also 6.2).

A further practical question also arises. Who should be classified as performers and in what sense, whether in assessing local art forms and traditions, thinking about performance skills, or making recordings?

Anyone able to give a reasonably connected and coherent performance might at first sight seem equally acceptable. But it cannot just be assumed (as such a conclusion might imply) that a given culture is homogeneous, that there is no artistic or cognitive division of labour, nor that texts have some single verbal form unaffected by the status, expertise or individuality of the person who performs them. It is surprising how often this point too has been neglected – perhaps because of the older image of verbal art and oral tradition as somehow existing independently of current social and political processes, and expressing communal tradition. But all the usual questions of anthropological research still need to be asked. For example, does the culture distinguish between expert performers and more amateur or ordinary ones? And if so, which is it in a given context and how does this affect the research? Is there any distinction between 'active' and 'passive traditors' and if so which have you got? Are some art forms or traditions the preserve of particular social categories? Are some individuals or groups thought better or more knowledgeable than others?

There are also more searching questions. The pre-eminent part in a performance is usually taken to be that played by 'the performer(s)' and this role has certainly attracted by far the most attention. But precisely for this reason it has also been taken for granted in ways which now need to be looked at more critically. The 'performer-as-primary: audience-as-secondary' model which has underpinned most recordings and publications of oral art/tradition is only one schema, for performers can interact, overlap or even coincide with other participants in many differing ways. It may be near-impossible to distinguish 'performer' clearly from 'audience' – a problem many studies slide over without mention.

The image of a single leading performer whose actions are the central focus for observation and recording is also related to the univocal or one-line model of verbal communication. This may be appropriate for written forms. But the words and actions of just one person (the 'author', the 'lead performer') are seldom the only component of any oral performance. Not only are meanings formed through the face-to-face interaction of several people (perhaps bringing different interests or understandings to bear), they are also often created through the active participation of several performers. Transcription and analysis has usually privileged just one of these as 'the' performer, screening out others. Whether or not this particular individual does indeed have the primary status in the performance needs to be investigated rather than – as is more usual – just assumed.

Merely describing someone as 'the author', 'the performer', 'the narrator', etc., is therefore not enough, for complex interactions and problems lie behind these simple-sounding terms. And since one of the most important points is to be alive to the interaction or the overlap between those in performing and those in more audience-type roles the complementary actions of other participants too must be taken into account – to be discussed in the next section.

5.2.2 Audiences and participants

The degree and form of participation – and of being an 'audience' – is a relatively neglected topic which repays detailed investigation. The following list indicates some differing relations between performer(s) and other participants, not as definitive categories – for they overlap – merely to open up some possible variations and challenge simplified distinctions between 'audience' and 'performer'.

1 *Clear distinction between audience and performers* (for example western concerts or Japanese No plays). This may be marked by a physical separation (the 'proscenium arch', separate stage), or by its symbolic equivalent or parallel. The role of the audience can still vary and thus need investigating (compare audience behaviour at a classical concert with that at a pantomime or rock event) but is basically conceived as separate from the performers.

2 *Audience and performers relatively separate, but without the clear barrier of* 1. The audience still takes little or no formal part in the sense of delivering any of the text, but may influence it by its presence and reactions, enough perhaps to affect not only the manner of delivery but the formulation of the text itself, as in the South Slavic epic performances described by Lord 1960 (for similar examples see Finnegan 1977: 54–5).

3 *General separation between audience and performers, but with some active contributions by those who otherwise perform an audience role*. The listeners may, for example, join in singing during stories or religious rituals, or utter arranged interjections (as by the 'replier' in Limba story-telling, Finnegan 1967: 67f). This can comprise a kind of 'secondary' performance. Such relations can be complex, and it may need careful enquiry to establish the local views and behaviour.

4 *Active participation by different participants in different roles or at different times*. A sequence of performers may come forward in turn to tell stories, or make speeches. Such participants are clearly distinguished from the audience while actually performing but at other stages take the role of audience, or, as described in Dégh and Vázsonyi (1976: 108), engage in counterpoint parts within the 'polyphonic' structure of legend-telling sessions.

5 *Little or no separation between 'audience' and 'performers'*, as in choral singing or joint declamation during rituals. There are likely to be complexities worth exploring within this at first sight simple-sounding category – which might in the past have been dubbed 'communal' and left at that – for even in such situations there are degrees in the amount or intensity of participation (certain people may be accepted leaders even if everyone present is more or less taking part, for example in the 'call and response' lyrics so common in Africa). Festival and carnival events are perhaps further examples where there may be not only mixed genres but also a great deal of *joint* activity to be studied (Abrahams 1985a, Babcock-Abrahams 1974, Bakhtin 1968). Joint participation may comprise one phase of a wider performance or take place in such a manner that other performers may also be a kind of audience at the same time as performing.

6 *Solitary performance with no apparent audience.* Rhythmic work songs while grinding corn or paddling a boat are instances of this, singing or declaiming while walking on one's own, or personal songs while herding cattle. Some might argue that absence of audience means that these are not 'real performance'. They may still be illuminating however in their contrast or comparison with 'full performance'. Sometimes too the 'same' songs *are* performed to an audience, and there may also be senses in which there is an actual or imagined secondary audience (see below).

5.2.3 Some other classifications of audiences

Looking at audiences in terms of their participation and/or differentiation from the 'performer' is not the only way of assessing their roles. Other proposed classifications include:

1 *Primary versus secondary audiences.* The overt audience may be of one kind, but there may also be others attending (or eavesdropping) in a different capacity. Sometimes this is the performers' intention, as when political songs are secretly directed to supporters while the supposed official audience take the words at their (misleading) face value; alternatively a group's songs can be apparently performed for one audience but deliberately meant as protest or comment to bystanders. The overt presence of a researcher, perhaps known to be making a recording, could be another example of secondary audience; so too could be the potential future audience which some performers have in mind

while making a tape-recording for example. Again, apparently solitary or small-group songs like laments may in fact be widely audible and known to be so, specially with outdoor performance. In such cases both kinds of audiences – or more – need investigating, and how people move between them (for further examples see Finnegan 1977: 221–2).

There is also the complex situation where some participants give fuller attention whereas others attend only partially, or only at certain points. Toelken speaks of the 'bystander audience' ('bystanders, tourists, paying customers', 1979: 108). Only partial attention is difficult to investigate – but it would be misleading to take ideal values (our own or others') as evidence that everyone is in practice equally attentive or shares the same expectations (on 'selective inattention' see Schechner 1988: 196ff).

2 *Integral versus accidental audience.* This distinction also brings out the variety of roles an audience may play, for, as Schechner puts it (1988: 193), 'the audience is not an either/or stagnant lump'. This overlaps the primary/secondary distinction, but lays more emphasis on the purposes of, and connections between, audiences. Schechner explains the difference through the example of theatrical performances:

> An accidental audience is a group of people who, individually or in small clusters, go to the theater – the performances are publically advertised and open to all. On opening nights of commercial shows the attendance of the critics and friends constitutes an integral rather than an accidental audience. An integral audience is one where people come because they have to or because the event is of special significance to them. Integral audiences include the relatives of the bride and groom at a wedding, the tribe assembled for initiation rites, dignitaries on the podium for an inauguration.
>
> (1988: 194)

As Schechner points out, 'artistic communities' develop integral audiences of 'people who know each other, are involved with each other, support each other' – or in some cases integral 'anti-audiences . . . who come especially to heckle or attack' (195). The two categories are not exclusive, for any one performance may include people from each of them.

3 *Homogeneous versus heterogeneous audiences.* This is perhaps a non-distinction for an audience is never fully homogeneous (unless an audience of one) but always includes different indi-

viduals and thus different interests and viewpoints. As Perelman and Olbrechts-Tyteca point out, not only may the audience itself be composite, but each listener may 'simultaneously belong to a number of disparate groups' (1969: 22), with different interests in play at different points. However, some audiences are *more* heterogeneous than others so the degree of homogeneity becomes another component for investigation.

4 *Mass or impersonal versus personal audiences*: again a relative rather than absolute distinction. Even the apparent extremes, like audiences for broadcasts in a large-scale society as against live performances by local performers to friends or relatives, need investigation as to how they work out in practice. How far are performers and audiences known to each other personally both inside and outside the specific performance, or at different points during it? Do their expectations and actions affect the actual meanings of even apparently impersonal performances (even mass media research now takes note of the constructive input of audiences)?

(For further comments on audiences and audience participation see Perelman and Olbrechts-Tyteca 1969: 17ff, Finnegan 1977: 214ff, Schechner 1988: 193ff; also below 5.3.5.)

5.3 OTHER COMPONENTS OF PERFORMANCES

Observing and analysing performance(s) clearly involves more than just listing the presence and actions of those participating. But its further study is not altogether straightforward, partly because this interest has been relatively undeveloped till recently compared to textual analysis, partly because of the unlimited number of possible components in performance given the variety of cultural, historical and generic conventions and the varying ways these are deployed. There are however some recurrent elements which it has proved illuminating to enquire into. The categories below may provide a preliminary stimulus.

5.3.1 Situation, 'framing' and organisation of performance

Performances take place in many kinds of situation, from highly organised and planned to quite informal or impromptu. It is important to be alert to this variety rather than just presupposing one model (most likely projected from personal preconceptions). The kinds of factor which often repay investigation include:

Time, place and spacing
Mode of 'framing' and organising
Participants and their behaviour
Local evaluation

Their combinations make up a complex series of continua rather than a single scale, but some provisional categories are:

1 *A differentiated and planned event* such as a concert or a festival. Such events are likely to have specific features (well summarised in Bauman 1989a: 265): scheduled (i.e. planned and organised in advance); temporally and spatially bounded; programmed, with a structured scenario or ordering; coordinated as a public occasion for people to come together and participate; recognised as a heightened occasion, often with formalised and elaborate artful performances set apart from the 'everyday'.

These properties are always worth enquiring into – as, too, are their apparent absence. The organising probably has precursors and follow-up, sometimes on a cyclical basis, so needs investigation beyond the temporal bounds of the event itself. Related questions concern who organises the events and in what capacity, how times and places are arranged, the degree(s) and conditions of temporal bounding, in what sense the events are 'public', and the structure and organisation of audiences. How events are 'framed' (to follow the terminology often used by performance analysts, following such writers as Goffman and, earlier, Huizinga) is another set of questions. This may include the features listed above, but there may also be specific markers such as music (or particular kinds of music); costume or other display and visual attributes; locale or spatial arrangements; mode of behaviour by various participants; the register or artfulness of the language used; and local terminology.

2 *Performance during some wider ritual or ceremonial occasion.* This overlaps with the previous, but can be broadly distinguished as not so 'staged' in its own right, but one element in a wider event. This is a common context for performance. Examples include songs or speeches during a wedding ceremony, or praise poetry at parties or court occasions. Laments too – for even when they are in one sense 'impromptu', individual lamenting often forms one recognised stage in a longer ritual sequence.

These performances too may be prepared for and accepted as artful and heightened forms. Many of the same questions as in the previous category can therefore be asked, together with what role it plays within the ceremony, how it is regarded, and how temporal or spatial boundaries are treated.

3 *Recognised contexts for the performance of verbal art or enunciation of oral traditions which are nevertheless more an accompaniment than the central focus of the occasion.* There is a whole range of such occasions, potentially perhaps the whole gamut of cultural activities, from songs accompanying dancing or repetitive work to 'background' singing or speech-making. Though shading into other categories, this is worth distinguishing in that it leads towards further questions about how far (if at all) such performances are regarded as artistic, in what sense they too are framed or heightened (or, indeed, attended to – and by whom), how they are organised (a 'natural' and spontaneous impression may conceal a degree of deliberate structuring), and the role of time and space conventions.

4 *Relatively impromptu and informal performances in some sense recognised as special and with some concept of boundedness*: another wide category, from funny stories in conversational setting (often extremely artful performances), to impromptu recitals or the interchange of songs in an evening gathering. Such performances are not pre-planned in the style of the previous categories, but are nevertheless not unexpected – indeed participants may in some sense prepare themselves or their settings for them. They may also have their own delivery conventions and means for introducing and (specially) for ending, as well as for audience participation.

5 *Performances embedded in other interactions and produced informally, with little or no overt planning and/or boundaries.* This applies particularly to conversational genres and modes of verbal expression like proverbs, rhetorical devices, word play in the course of conversation. The apparent informality and openness can conceal conventions which it may be interesting to explore, as are local assessments of such performances and their skills.

In all these cases (but perhaps particularly the less formalised ones) it is worth being alert to verbal features which (often of course in conjunction with other auditory or visual cues) frequently mark out utterances as in some sense 'performance'. Bauman usefully lists such recurrrent elements as: special codes; figurative language; parallelism; special paralinguistic features; special formulae; appeal to tradition; disclaimer of performance (Bauman 1977a: 16; see also 8.4 on verbal style).

These categories shade into each other, particularly if one takes the sense of performance as one aspect of action and expression rather than a specific event. They therefore provide the start rather than the end of the investigation. Apparent 'exceptions' and 'problem' cases will be especially worth enquiring into (for example the artful but in a sense unbounded Yoruba *oríkì* performances in Barber 1989). It is important to be alive to the recurrent but differing patterns, for it is otherwise easy to fall into the facile assumption either that there is nothing to investigate, or that the framework of performance is inevitably of only one or at most two kinds, the most favoured models being the differentiated 'artistic' or 'entertainment' event or, alternatively, the 'communal' rituals supposedly typical of 'primitive society'. In practice there is far more variety.

5.3.2 Internal organisation

This is an extension of the previous questions, but emphasises the internal programme of performances. The expected sequencing is often a significant component of generic conventions which needs noting even if (perhaps particularly if) part of the art concerned is to *play* with or manipulate that expected programme. This applies to 'festival' and composite as well as single-performer events (for further discussion see Toelken 1979: 129ff).

5.3.3 Performance media

Until recently most interest in oral traditions and the verbal arts has focused on verbal communication, with the spotlight on the principal speaker of the words. Verbal channels are of course important. But, even if the prime concern is only to understand the words fully, let alone a performance as a whole, other communication media too may need attention. These are noted below, with the proviso that while it is convenient to separate them as an *aide-mémoire* there are overlaps and continuities both in theoretical terms and in practical application (how and whether such distinctions are observed could itself be a question for research).

Since the 'main' performer has so often formed the centre of observation and analysis, it may need a special effort to remember also to document the use (or non-use) of all or any of these channels by the other participants too.

1) *Acoustic*

a) *Verbal.* The most obvious acoustic medium in the context of oral performance is indeed that of words (though in some traditions words might seem to be equally or better classifiable among visual media). In the context of performance, however, there is more to words than just the voiced equivalent of written forms. Where and when they are pronounced, by whom and why may be highly significant for the meaning or quality of performance. This of course applies to all media in performance, but is somehow easier to forget with words. *How* they are delivered can transform the meaning and impact of the 'same' words almost out of all recognition. 'Oral performance has pauses, stress, pitch', as Chimombo puts it of Malawian performed narratives (1988: 46), or, to take the summary statement by Sherzer and Woodbury:

> The use of basic features of the voice is totally unique to the creation of oral text, manifesting itself in the use of pauses, pitch, and tempo, and the imitation of human and nonhuman voices and noises.
>
> (1987: 10)

Both formulations sound simple, but refer to crucial and too often unnoticed elements of oral performance.

There is much to be investigated here. Some aspects are straightforward: the formal medium in relation to the use of, for example, the speaking, chanting, wailing or singing voice and their variations; other auditory forms used for delivering words (such as drums or whistles); the verbal interactions between chorus, individual singer(s), and other participants. More difficult to document but equally important is how the words in a story or a song are presented. Their tempo; volume; dynamics; emphasis; timbre; dramatic quality; intonational patterns; vocal weighting; prosodic features, including rhythm, parallelism, rhyme or tonal patterning; play on different registers or accents; forms of onomatopoeia (including ideophones, so effectively used in African narrative performances); alternation of words and silence – all these and more are integral rather than merely marginal facets of the words in performance.

Such auditory aspects of verbal performance have received minimal attention by scholars compared to the denotative or grammatical properties of words. However there has been increasing interest in such topics and several works which can be consulted for examples (D. Tedlock 1971, 1972, 1977, 1983; Sherzer and Woodbury

1987: 103ff, Finnegan 1967: esp 77ff, and, on ideophones, 1970: 64–6, 71–2, 384–5; see also discussion on music below, and, on presentation of texts, 9.3).

b) *Musical features.* The varied forms of musical setting or accompaniment for oral art and tradition are in part a specialist subject of their own. Music however is so often an aspect of oral performance that it cannot just be dismissed as marginal or belonging to some 'other' discipline. Researchers into oral forms may thus need to note the role played within performance of various instrumental combinations (including the various modes of the human voice); playing style; deployment of volume, tempo, dynamics, and timbre; the intersection of text and tune; and sound symbolism (for further discussion and examples see Karpeles 1958, Merriam 1964: 187ff, Herndon and McLeod 1983, Feld 1982, Seeger 1986, and such periodicals as *Ethnomusicology, Popular Music* and *Yearbook of Traditional Music*, also 7.2.1; for cooperative work between anthropologists or linguists on the one hand and ethnomusicologists on the other see Firth 1990, Innes 1974).

c) *Other acoustic elements.* Other non-verbal – but still auditory – effects also need noting. Some genres have coughs, pauses, sobs, shouts, or other non-verbal interjections. There may also be sound effects by performers or audiences like tapping time, clapping, clicking fingers; perhaps seeming merely fortuitous, but in some cases an expected convention.

2) *Visual and material*

Visual elements can also be important, in some cases part of the definition of the genre, in others a valued aspect of good performances.

Some common components are: colours; costume, dress, hair, jewellery; other accoutrements and equipment (sceptre, wand, animals, etc.); musical instruments; spatial arrangements (see also on proxemics, below); sign systems; local symbolisms relating to visual or material objects such as a temple, icon, flag, sculpture. There may be recognised links between visual or material signs and spoken performance, as in visual representations linked to Indian epics, South Pacific string figures/stories, Australian sand drawings, mediaeval stories in verbal *and* visual media, written words and symbols, and illustrations in books designed to be read aloud. Links between oral performances and physical texts are sometimes important, like the ceremonial handling of manuscripts during Old Slavonic church singing, or the audience consultations of written copies during Japanese No plays.

Such aspects may seem extraneous to the 'central' verbal component but may in fact be an expected part of the performed art form and fortunately are, now, becoming of greater interest to anthropologists. And even where they in some sense supplement rather than constitute the performance they may still be significant. It could be argued that some cultures, as in East Asia or the South Pacific, and some genres lay greater emphasis than others on the visual and material aspects in performances (Finnegan and Orbell 1990: 175–6, Carrier 1990); or, on the other, that such interactions are in fact more significant in western cultures than sometimes recognised (on the interactions of verbal/visual languages see the journal *Word and Image*, and, for further discussion of visual and artifactual elements, Fine 1984: 118ff; on visual anthropology generally see references in 3.3.3).

3) *Kinesic and proxemic*

The term 'kinesics' draws attention to the importance of communication expressed in body language, gesture, facial expression, and other forms of non-verbal expression involving movement. Proxemics is closely related to this, being concerned with spatial relationships. Such components are often integral to performance but tend to be elusive to record, both because of the absence of a standard language for documenting them and because they are sometimes below the level of consciousness. However for the purposes of a practical checklist, important elements to note include:

a) *Local body language and its conventions*. These may not be confined just to framed performance and be more explicitly developed in some cultures than others.

b) *Specific movements*, such as gestures or facial expressions, used as part of performance art and expression, often but not always overlapping with those of 'ordinary' communication. This sometimes reaches the level of a specially developed and expert form, specifically in dance (on ways of representing these through e.g. photographs, film or special notations, see 9.3.3).

c) *Proxemics*: cultural conventions concerning nearness, distance and placing (see Fine 1984: 131ff, E.T. Hall 1966, 1974, Goffman 1971; on kinesics more generally see Birdwhistell 1970, Kendon 1981, 1989, Blacking 1977, Brandon-Sweeney 1972/3, Moore and

Yamamoto 1988, Poyatos 1983, Scherer and Ekman 1982; on dance Spencer 1985, Blacking and Kealiinohomoku 1979).

4) *The senses*

The list of communication channels above, no doubt based on western perceptions, does not cover everything. Taste and feel seldom enter into western scholarly analysis, so it needs a special effort to enquire about the possible role of tactile or olfactory channels, indeed *all* the senses in performance (see Fine 1984: 133, Stoller 1989; also, on multi-sensory approaches to aesthetics, Feld 1988, Moyo 1986, Tedlock and Tedlock 1986; on the anthropology of the emotions, Lutz and White 1986, Lutz and Abu-Lughod 1990).

5.3.4 Performance skills and conventions

A full account of this huge subject would quickly lead outside anthropology (in the narrow sense) to such fields of study as dance and body notation; specialist work in kinesics, non-verbal communication, and proxemics; and psychological studies of personal interaction. Some will want to follow up these wider fields, but at the least some minimal attention to such aspects should be possible for anyone with some interest in oral expression as performance.

The first point is that performance skills and conventions may exploit any or all of the channels of communication discussed in the last section, so all of these should be considered. This needs saying, since the long dominance of scriptist models means that non-verbal elements have received less attention than content or words. Fortunately audio-video technologies for capturing performance qualities have helped to supplement older methods and made non-verbal performance techniques more visible.

Second, whatever the details there will always be *some* performance skills and conventions to record. It is true that local conventions sometimes seem to place little emphasis on individual flamboyance. The Rwanda historical reciter, for example, might seem at first sight to be lacking performance skills:

> Contrairement à l'amateur, qui gesticule du corps et de la voix, le récitant professional adope une attitude impassible, un débit rapide et monotone. Si l'auditoire réagit en riant ou en exprimant son admiration pour un passage particulièrement brillant, il suspend la voix avec détachement jusqu'à le silence soit rétabli.
>
> (Coupez and Kamanzi 1962: 8)

But the point, of course, is that his art lies precisely in conforming to *this* performance convention – one which has to be learnt. Such conventions are as important to note as the more dramatic skills of other cultures or genres, and apparently 'negative' features may turn out to have positive significance.

The form of the delivery often turns out to convey much of the meaning. Indications of time and place, for example, of atmosphere, humour, foreboding, irony, paradox, allegory and so on and so on can be conveyed in performance without needing words. So too with the communication of characterisation or of individuals' inner feelings, where it is sometimes thought that oral forms are deficient in contrast to the explicit exposition of written literature: these can in fact be directly represented through the dramatic art of the performer, often through the use of such techniques as direct speech, gestures, or dramatisation:

> The characterization may seem to the reader of African oral narratives to be flat, undeveloped. But this is a problem for the reader, not one for the member of the audience during the actual production. The performer is himself the characters, he gives them life and fullness, and his *body* gives them dimension. He need not tell in any verbal way how his characters looked or frowned or laughed or grimaced, because he is himself doing all this.
>
> (Scheub 1971:31, cf Finnegan 1967: 52)

The application or otherwise of these or similar features of performance are always worth enquiring about. They cannot, however, just be assumed in advance, for performance skills and conventions vary between cultures, historical periods, and genres, as well as in the ways they are deployed in different situations or by different categories of performer.

Oral performances usually involve several participants in varying roles so delivery skills and performance conventions will probably not be confined to the 'frontman'. Even the most apparently passive 'audiences' may be deploying learned conventions of audience skill which play a crucial role in a successful performance (see Finnegan 1989: chap. 12, Stone 1982: 29–30, Blacking 1973). This particularly applies to multi-performer situations or actively participating audiences, like those in many African story-telling performances.

Another question to investigate is the amount of 'variation' or 'embellishment' allowed within particular genres or to individual performers, for it cannot be assumed that all performers or performances are uniform. Putting it this way perhaps suggests a model of 'text' as basic, 'performance' as contingent – so this assumption too would need to be investigated in the light of local practices and perceptions.

Audio and/or video recordings might seem to solve the problems of the observation of the multi-faceted arts of performance and their documentation for later analysis. This was well foreshadowed in an early account of Lamba story-tellers' performances:

> It would need a combination of phonograph and kinematograph to reproduce a tale as it is told . . . . Every muscle of face and body spoke, a swift gesture often supplying the place of a whole sentence . . . . The animals spoke each in its own tone: the deep rumbling voice of Momba, the ground hornbill, for example, contrasting vividly with the piping accents of Sulwe, the hare.
> (Smith and Dale 1920: vol. 2: 336)

Certainly by now few scholars would embark on a serious study of performance without making at least some audio recordings (and in some cases video/film too). However these present problems as well as opportunities, and audio-video recordings can be problematic in capturing at once too little and too much. Any one recording (specially video) is inevitably selective: if the performer(s) is being recorded, the audience cannot be (or at any rate not so fully); and if the audience, *which* members? Because the performance event has apparently been thoroughly captured in the recording – perhaps after some difficulty in the case of video – it is tempting to assume that one therefore has captured it all. A second danger is of recordings becoming ends in themselves, cutting off rather than leading to analysis. In the context of the study of performance, such recordings are the illustrative vehicles for its analysis and investigation, rather than themselves constituting that analysis (see also 3.3.3).

5.3.5 Performance as the interaction of many participants

There are many different forms of interaction between the participants in a performance – the actors, that is, in both 'performing' and 'audience' roles. It is thus hazardous to generalise about this interaction; there is for example no such entity as '*the* oral audience'. There will always however be *some* such interaction in the context of the dynamics of any performance, and a number of questions to investigate.

The various participants and their actions mould the performance.

This may be true even with remote mass audiences, but is even more obviously so with live performance. Xhosa narrations partly depend on the listeners filling the (apparent) gaps in the narrator's exposition (Scheub 1971), Yoruba narrative-performances on the performer's 'manipulation of audience emotion' (Sekoni 1990: 145), and Limba story-telling on the audience's role in taking up – and thus helping to create and intensify – the atmosphere of humour, scandal, horror, philosophic comment, irony or tragedy by their exclamations, gestures, or emotive reactions (Finnegan 1967, see also Okpewho 1990: 160ff). These and similar interactions need investigating in their own right and may mean challenging traditional definitions of 'the audience' as separate from, and inferior to, the 'performer' or 'author'.

The traditional western model of the performer as dominant implies that, provided that a performer *has* performed, the performance has been successfuly realised. But in any given case this may need questioning, if only because the lead performer's actual (or presumed) aims may not be the whole story. It cannot be presumed, either, that those labelled 'audiences' from one viewpoint always consider themselves so in every sense, and the relations between participants may not be smooth or straightforward. There may be 'flaws' in audience–performer interactions or 'risks in verbal art performance', as Yankah has it (1985), and relative failures in engaging a group into an 'audience' role. Similarly it is worth questioning how far the behaviour of those present is always consciously directed to an 'audience role' or perceived in the same terms as the performer's, and whether questions of control may be as relevant as 'pure' artistic shaping (see for example Bennett 1990). Furthermore performance may be relative process rather than absolute unit, and may emerge not from some prior plan but also in and through the event itself – another reason for considering the interactions of all participants (and at different phases in the action too), and not just the definitions of outside analysts or of only certain parties in the transaction.

It could be argued against this emphasis on the dynamic interactions within a performance, that verbal expression conveys cognitive messages as well as affective meaning, and that for the former the verbal text should be primary. But this meaning itself may be constructed through the interaction of all the participants in a performance – and quite likely a plurality of meanings for this very reason. There are of course controversies here, not least about the nature of 'meaning', but one widely-held view would be that there

can be no real meaning without interchange between several participants, where in one sense an audience has the last word. As Perelman and Olbrecht-Tyteca argue in their study of rhetoric: 'It is
indeed the audience which has the major role in determining the
quality of argument and the behavior of orators' (1969: 24, see also
14ff).

Conventions of audience composition and behaviour thus need
noting, together with the dynamics through which these are
expressed (for some examples see Béhague 1989: 115, Finnegan
1989: chap. 12). Even the apparent *absence* of physical participation
by listeners or observers is worth attention, for this too affects the
performance, moulded as it no doubt is by shared conventions
about how participants should act or about what a performance is
and should be. So too is the question of how far such conventions
are followed, or whether they are contested by certain groups or
individuals: disruptions can be illuminating too.

Any full account of performance, therefore, needs to take
account of the many participants involved and their interactions –
not just the 'star' performer or the 'obvious' audience but also all
the other roles and contributions (including the apparent 'interruptions' or lapses that tend to be screened out in traditional textual
and performer-oriented models) and how they change or are re-
defined over time. Only with this full understanding can the actu-
ality of oral performances be appreciated.

This applies most obviously to the observation of oral performance in the field. But it can also be useful to remember in studying
archive texts too, in some ways chiming in illuminatingly with recent
literary theory. John Miles Foley puts this interestingly, in the
context of intertextuality in mediaeval texts:

> I like to think of the 'formulas' and 'themes' of a narrative poetry
> . . . not as necessary evils for the poor oral dullard, or as simply
> generic stop-gaps with boiled-down 'essential ideas', but rather
> as highly echoic *metonyms* that comprise a referential code. . . .
> By a special kind of synecdoche, each phrase or scene or tale-
> type or 'flat character' reaches out actively into the audience's
> experience to enlarge the present moment, to fill it with life, to
> convey meaning not properly present in the physical text at all.
>
> (1988b: 478)

6 Production, functions and ideas

Any cultural product needs to be set in its wider social and economic context for full understanding – including how it is produced, transmitted and supported. In a way this whole book is about such questions, for social processes underlie every stage of the creation and analysis of oral tradition and the verbal arts, and the possible lines of enquiry about them are endless. This chapter does not attempt to cover them all but merely draws attention, in the briefest possible terms, to some specific questions. The aim is to indicate variants and problems in what might otherwise be assumed to be self-evident, rather than provide a comprehensive account of these subjects.

6.1 COMPOSITION, TRANSMISSION AND MEMORY

Composing, transmitting and remembering are often held to be key processes in oral tradition and the verbal arts. They are treated separately here (and have often been kept apart in the literature), but a full ethnographic analysis would eventually need to bring them together and elucidate their interactions.

6.1.1 Transmission and circulation

Transmission has long been a central idea in studies of oral forms. Older approaches often rested on searching for origins of various kinds or, as in the historical-geographical method, tracing the paths of particular stories. There are also long-standing arguments about the mechanisms of transmission (on whether, for example, certain forms are 'degenerating' or developing, filtering down or rising upwards) and about possible 'laws' of transmission, or concepts such as 'active' and 'passive' traditors.

Such questions still have some influence, but much recent work has moved away from a preoccupation with generalised historical questions or the transmission of fixed entities from the past. As Georges puts it:

> The development of an awareness that tales can change or be altered as they are transmitted from person to person and from place to place, and that variability might be common rather than anomalous, motivated some investigators to shift their attentions from *the stories people tell* to *those who tell tales* and to *the act of telling stories*.
>
> (1976: 161)

To this can be added the increasing interest in the processes of composition, transmission and circulation as created and re-created in the present, subject to all the social, political and personal pressures of social life. These pressures may well include the activities of contemporary educational, commercial or religious institutions, and developing local and international networks – part of the current situation, much though some traditional scholars might prefer to ignore these 'newer' influences.

The older questions do not all go away, however, and still stimulate new work, if in a different vein from the past. There is, after all, evidence of a sort that certain forms of stories, ballads, or nursery rhymes have come down through the generations in relatively unchanged form or are distributed widely throughout the world. It still makes sense to ask about the basis for these striking continuities or stabilities – notable despite the variations. Are we to look, as often in the past, to inert tradition; memorisation; re-creation; a greater role for writing than sometimes supposed? Or are there no *general* answers, but only specific questions to be explored for different contexts or historical periods?

Many interlocking factors will no doubt be involved in any given situation, but the following questions are often worth following up:

What are the local concepts about change, stability and transmission in verbal expression, and how far do these concepts or values fit with what actually happens? Do they differ for different genres, or at different periods?

Who is responsible (and in what sense) for circulation, transmission or preservation, and is this changing? What are the social, artistic and political processes relating to this?

How stable or crystallised are the genres in question (probably varying among themselves) and what is the evidence for this?

What historical evidence is there for earlier precursors of contemporary forms, and in what sense?

What are the accepted occasions for performance, publication or other forms of circulation, and who is involved?

What are the interactions between oral, written, printed and/or audio-visual media in the context of circulation and transmission? In particular what are the implications of the mutual influence between 'Great Tradition' in the form of written or élite literature, perhaps with international links, and more localised and/or oral forms (there are almost certain to be some such interactions and divisions)? What is the role of local broadcasting or local publishing (once again there is almost certain to be some – ignored though this often is) or of local schools, churches or festivals?

Do the answers to such questions differ according to specific genre: date; location (centre/periphery questions might be relevant); age, status or education of those involved; individual personality?

(For further discussions and references see Dundes 1969, Georges 1976, Honko and Voigt 1981, Pentikäinen 1978b, Pentikäinen and Juurikka 1976, Ben-Amos 1984, 1985, Finnegan 1977: chap. 5; see also 1.3.2, and, for earlier background, 2.3, 2.4.1–2, also below on memory.)

6.1.2 Memory and remembering

Theories of transmission usually implicitly assume some theory of memory. The earlier model was often a somewhat passive one: stories pictured as coming down automatically irrespective of human agency. Insofar as the 'traditor' had a role, it was that of recalling items lodged in the memory through a generalised and non-culture-specific process. This approach also sometimes drew on assumptions about the 'traditional' and 'past-bound' nature of non-western societies, with the conclusion that people's memories in this 'primitive' state must necessarily – and naturally – have been vastly better than in literate societies.

Recent thinking however has made some of these notions more controversial. One set of debates is between associationist views, often invoking a search for scientific laws of memory, and the branch of memory theory arising from Bartlett's work on 'remembering' (1932), itself partly based on experiments in the transmission of stories. This latter view moves away from the idea of storing verbatim memories to one of people reconstructing and organising on the basis of what they know and do, so that remembering means not drawing on rote memory but a creative and organisational activity by the user. This second view shifts interest from memory content to the processes of remembering and those doing the remembering. As Wingfield puts it, 'modern memory theory has come to learn that we are not studying the dream, but the dreamer' (1981: 47), relating this to work in psycholinguistics in which 'story grammars' involve not passive memorising but 'scripts' through which people actively structure and manipulate conceptual elements within a narrative organisation.

This puts a different complexion on transmission, for it directs attention to the active part people take in transmitting – but at the same time creating and re-enacting – forms of verbal art and oral tradition. This in turn can be brought into conjunction with more recent moves in the study of tradition which envisage tradition not as a piece of dead baggage from the past but as something constantly in change and continually needing to be actively renewed (see 2.5).

Such arguments stimulate attention to memory as a *social* process and to the related cultural conventions. Some cultures, like the Somali or the Maori, do indeed emphasise word-for-word memorising, at least for certain genres or pursuits (Andrzejewski 1981, Finnegan 1988: 103); others lay more stress on visual aspects of memorising (see Küchler 1987, Carrier 1990) or are concerned with social practices rather than verbalised beliefs which could be the subject of cognitive transmission (Brenner 1989). Yet others have highly developed techniques for training and enhancing memorising. Frances Yates' *The Art of Memory* explains the classical and mediaeval devices which enabled speakers to deliver long speeches from memory:

> In the ancient world, devoid of printing, without paper for note-taking or on which to type lectures, the trained memory was of vital importance. And the ancient memories were trained by an art which reflected the art and architecture of the ancient world, which could depend on faculties of intense visual memorisation which we have lost.
>
> (Yates 1966:4)

Not all 'oral' cultures need to be envisaged as precisely like classical

Greece to bring home the point that such cultural mechanisms are neither just a matter of individual intelligence nor of universal laws discoverable through psychological experiment. Rather, the processes of remembering are likely to be socially shaped by the particular devices and values developed in specific societies.

Because it is so often just assumed that 'memory' is some psychological fact of nature or, alternatively, that 'good verbal memory' and absence of literacy automatically go together, there has until recently been relatively little culture-specific work on social strategies relating to memory or the ways in which particular kinds of remembering are sanctioned (or not, as the case may be). The newer theoretical approaches to memory form a useful background, but the issues they point to also need to be explored by ethnographic investigation (so far relatively little detailed ethnographic work has been reported on this topic, with the exception of a growing corpus of work on Melanesia: Küchler 1987, Bateson 1958: chap. 15, Battaglia 1990; see also Hymes 1985, Andrzejewski 1981, 1985: 36ff, J.D. Smith 1981).

The kinds of questions that could be taken up include:

What kinds of processes and ideologies are recognised for the preservation of records and memories without writing, and how are they valued and sanctioned?

Is there a stress on verbatim memorisation (this can*not* be taken for granted) and if so in what sense(s) and what is it applied to? Is there a contrast between word-for-word memory and memory of content or style?

Are there observable institutional links with the processes of remembering or forgetting and how do they relate to the articulation of verbal art and tradition?

Are there recognised ways in which people are explicitly or implicitly trained to remember – or to forget? What kinds of mechanisms are involved, and memory of what?

Are such devices – and the content of what is remembered – necessarily all verbal or are other media, images, and/or active performances additionally or alternatively involved, and if so what is the interaction between these?

(For further discussion, see, besides references already given: for the (mainly) psychological debates: Gorfein and Hoffman 1987 (esp. Reder 1987: 203ff and Bahrick 1987: 394–5), Bartlett 1932, Wingfield 1981; for general discussion or references: Finnegan 1977: 139ff, Mayer 1989, R. Thomas 1989: 13, Hoppál 1981, Baddeley

1976; on oral history: Henige 1982, Oral History Society 1990, Grele 1985: 249ff; on social and performative practices: Connerton 1989, Middleton and Edwards 1990.)

6.1.3 Composition

The earlier focus on transmission has in many circles now given place to questions about how oral forms are composed. Such investigations are not simple, however, for composition, whether written or oral, is a complex notion. The relation between tradition and individual creation can extend to many different dimensions, varying in different cultures and for different genres, such as verbal style, content, music, plots, ideology, and performance modes: all these and their relationships may need separate enquiry. And even if you know the collective conventions it may be a subtle and elusive matter to discover just what the roles of individual composers (or composer-performers) are, or the degree of personal flexibility or innovation.

Such questions need empirical investigation, for the answers are *not* already given by the fact that a particular form or process has the term 'oral' attached to it. It is true that one approach has been to look for universal – or at least broadly cross-cultural – rules of composition. Much recent research, however, has taken the line that while there may be recurrent patterns, answers also have to be sought through detailed research into specific cultures, historical periods and genres (for some account of earlier theories and findings see Finnegan 1977: chap. 3).

Against this background, several kinds of questions can be asked about composition. Some relate to the final product, not just to composing as such, for without some idea of the former it is difficult to be clear about the latter. Most questions furthermore need following up for *each* genre to be studied (as in Feld 1990, Sherzer 1983), for we can no longer make the easy assumption that all are the same. Although the study of composition is less susceptible than most to being compressed into a delimited list, for it will interpenetrate almost every aspect of cultural and personal experience, an aide-memoire of possible questions might include:

Who is involved and in what capacity? The western model of the solitary writer may need to be replaced by the idea of composers working in a group, of joint processes of composition and performance, of memorising assistants to a composer, of direct input from the audience, or of a series of stages by which a composition comes into being, perhaps with no single final and correct product.

What is the relation between composition and performance? For example, is composition prior to, separate from, and fully completed before performance, or gradual and/or dependent on rehearsals? Is the final performance fixed and memorised, or flexible, and in what respects (there may be a mixture, as in the variable spoken sections as against more fixed sung or poetic portions in Somali plays or Cook Islands dance dramas – Mumin 1974: 30, McMath and Parima 1990)? Is there improvisation during performance and if so in what sense?

Are there experts or specialists and if so in what roles, and how are they trained and recognised?

Is there an explicit or implicit 'career' or artistic life cycle for composers?

What is the ideology of composition and its relation to memorisation and repetition, or to the idea of the self; and how far does this accord with what is actually practised? Does the concept or practice of possession or trance enter in?

Are composers' names and/or rights of ownership or control attached to specific compositions or skills, and if so in what way?

In what sense(s) can one speak of 'authorship'? Is it in any way multiple or staged?

How far does the specific genre being studied give freedom for (perhaps demand) individual variation and innovation, and in what sense and in respect of what elements? Where does it fall along the possible continuum between 'fixed' and 'free' texts?

Can specific compositional techniques be detected (e.g. on the basis of formulae, topoi, schemata, expansible images, or recurrent plots or characters)?

How far does composition eventuate in a bounded text, how far in more undefined series of utterances?

Since so many studies of oral composition have arisen from the oral-formulaic or 'oral theory' this needs a special mention (for general account and references see 2.4.9). The model of oral composition as a distinctive oral mode by which each composer, in the act of performance, draws differently and uniquely on a store of traditional formulaic material has been enormously influential. Among many scholars, specially those studying early or mediaeval European texts, it was for long the accepted view of oral composition (that this is the *only* possible mode of oral composing has never been universally accepted, however, specially among anthropologists – who tend to look to cultural variety rather than single-model universals). It is worth taking some account not only of the theory's original insight but also of recurrent controversies and recent developments. These focus around the following questions:

1 How widespread is the specific compositional process discovered through oral-formulaic analysis? Earlier scholars sometimes assumed that the composition-in-performance model (usually with the associated features of textual variability, no concept of a single correct text, and absence of prior composition) was *the* oral form. Some of the older oral-formulaic work also aimed to apply the theory very broadly ('to all oral poetries' in Parry and Lord 1954: 4), extended by some, but not all, analysts to almost every conceivable genre, sometimes including prose; others confined it to oral narrative heroic poems or to 'traditional' oral forms. Recent work by leading oral-formulaic scholars, however – as in comparable work by anthropologists and folklorists – encourages attention to diversities as well as to similarities (for earlier critiques see J.D. Smith 1977, Finnegan 1976, 1977: chap. 3, 1988: chap. 5; for recent discussions or approaches: Foley 1988a, 1990a, Lord 1987, Feld 1990).

2 What is covered or implied by 'oral'? This has been a controversial term, not least because it has sometimes been limited only to works resulting from composition-in-performance through the oral-formulaic mode: thus texts memorised and preserved word-for-word 'could not be *oral* in any except the most literal sense' (Lord 1960: 280) and 'oral' poetry is defined as 'poetry composed *in* oral performance' (Lord 1974: 591). This restriction has been challenged by others, given the documented cases of prior and memorised composition without writing (see references above). More recently Lord has laid more weight on the additional concept of 'traditional', rather than just 'oral' (1987a and b).

3 What is the 'formula' and its significance? There have been continuing controversies over whether this is a valid unit for counting or comparison across different languages and literatures and whether formulaic expression is really a differentiating factor between oral and written composition, and in what sense? An early aim was to differentiate the characteristics of oral style, one suggestion being that a high proportion of formulae was evidence of oral composition. This has been disputed, not least because

of the appearance of formulae in written literature. Many oral-formulaic scholars now no longer assume that formulae can be simply counted or that formulaic density can be used 'as a reliable index of the actual circumstances of composition of particular ancient or mediaeval texts' (Renoir 1988: 56) but instead speak of oral-influenced rhetoric within otherwise written texts (see Renoir 1988: 54ff, Foley 1987a, b, Lord 1986b). Current writings increasingly face up to the problems of definition or application (see Foley 1987a, also Stolz and Shannon 1976 and references there).

4 Can there be 'transitional' texts or compositions? The original view was that oral and written techniques of composition were 'contradictory and mutually exclusive' (Lord 1960: 129) and that the typically literate concept of a correct text meant the 'death knell of the oral process' (137). 'Transitional' texts in the strict sense were thus impossible – an influential viewpoint perhaps reflecting and reinforcing assumptions about a divide between pre-literate and literate culture. Many oral-formulaic scholars now question this, at least in its literal sense (see Lord 1986: 19ff), and are studying 'transitional' texts in the sense of forms involving both oral and written elements (Foley 1986, 1987b) or challenging the earlier categories (see Bäuml 1984).

Recent analyses thus now more often use the insights of the Parry-Lord approach to highlight aspects of complex compositional processes rather than as providing definitive instances of some universally-applicable generalisation. While the earlier oral-formulaic work mostly emphasised cross-cultural *similarities* in oral composition, the present tendency is to attend to diversities and to cultural specifics in terms of differing poetic traditions, genres and texts – a trend which now brings it closer to the ethnographic concerns of anthropologists. (For new directions in oral-formulaic studies see Foley 1988a: 108ff, 1990a, b, and recent issues of the journal *Oral Tradition*, also references above and in 2.4.9. For some recent stimulating or informative analyses of composition generally see Sweeney 1980, 1987, Cancel 1989, Feld 1990, Thomas and Tuia 1990.)

6.1.4 Repertoire, composition and individual creators

A further set of questions arises from studies of individual singers or narrators and what can be concluded from these.

Earlier communal-based theories about origins meant little interest in *individual* contributions and till recently anthropologists have paid little attention to personal artistic or intellectual repertoires. There has long been an interest in this topic within the discipline of folklore, however – though even there, it has been argued (Dégh in Pentikäinen 1976: 275) that it is only since the late 40's that researchers have conducted in-depth studies with *individual* narrators and their repertoires. These have involved both collection and analysis, and have linked with changing theories about the nature of transmission and of 'folklore' (see Pentikäinen 1978: chap. 1). Earlier collections sometimes take the form of merely amassing quantities of annotated items. But even they can throw light on individual characteristics. As Holbek points out personal traits emerge even in the bare hand-written summaries collected in the last century, while 'recordings made with modern equipment reveal even more diversity and individuality' (1987: 576). Recent work has taken a wider scope – looking to the processes of composition or performance rather than just their products and relating these to wider questions of genre patterning, individual creativity or change.

The kinds of questions that have been investigated or debated include:

How are individual repertoires developed (or changed) over time? How does this link with such topics as apprenticeship, learning or the domestic life cycle, whether in individual pieces or in personal skills or ownership?

How does an individual's repertoire differ from or resemble those of others?

What is the significance of existing poetic conventions and the ways individuals may or may not manipulate these? And what light can this throw on more general questions of the relation between 'individual and tradition'? Discussion of these aspects now usually includes reference to performance features, not just words.

What is the individual's position in the wider poetic or cultural traditions, whether in continuing, developing or in some cases changing the accepted oral forms? How much emphasis is there on *personal* roles and/or ownership, and how is this expressed and mediated? (Cf. the Shoshone concept of individual 'songprints' (Vander 1988) or Siikala on 'egodistance': the gap between the tradition and the story-teller's self concept 1980: 168).

How has the individual artist developed over time?

What is the best way of analysing and appreciating a particular individual's repertoire/compositions, including both the relation between these and his or her personality, life and experiences, and that between different elements within the corpus?

The normal model in discussing repertoire or corpus is of an individual peformer/composer, but there may also be questions to be explored about the joint creations of two or more individuals and how their roles inter-relate (see also 5.2 on categories of performers).

(For further discussion or examples see Abrahams 1970b, Holbek 1987: 576ff and *passim*, Pentikäinen 1976 (and following commentary by Dégh), 1978a, Russell 1986, Siikala 1980, Vander 1988; also, for further examples of individuals and their works, references in Finnegan 1977: 170–88 and on 'personal narratives' in 7.4.5, also on composition, transmission and memory above.)

6.2 SOCIAL AND ECONOMIC POSITION OF PARTICIPANTS

The standard sociological questions apply as much to the producers and consumers of artistic and linguistic forms as to those in any other sphere of society. Though this should go without saying it has often been neglected, not only because of the view of 'art' as somehow a-social but also because of still-influential assumptions about the 'natural' or 'communal' status of 'oral' or 'folk' forms. So it needs to be asserted that there are *always* questions to be investigated about such topics as the local division of labour, training, status or means of support.

One main focus in research on oral – or indeed any – art has consistently been on the producers. These do indeed have an important role, and the questions below need to be investigated for the poets, singers, historians, story-tellers and others responsible for creating or performing the forms under research. But these are not the only participants and similar questions should be explored about *all* those involved in composition, performance, consumption or support. Ideally this should also follow the holistic tradition within anthropology in including research on the social framework in general, and probe such familiar topics as the economic and power relations within the society, family structures, the nature and organisation of communication and expressive art generally, or the ideological and value systems, whether agreed or disputed. Such questions are already well-known, however, so though a full understanding must include them, the following concentrates on specific questions about those participants more, or less, actively and directly involved in oral arts and traditions.

Even here, the list of possible questions is endless, and varies according to the particular society you are studying. The following represent some of the main topics.

1 *Division of labour*. This is the broadest question, including both the social framework generally and divisions relating particularly to artistic processes. It could be broken down into sub-questions such as:

How is the overall division of labour conceptualised and how does it relate both to broader economic and political patterns and to artistic divisions?

Who is responsible for the production of particular forms of artistic (or other) verbal expression, and in what capacity? If there are special individuals or groups for certain roles (probably in regard to some but not all genres) how is this organised, how far hereditary (and in what sense), how related to wider stratification and economic patterns? How expert are the producers (or other participants), how far exclusive or esoteric, how rewarded?

What role is taken by audiences, consumers and/or those who participate in less leading roles? How far are *they* expected to learn such roles? What is their economic and power relation to the performers?

How are these patterns changing?

2 *Social characteristics of performers and other participants*. The standard questions apply: age; gender; domestic circumstances (some poets may consistently be celibate, for example, or widows); hereditary background; degree of expertise; status (not necessarily 'high' in every respect – poets are sometimes regarded as low in one scale while powerful in others); economic or political power; stage in artistic 'career' or life cycle; education; wider experience (e.g., of travelling); social or psychological 'marginality' in some sense (often claimed to be characteristic of poets); personality (both in the sense of the 'expected' persona for a particular artistic role, and of how individuals manipulate or develop traditional resources). Similar questions may need to be asked about 'secondary' performers and participants, and about various categories of audience members (see 5.2).

Exploring these questions should elucidate general patterns, but can often be further illuminated by case studies in more depth.

3 *Recruitment and training*: once again worth enquiring into, contrary to the older picture of art as somehow bubbling up 'naturally' in non-literate or in 'folk' contexts. How do experts – or non-experts – get started: are there special ceremonies (whether personal or public); particular images, experiences or expectations; specific sanctions or barriers? Do family or other relationships help? Is status achieved or ascribed, and in what senses? What are the socialisation patterns (and for audiences as well as performers)? Are there implicit or explicit artistic 'careers' or life cycles? Are there formal systems for training and if so how do people enter and progress? What role is taken by modern educational institutions and how do these relate to more 'traditional' forms? How expert or distinctive are particular categories of performers? Are there sanctions, stages, examinations, or barriers to recruitment and accreditation. After all closed shop and self-perpetuating professional groups are not just western institutions.

4 *Patronage, support and exploitation*: also relates to questions about the political and economic relations of performers, consumers and their supporters in various roles. How far can the (various) participants be regarded as 'amateur' or 'professional' (a tricky area, usually a continuum rather than clear divide, but always worth exploring)? How are they rewarded, whether in material or other terms and by whom? Is their work in any way commercialised (as 'folk industry', as 'popular culture' or in any other form) and what parties are involved? What role is played by government, tourism, researchers, foreign record-companies, 'folk festivals' or local broadcasting, and who makes what payment to whom and for what? How is patronage exercised both now and in the past and by whom: traditional chiefs or kings; government; educational authorities; religious institutions; local notables; tourist boards; collective 'self help'? Is there a local concept of intellectual property rights, in the sense of individual (or group) 'ownership' of particular works, techniques or knowledge, or of wider (e.g., national) rights to local products, and how is this translated into practice?

(For further general discussion see also Finnegan 1970: esp. chap. 4, and 1977: chap. 6.)

6.3 VERBAL ART, ORAL TRADITION AND FUNCTIONS

The question of function is probably the most difficult of all to get a grip on. For though some aspects are relatively easy to observe, understanding the 'real' or inner roles of some piece of art or tradition in any deep sense is no easier for oral than for written forms. A list of possible headings would need to encompass the world! Nevertheless this question, like that of the related topic of 'meaning' (see 8.7), is one which continues to fascinate both researchers and participants.

Some preliminary points can be made. One is that there are as many functions as there are theories. As with the quest for meaning, what you find partly depends on what you think important to look for – social charters, symbols, psychological functions, social interactions, personal artistic expression, power relations, ideological reflections or whatever; and the results will be interpreted according to your assumptions about the nature of humanity, of history, or of art and its relation to society. There are a host of possible insights to draw on (among them the perspectives in 2.4) – but, correspondingly, definitive assertions about *the* function of oral forms in either particular or general can be regarded with scepticism.

So much should be obvious. But there is a further corollary. This is that there can be multiple co-existing functions, for verbal formulation can take on an infinity of forms and purposes: as many roles indeed as communication itself. This equally obvious point is also worth stating. For the sequential dominance of this or that theoretical position has, each in its turn, led to assumptions that only *certain* functions are significant. At some periods it was believed that only 'communal' or tradition-conserving functions were fulfilled by oral forms – and there was thus no point in looking for personal creativity, social manipulations or inducement to change – while at others the focus was on the function of verbal formulation as 'testimony' (but not 'art') or on the unfettered expression of enduring symbolic truth with no hint of competing or changing social constraints. So whatever your focus, do not close the door too firmly on the range of roles which some or all of the forms you are studying may also fulfil.

Despite the complexities – of which more later – commonsense enquiry into specifics, whether through field ethnography or detailed investigation of the social and historical context of archive materials, should remain a central strategy. It is essential, if difficult, not to *assume* functions in advance but to examine the actual occasions on which differing forms are performed, how people behave during such events, and how their behaviour relates to what they say about it. Some quite straightforward but nonetheless informative conclusions can be reached from such investigations: the differing roles of, say, some conversational genres as against 'set piece' performances, or the place of 'special occasion' forms like laments, lullabies, wedding songs, speeches or panegyric (how far these *are* tied to these occasions might also need investigating, for they may be neither fully 'spontaneous' nor purely utilitarian). Common roles and occasions that are always worth looking for, if at different levels, include work, dancing, lamenting, divination or possession, praise, duelling, competitions, political pressurising, entertainment, religious rituals, and rites of passage. But there are also countless variations, interpretations, changes and contradictions, even within one culture, so *each* form and *each* conclusion needs to be investigated in its own right and against the specific ethnographic evidence.

Investigating these overt specificities must always remain the basis. However there are also complications which need further consideration.

The multifunctionality of verbal expression needs remembering yet again here. This rests on more than just the existence of different genres, cultures, situations or historical periods – important though these are in reminding us of the dangers of generalisation. More significantly, there can be multiple uses at *every* level. Not only the same genre but even the same performance can work differently for different participants or in different phases, and a form which has one role for certain categories of people – in terms, say, of age, gender, education, status, religion, language – may be doing something different for others. Again, a work performed or recorded in one situation may be used differently by those who read or hear it elsewhere. Sometimes multi-meanings are deliberate, sometimes implicit only but still a potential resource for hidden negotiations or misunderstandings between performers, hearers or supporters. Furthermore – an obvious but somehow over-looked point – several things may be going on at the same time even for the same people: making money, perhaps, as well as aesthetic expression, satirising in the same breath as praising, propagandising together with entertaining. Whatever the 'overt' function, there will almost certainly be further questions to investigate.

A second complication is the well-known problem that 'functions' can be more, or less, explicit: just where to draw the line between 'purpose', 'interpretation' and 'social role' is seldom clear. So it is worth enquiring into *who* is attributing the functions, *for whom*, and *how far shared* by which participants or interpreters, even where the answers cannot be fully ascertained. Local participants in oral forms – as in any other – may be blind to certain implications of what they do. But equally they may not; and some dialogue with the range of (doubtless varying) local reflections on functions and purposes may provide new perspectives on what at first looked a 'simple' function.

Such dialogues are now recognised as both relevant and complex. This partly results from the greater current awareness of the inter-active role of researcher and researched. Most scholars have also moved away from concepts of the 'pure and uncontaminated folk' as the locale for discovering the 'real' functions of oral tradition etc. (the idea behind the old contrast of 'folklore' and 'fakelore'). Since, it is now realised, many actors enter into the creation and codification of oral forms – researchers and nation-builders as much as rural 'traditional' singers – the attribution of functions must consider *all* these parties and their interrelationships. These may include intellectuals or experts in any given culture, themselves holding views about the actual or the desirable functions of particu-lar genres, or locally-based participants involved in publishing, broadcasting or the record industry. In every case local people (not just 'outside' scholars) reflect on and interpret what is happening, and interact with a range of perspectives – and change their views too. In these wheels within wheels, and interpretations within inter-pretations, the superficially serviceable contrast between local views and purposes on the one hand ('emic') and outsiders' interpretations on the other ('etic') ultimately breaks down.

Equally worth noting is the particular characteristic of the field under study: formulated verbal expression. For here *already* there is verbally articulated analysis, abstracted in some sense from the flow of human activity, a meta-comment on human and social experience. Literary forms in themselves represent a kind of reflec-tive interpretation in words. In the sphere of verbalised art and tradition, local interpretations and reflections are thus already making their input: in a sense the art form is itself a formulation of the function or meaning, whether of the specific occasion or of some aspect of the human condition.

The most general point to make, then, is that verbal formulations – whether regarded as 'oral tradition', 'verbal art', 'folklore', 'narra-tive' or whatever – can have a near-infinite range of functions, different too depending on where and to whom you look, and at what level. They can be used for upholding political authority or for attacking it, for passing on tradition or for challenging it, for satirising, propagandising, showing off, framing rituals, expressing love or beauty, complaining, saying or veiling the unsayable or even the unthinkable, standing aside from the pressures or commitments of 'real life', self discovery, indirection, mediating the human psyche, joining people or separating them, finding a place to stand amidst chaos, entertaining modern tourists or traditional chiefs, providing a detached, or a self-interested, or an allegorical perspective, letting off steam, making a living, parodying, scandalising, entrancing, dreaming, consoling – and a hundred other things.

Any attempt at a list, even just of questions to ask, could only be misleading in its implications that other functions were off the agenda. But, purely to give some random but perhaps stimulating illustrations, the following are some of the many ways in which some recent scholars have looked at the questions (these are neither mutually exclusive nor systematic, and employ varying terminologies – at times elusive).

The function of constituting a charter or validation for existing social arrangements is still often stressed. Cruder reflection or structural-functionalist versions focusing on limited and somewhat literal aspects are less popular. But there *are* still questions to be pursued about the role of verbal formulations in upholding and expressing values or power, in socialisation and education, and in both creating and mediating social experiences (for new looks at older questions see Järvinen 1981, Abrahams 1985b; for comments on Marxist and feminist critiques stressing the functions of verbal art in maintaining – or in some cases challenging – existing ideologies see 2.4.6, 11).

There is also the part played by oral forms (and written ones too) in the creation or maintenance of identity and the validation of experience. The claim – whether in every sense justified or not – that something is 'old' or 'traditional' may carry great weight. This was a strand in both earlier and contemporary nationalist movements but can also be extended to sectional, ethnic, local or personal identity and experience: for example the role of personal narratives in locating oneself or validating one's life and experience (see Johnston 1976, Bornat 1989, Samuel and Thompson 1990) or the place of art forms in the consciousness of marginal or emergent groups (as in Ostendorf 1975 on 'black poetry'). Fairy tales – and other forms too? – can function as a 'paradigm for understanding the community and for determining and developing individual behavior and personality in that community' (Bottigheimer 1986b: xii). Lüthi speculates still further on the deeper role of folktales:

> People who find themselves hurled into a threatening world whose meaning they do not know . . . experience the transform- ation of this very same world in the quiet, epic vision of the folktale . . . . The folktale envisions and depicts a world that unfolds before us as the antitype of the uncertain, confusing, unclear, and threatening world of reality . . . . At the same time as the folktale leads us into the midst of the rich nuances of the life of the folk and the individual, it leads . . . us to the great constants of the human condition.
>
> (Lüthi 1982: 85, 125)

There is also the cathartic function of verbal expression in relieving social tensions or in alleviating overwhelming sorrow. There can be differing interpretations here too. As Feld argues in the context of Kaluli ritual wailing, another view could be that rather than a mere 'bursting of the dam',

> The key affective quality . . . is a creative 'pulling together' of affect . . . [which] serves . . . to centrally display and focus the aesthetics of emotionality, and to positively value these social articulations as organized, thoughtful expressions of personal and social identities as deeply felt.
>
> (Feld 1990: 257)

The role of expressing underlying preoccupations and ideologies – whether or not consciously – has been stressed in recent French studies of oral literature: thus Görög-Karady's comparison of con- cepts of inequality in Hungarian and African stories about Eve's children so as 'to apprehend *different ideological patterns in the elaboration of an identical narrative subject*' (1982: 32, italics in original). These go further than comparative indexing of motifs or tale types to try to reach some deeper understanding of the stories' implications for intellectual conceptualisation in the society in which they are told.

Recent interpretations stressing cognitive functions are related to allegorical, transcendent or psychological aspects rather than just narrowly intellectual ones, and extended to the wider roles of ritual or performance. As Cancel expresses it, 'The creation and perform- ance of oral narrative become a social form of thinking aloud. Allegory on various levels approximates or parallels cognition itself;

sense-making in public becomes world making' (1989: 207; cf. Feld 1989, Turner 1982: 13, Finnegan 1989a: 337ff).

Oral literature and verbal art can also be regarded not just as 'mere' verbal expression but as one form of social activity: of people engaging in performance, and in sociability and collective action (see Becker 1984). In the case of poetry at least – but perhaps also of all verbal expression – this can go further too:

> 'People doing things' does not just refer to the outward and observable acts by which people organise poetic activity or use poetry to achieve political power, economic reward and cooperation, religious satisfaction, aesthetic pleasure. . . . What is involved is not the passive repetition of externally determined words – artistic or ritual or utilitarian or whatever – but people actively moulding the world around them: the world of symbols which, ultimately, constitutes the world we experience and live in. It is through poetry – not exclusively, certainly, but surely pre-eminently – that people create and recreate that world.
>
> (Finnegan 1977: 273–4)

The roles stressed in traditional literary or artistic scholarship are not irrelevant either. Admittedly simplified concepts of 'art for art's sake' could be queried or, at the least, need specific ethnographic foundation. But that aesthetic appreciation, entertainment, or personal creativity form at least aspects of what verbal expression is about is a common, if sometimes unstated, assumption of many interpretations. Thus terms like 'artistry', 'playing with language', and 'delight' enter in, and the analysis of poetics, metaphor, layers of meaning, or the beauty of words, performance, rhythm, and music often seem to be taken as a mark not just of formal stylistics or surface meaning but of some deeper social or personal import. It is not only in Apache speaking with names that, as Keith Basso puts it, 'on the pictorial wings of placenames imaginations soar' (1988: 123).

Finally, though these and similar approaches can provide illuminating pointers to possible interpretations, they cannot replace detailed investigation into specifics. It is tempting to spin seductive intellectual webs which might not in any way be recognised by the people concerned. Indeed it is probably fair to say that the most stimulating and influential recent work has been based on an interaction between acquaintance with the comparative literature and its debates on the one hand, and detailed ethnographically-informed investigation on the other. The results take the form of more subtle and open-ended analyses than in the past, with a sensitivity to a range of interpretations from both participants and scholars – and a recognition that these are not always different (e.g. Feld 1982/89, Cancel 1989, Briggs 1988, K.H. Basso 1984, 1988, Abu-Lughod 1986; for further discussion or references see McCall 1989, Rooth 1976 (story-telling); Willis 1981 (symbolic and ideological aspects of myth as root metaphor); Brenneis and Myers 1984 (political roles of 'dangerous words'); Finnegan 1977: 241ff, 268ff (oral poetry); Holbek 1976 ('games of the powerless'); Hymes 1991 (myth); K. Stewart 1988 (nostalgia); S. Stewart 1979 ('nonsense'); also 8.7 on 'meaning').

6.4 LOCAL AESTHETICS AND THOUGHT

Questions about the nature and significance of locally developed aesthetic theories are ultimately inseparable from the previous discussion. However, they call for some specific treatment in that, though in the past usually subordinated to the collection and analysis of textual material, the subject is now starting to be discussed in its own right. Its emergence fits not only with anthropological interests in local perceptions, but also with the increasing visibility and influence of locally-based researchers in African and other cultures that were in the past only too often regarded as merely the 'object' for outsiders' research (at best providing 'informants' or assistants in an endeavour defined by others). Whether or not these questions are central to your particular research, it is worth remembering their significance and being open to such evidence as is available.

There are relatively few studies directly on this aspect – many of course touch on it in passing. Some move at a high intellectual level, as much about general symbolic structures as about verbal art specifically (like Calame-Griaule's influential analysis of the Dogon (1965), or, at a more generalised – and arguably unhelpful – level, Tempels 1959 on 'Bantu philosophy', or the *Négritude* and *Présence africaine* writers on Africa). Such writings have been criticised for not taking enough account of specific artistic practices or for imposing an over-systematic and coherent framework, itself arguably derivative from western intellectual assumptions; they are interesting nevertheless if only because they in turn have shaped the perceptions of local (and other) scholars. There has also been the recent more sophisticated work on 'black aesthetics' (see Johnson 1982, and references in Chimombo 1988: 77–8 and Barber and

Farias 1989: Part 2), and assessments of oral style which, while still cast in a comparative mould, move from earlier generalising abstractions to seek new sensitivities to oral aesthetics (Foley 1988b). Scholars and poetry-lovers inspired by 'ethnopoetic' approaches have argued strongly for an appreciation of local aesthetics, in particular the need to give more weight to the creative aspects of performance (see Hymes 1981, Rothenberg and Rothenberg 1983, D. Tedlock 1977, 1983, 1989, *Alcheringa–Ethnopoetics*, also 2.4.10 above).

More recent analyses include Chimombo's intriguing account of Malawian aesthetics. He points out that work on 'indigenous aesthetics' is in its infancy, for it is only with 'recent trends in black scholarship (African and Afro-American) that local academics have started looking in this direction' (1988: 64). His aim of articulating these local aesthetics for Malawians themselves might seem yet another piece of intellectual and nationalist image-building (always a hazard in this area, for insiders as much as outsiders), but is in this case supported by specific empirical evidence, covering not only the local terminologies for the various art forms but also detailed accounts of local practices and performances. Feld's innovative work among the Kaluli of Papua New Guinea Highlands has also illuminated in some detail how 'Kaluli song terminology and conceptualization of musical form relate systematically to the terminology of waterfalls, water sounds, and water motion . . . . Waterway terms in Kaluli are visual metaphors for forms of sound' (1982: 164–5). Finally, at a more comparative level, there are the questions raised in an important paper by Olabiyi Yai on forms of oral criticism.

> To be able to understand the oral poetics of oral poetry, we must dismiss any theory which presents this poetry as a 'product' or 'work' that has the features of finitude and closure as implied by these concepts. Instead, we should talk of uninterrupted 'production' . . . . In the case of an oral poetics, what happens during 'performance' is as significant as what goes on before and after . . . . Unlike the criticism of writtenness which is in essence a criticism of mediation, oral poetics is indivisible with its poetry; it is self-productive . . . . From the point of view of oral poetics, oral poetry strictly speaking should not even be described. We know it by practising it and by contributing to its making.
>
> (1989: 63, 65)

In investigating this topic, many of the same problems arise as in the last section: of differing and changing voices, perceptions, and interpretations even within 'one' culture; and of the interaction of insiders and outsiders, of old and new, and of concurrent ideas even at the same time and place. Similarly it is hard to elucidate how far such views are or should be explicit or coherent, and general ideas – *wherever* they originate – cannot be just assumed but have to be investigated on their own merits. However there do seem to be some recurrent factors (each no doubt with their own local elaborations) – or at any rate recurrent questions to follow up. Among these are:

What are the local concepts, divisions and relationships of art forms/ genres – or is there perhaps not one systematic taxonomy? Do their divisions or evaluations differ from those elsewhere (as for example in the Limba assessment of drumming and dance as higher and more specialist than (literary) narrative – Finnegan 1967: 25ff)? How about local ideas on wider divisions such as prose/poetry, speech/song?

What is thought to be the nature of poetry, narration or verbal composition generally? How does this relate to such concepts as, say, inspiration, dream, tradition, ancestors, and what are the local terminologies?

What are the artistic canons of composition and of performance, and what is the vocabulary and practice for evaluating these (different for different genres perhaps), and for conceptualising the underlying processes?

Does 'literary criticism' or its equivalent in any way emerge *during* performance (for example from pre-performance pressures, by audience behaviour) rather than, or in addition to, being a separate phase after the event?

How is the role of memory conceived – or of transmission, accuracy, composition, style, or indeed any or all of the topics discussed in this or the following two chapters?

What views have been developed about the relation between written and oral forms, or the evaluations and expectations relating, variously, to the canons of western high art, local publications, or the broadcast media?

For all these questions, finally, it is essential to be alive to multiple and overlapping answers. There will probably be no such thing as 'the pure indigenous system' untouched by wider interactions, the views of local intellectuals may or may not accord with those of others, and there may be contending groups with differing artistic practices and ideologies. If only for this reason any full study would also have to relate these views to other ideas, arts and institutions in the society. (For further examples or references see also Finnegan 1977: 235–41, Krupat 1982, Feld 1982: esp. 163ff, 1988; Dundes 1978: 38ff, Deng 1973, Moyo 1986.)

7 Genres and boundaries

Classification no doubt enters into all branches of scientific study. It has been particularly prominent, however, in the field of oral arts and traditions. The construction of typologies played a central part in many earlier studies, and in turn linked with the notion of genre, a deeply influential concept within linguistic, philological and literary study, as well as in anthropology, history and folklore. As a result categories such as 'myth', 'folktale', 'epic', or 'proverb' take on the air of real and permanent objects in themselves, seemingly the unquestioned basis for scientific taxonomies and the representatives of pure and enduring types. Such classifications, and in particular the concept of genre, have been productive ones, and certainly need to be noted by anyone involved in research on verbal art. As will appear, however, they also involve complexities and controversies of a kind which accord well with recent trends within anthropology to question traditional single-factor classifications and realist definitions.

(For general discussion of classifications in oral forms see Abrahams 1981b, 1985a, b, Bauman, Irvine and Philips 1987, Bausinger 1968, Ben-Amos 1976, Honko 1976, 1989b, Jason 1986, Pentikäinen and Juurikka 1976, Perić-Polonijo 1988; for varying treatments of genre within literary theory, Wellek and Warren 1949, chap. 17, Dubrow 1982, Fowler 1982, Derrida in Mitchell 1981, Todorov 1975, 1977, Bakhtin 1986, Rosmarin 1985.)

7.1 APPROACHES TO CLASSIFICATION

Analysing verbal expression and its conventions raises dilemmas which will be familiar to all anthropologists and other scholars concerned with cross-cultural research: the desire, on the one hand, to have general terms to facilitate translation and comparative understanding and, on the other, to represent specificity. The tensions are particularly stressful because of the subject matter here, with its value-laden implications for how we see ourselves as human beings partaking in shared (and universal?) expressive forms of human culture. Nevertheless some strategies have to be devised to cope with such problems. In the past these have often connected with the concept of 'genre' or of pure and supposedly culture-free types, and have ranged from the invocation of scientific typologies (albeit based on a series of differing criteria over the years) to ethnographically-based vernacular classifications in more recent writings.

The varying approaches not surprisingly follow the familiar sequence of theoretical perspectives. Evolutionist scenarios classified forms in historical or origin terms: 'epic' (or sometimes poetry generally) as early in a culture's history, non-heroic narrative, personal lyric and prose as later; so too the Chadwicks' more empirically-based – but still sweeping – theory of epic as attached to the 'heroic' stage of society (1932–40), or Marxist recyclings of nineteenth-century evolutionism in some East European folklore studies (on evolutionary approaches to classification see Ben-Amos 1976: xxff; Edmonson 1971). Most functionalist approaches by contrast classed any narrative interpretable as upholding the status quo under the label of 'myth', the point being its function rather than form or content (see Finnegan 1969a: 63ff). Other approaches took psychological role or cognitive structure as the basis, again often labelled 'myth'. The historical-geographical interest in content resulted in cross-cultural categories such as 'animal tales' together with their various subdivisions in terms of plot, actors or motifs, while structuralists differentiated contrasting types of narrative in terms of their structure (see 8.2, 8.3). In many of these approaches, and in particular in the influential nineteenth and early twentieth-century folklore studies, there was heavy emphasis on the importance of classification and of allocating items to their due classes as the basis for scientific collection and study.

The study of genres also had its own history within literary scholarship which complicated matters further. The classical Greek terms ('epic', 'tragedy', 'lyric', 'myth') long held a special position. These have now been supplemented by later genres like the novel and (sometimes) categories from the so-called 'folk' genres. In the past such genre terms were sometimes used as the basis for prescriptive models for writers or as representing somehow absolute and enduring entities. They often cut across other theoretical divisions and are still commonly used to present or sum up observed textual regularities.

However, useful though such terms will continue to be for some purposes, recent writers in a number of disciplines have been moving away from the idea of fixed genres. One approach is to look more to the dynamics of performance and practice. Exploring the processes through which generic expectations are played on by performers and audiences has led to alternative views of genre as 'a resource for performance, available to speakers for the realization of specific social ends in a variety of creative, emergent and even unique ways' (Bauman et al. 1987: 6). This is particularly effective for analysing multivocal or recently synthesised tradition (like St Vincent tea meetings or concert parties in Africa with their series of different forms, Abrahams 1985a: 93), or for considering fluid and changing genres.

It can also lead to the radical approach, in keeping both with current post-modernist concerns and with ethnographically-focused performance studies, of directly challenging earlier preoccupations with fixed, normative or 'pure' genres. Certainly there are conventions in all accepted forms of linguistic usage; we find 'speech genres' in everyday dialogues as well as in the classically recognised literary genres, each developing 'its own *relatively stable types* of these utterances' (Bakhtin 1986: 60). But these generic conventions have to be enacted in practice. And such enactments and the divisions they arguably represent are not always fixed and definitive but overlap, provoke explicit or implicit disagreement among different participants, vary at different times, develop differently in particular situations, and are subject both to participants' expectations and to the wider interplay of social and ideological forces (see Medvedev 1978, Bakhtin 1981, 1986 and discussions in Dorst 1983, Abrahams 1985a, b, Bauman, Irvine and Philips 1987). This approach looks not just to stabilities, as in earlier studies, but also to change and ambiguity, taking account of 'emergence, transformation, obsolescence, and so on as positive realities of genres, that is, as active processes to be treated in their own terms and not merely as forms of defect or breakdown in generic order' (Dorst 1983: 413).

There are thus now challenges to the long-influential views of genre as representing something unambiguous, timeless, mutually exclusive or universally accepted. If genre-enactment is looked at in terms not of ideal models or fixed types but of social practices, different questions arise. Certain settled boundaries and conventions may indeed be detected – 'more or less fixed pre-existing forms into which one may then pour artistic expression' as Bakhtin well puts it (1981: 3) – but equally they may not be agreed even by their own first-hand executants. It is also necessary to look beyond surface consensus to the processes through which the participants (or some of them) themselves realise, manipulate, play with, quarrel about and perhaps transform their art forms.

Increasingly important too is the ethnographic perspective which stresses cultural specificity and the importance of building on local classifications and experience rather than outsiders' categories. Stated simply this view will appeal to most anthropologists. It too has complications however, some only too famL'ar from other subjects of anthropological research, some more directly related to the subject matter of this volume.

In the first place, there may not be a fully coherent or explicit local taxonomy – and this may be due neither to incomplete research nor to some 'lack of development' but part of the situation to be recorded. If so, you may find yourself taking a more active part in classifying than you realise. It is always tempting to start either from one's own cultural genres or from hazy popular preconceptions (for example assuming that all non-literate cultures 'must' have an 'epic' or a 'myth of origin' and so 'finding' such genres) and so present the transcriptions accordingly (see 9.2).

Further, even if some verbal formulations are distinguished in an articulate taxonomy, others – perhaps equally pervasive – may not surface in local terms at all. The outsider's eye can then sometimes point to conventions which are indeed obligatory in people's practices but not consciously recognised. To represent the reality of local practices you may have to go outside local terminologies.

Local terminologies themselves are not always non-controversial. Participants may categorise performances in several equally valid ways, there may be changes over time, and more, or less, explicit terminologies. *Which* people you observe or consult, or *when* or *where*, may turn out to be crucial – and political – issues. You may end up describing differing viewpoints or selecting between them, rather than positing one agreed taxonomy.

Even where the local generic terminology is quite explicit, there is still the question of how to present it, particularly if you want not only to document local ideas but also to communicate them to outsiders or draw comparisons which themselves cast light on cultural specifics. Translation *within* a given culture may even be needed too, with sensitive political decisions lying on the researcher.

The tensions represent old problems in anthropology – and in the social sciences generally – but are no less difficult for that.

One option, increasingly acceptable as certain areas of the world become better known, is to use the local words. Thus 'terms like Zulu *izibongo*, Xhosa *intsomi*, Yoruba *ijala* and Somali *heello* are beginning to acquire wide currency' (Andrzejewski 1985: 45) and entering the scholarly literature in their own right. In such cases researchers no longer always give English translations (though explanations and commentary may be needed), far less 'reduce' local forms to English-language genre terms – an approach that overcomes some, but perhaps not all, of the problems.

Whatever the final position, you do eventually need to adopt some strategy for considering and presenting the classification of 'genres' or other conventions – or perhaps a series of strategies for different purposes. Starting from local terminologies and practices might well be one guiding principle. But just how to interpret or present these and relate them to the wider theoretical and comparative literature remain complex issues.

7.2 SOME CRUCIAL BOUNDARIES: OR ARE THEY?

Certain rather general boundaries have sometimes been used as the basis for classifications which, though less discussed than those relating to genres, also have their own influence. These are described briefly below before going on to the discussion of specific genres. While each can have a role in understanding and describing verbal forms, the terms can also be used simplistically and may repay some critical analysis in the light both of cross-cultural relativities and of the growing doubts, post-modernist and other, about suggestions of absolute and objective boundaries.

7.2.1 Speech and song

The distinction between 'spoken' and 'sung' modes is often invoked, with particular art forms using one, a combination, or alternations of the two. It is more complex than just a single equal division between speech and song however. Threefold distinctions between spoken, intoned (or chanted) and fully sung are also made with differing gradations and emphases between these, while in some genres sobbing or weeping plays a significant role, feeding into, but going outside, the spoken/sung dichotomy. So too does the delivery of poetry through drums or other instruments (Finnegan 1977:

119ff, 1970: chap. 17). And in some cultures generic differences may be much more complex than a simple speech/song distinction (see Seeger 1986).

A further complexity is the relation between words and music within particular genres and/or performances. Are they thought of as distinctive or self-standing? If so, which, if either is the essential defining component? The answers may differ in different cultures and genres, in some cases the music being dominant, in others, as in some Fijian songs, the *verbal* text being regarded as in some sense prior and with an independent existence away from its tune. The detailed interactions between music and verbal text can also be significant (see List 1963, Sherzer and Wicks 1982, Beissinger 1988, Feld 1982, Fischer 1959: 47–8, also Fig. 7.2 on p. 155 below and for references on music generally 5.3.3).

Distinctions based on the speech–music relation are often used in classifying verbal forms. They can also be a factor – perhaps among others – for presenting and translating particular items under the head of, say, 'songs', rather than 'poems' or 'texts'. Such boundaries are multi-faceted and relative, however and – the important point – always need detailed justification rather than prior assumption.

7.2.2 Prose and poetry

This distinction too is more complex than it looks – 'looks' being the operative word here for in the context of writing we label a poem through its visible layout on the page. How is this to be applied to unwritten forms? The answer is not self-evident, though written transcriptions regularly make it seem so by imposing either a 'verse' or a 'prose' layout.

For oral forms researchers have looked to such features as marked and repetitive rhythm, music, lineation, strophic form, metaphorical expression, or local evaluations to decide whether to label any given case as 'poetry' or as 'prose'. The conclusion is often an approximation rather than wholly given in the form itself – and sometimes a disputable approximation. Arguments about African 'epic', for example, partly turn on whether certain narratives are to be regarded as 'verse' or 'prose', while the prosodic and structural features of American Indian narratives previously published as prose have led some scholars to reclassify them as poetry: 'All the collections that are now in print must be re-done', writes Hymes, 'they do not show the structure of the texts they present . . . . Hidden within the margin-to-margin printed lines are poems, waiting to be seen for the first time' (Hymes 1987:19). The apparent boundary between prose and poetry, recognised in some cultures' typographical definitions, thus relates to a series of relative and elusive factors and in some cases may not be appropriate at all (for further discussion see also Tedlock 1972, 1977, Bright 1979, Hymes 1977, 1981, 1987: 18ff, Sherzer and Woodbury 1987, Finnegan 1977: 107ff).

7.2.3 Oral and written

The difference between oral and written is in some approaches taken as the basis of all further classifications (implied indeed in the title of this volume, as in many others). This convenient and widely used differentiation, however, also conceals many problems and controversies and some established genre-terms (epic, legend, myth, riddle) cut across the apparent distinction. Many scholars now see the contrast as at best a relative, many-faceted and perhaps changing continuum, rather than an absolute divide (see 1.3.1, 8.5), and in any case not to comprehend all facets of communication.

7.2.4 Art, non-art and play

One commonsense basis for classification invokes distinctions between 'artistic' as against 'ordinary' or 'utilitarian' forms; parallel arguments similarly put 'play' in the first rather than second of these categories. Up to a point this works for some situations or cultures. But it also conceals some notoriously intractable problems. Most of these apply to any study of 'art' or of 'play'; but the question of what makes something 'artistic' is perhaps especially elusive in the case of *oral* forms: they are both in one sense ephemeral and also without the boundary which expression in writing (or print) can interpose between 'everyday' language and forms marked out as distinctive. Large-scale and clearly framed genres like epic perhaps present fewer problems, but shorter forms like proverbs, riddles, or word play are difficult to deal with. There may be other framing devices however that can be considered (see discussion and examples in Ben-Amos 1972, Bauman 1977a, Babcock 1977, Finnegan 1988: 65ff, S. Stewart 1979: esp. 21ff also discussion of performance in 5.3 and of style 8.4). A different line is to bypass such boundaries in any *general* sense – the concept of art at least is not always useful – in favour of more specific analyses; or to regard artistry or play as relative or emergent consitutents that enter, more, or less, into all forms of verbal expression. (For some relevant dicussions see, on 'literature': Fowler 1982: chap. 1, Krupat 1982: esp. 332ff, Wellek and Warren 1949: chap. 2, Hernadi 1978, Eagleton 1983: chap. 1, Finnegan 1970: 22ff, 1988: chap. 4; on 'art': Dissanayake 1988, Layton 1981, Forrest 1988, Zolberg 1990; on 'play': Huizinga 1970, Turner 1982.)

7.3 DIFFERENTIATING AND STUDYING GENRES

Whether consciously or not, most researchers get involved at some point in differentiating the kinds of spoken or written conventions that can be broadly summed up in the notion of genre; or, at the least, in using genre or genre-like words to convey their findings or interpret those of others. It is useful to be aware of the issues here, and of the range of genre-terms commonly used or argued over.

It is always worth trying to investigate local conventions and taxonomies. This obvious point needs stating in view of the older idea, reflected in Greenway's still-read *Literature among the Primitives* (1964: 35), that in oral contexts a 'literary taxonomy' is the exception, and that any implicit classifications will need formulation by outside observers in terms of their own cultural canons. It is true that local classifications are not always intellectualised or systematic, nor do they necessarily coincide with outsiders' divisions: the Limba *mboro* for example covers not only stories but also riddles or proverbs (Ben-Amos 1976: 236, Finnegan 1967) while the – to us – 'obvious' distinction between myths and legends is seen differently in some other cultures (see 7.4.1 below). But there are now many field-based studies to exemplify the occurrence of complex literary taxonomies (Chimombo 1988, Sherzer 1983, Feld 1990, Finnegan 1970: 79 and references there).

Taking account of these regularities is essential for a full understanding of the ideas and practices of any local art form, if only to place them in context and elicit their peculiar features. As Roger Abrahams put it

> We point to genres because by naming certain patterns of expression we are able to talk about the traditional forms and the conventional contents of artistic representation, as well as the patterns of expectation which both the artist and audience carry into the aesthetic transaction.
>
> (Abrahams 1976: 193)

The precise delineation of these genres is seldom straightforward, however. One constant problem is how quickly, if at all, to move to comparative genre-terms. Most existing collections and analyses *do* use such terms, useful vehicles both for understanding your own findings and communicating them to others. But the ethnographic data must also exert their pull, the more so that comparative terms accepted at any one time do not have any absolute or eternal validity.

A further issue is what criteria to use in differentiating genres – if this is thought desirable – and how to express these differences. This is more of a problem than it may seem, due to the confused basis for many generic classifications. There is often a cluster of heterogeneous, sometimes self-contradictory, criteria behind even apparently established words. Sometimes all or most of the following commonly-used criteria go together – but sometimes they do not, and you will have to come to an arbitrary (preferably conscious) decision:

1 *Stylistic or formal features*: including length, form of expression (prose? poetry? a mixture?), prosody, structure, type of linguistic expression ('everyday' as against symbolic or obscure language?), 'unity' or otherwise, and manner of treatment (as in Lüthi's concept of 'abstract style', 1982). Such criteria have a long history in literary theory, sometimes divided into 'outer form' (metre or structure) and 'inner form' (tone, attitude or purpose, as in Wellek and Warren 1949: 231).

2 *Subject matter*: another commonly used indicator. Thus 'heroic poetry' is sometimes defined as 'about heroes', and 'myths' differentiated from 'legends' because about gods or origins. Narratives are often similarly subdivided, as in the many collections separated into 'animal tales', 'wonder tales', 'stories about people', 'trickster tales', 'stories about supernatural beings', etc. (e.g., Nicoloff 1979, Finnegan 1967), or classified in terms of plot or theme (see 8.2) – convenient divisions but ones that may or may not coincide with stylistic differences. Such basic human subjects as, say, love, mourning, or the origins of the world also lend themselves to corresponding classes of oral art (useful for anthologisers).

3 *Occasion, role and context*: when and why a text is produced. Yoruba *ijala* poetry, for example, is defined through being performed by and for hunters at their gatherings, and songs sung at funerals, during drinking, or in interchanges between lovers are

often classified as laments, drinking songs and love poetry respectively (not necessarily the same as songs *about* death, drink or love). Similarly with lullabies, children's play songs, funeral oratory, and so on. This apparently simple feature is not always easy to discover and in practice context or role have often just been assumed without detailed investigation (attribution of function is a complex process, only too easily based on theoretical preconception rather than empirical observation, see 6.3).

4 *Performance characteristics*: sometimes an essential element in stylistic conventions rather than an optional frill (as it might be with written forms); indeed for some genres valued above the purely verbal elements. So how a particular form is performed, in what style, or the role of music or dance become central aspects to investigate (see chapter 5, also Finnegan 1977: 121ff.). The precise relation between text and performance can also be relevant, linking with questions about how far particular texts are crystallised or fixed, or how much variation is expected between performances of the 'same' work.

5 *Local terminologies and taxonomies*: now often emphasised, whether in the form of special terms or of an aesthetic critical vocabulary. Local terminologies may be more complicated than they seem in many published accounts, however, for the (arguably) crucial terms may not be known to everyone, and may be changing or disputed. Idealised or prescriptive terms, too, do not always correspond to what actually happens on the ground. Comparative words like myth, epic, folktale and so on may themselves play a part in local classifications for it is rare indeed for any culture, wherever it is, to be unaffected by wider scholarly discussion. Indeed it is not uncommon for local intellectuals to play the key role in collecting and shaping the corpus of material with direct feedback on the performers' interpretations. Some deplore such interactions as 'artificial' or 'fakelore'. Perhaps in some cases this is a fair assessment. But if and when these generalised and perhaps foreign-language terms do play a part in moulding people's consciousness this is surely merely part of the complex reality the researcher has to comprehend.

6 *Specifics of time, place and environment*: what initially look like recognisable genres may in practice vary not only between cultures, but also at different times and places within cultures, deployed differently by different individuals or interests. There can be emergent or variable forms whose formulation and enactment can be studied as dynamic historical processes rather than

neutral synchronic units. Apparent genres can also change over time as individuals exploit accepted frameworks in developing ways (see Vander 1988: 287ff), while older conventions can take on new forms, or new genres be created.

Genre classification can in principle build on any or all of these criteria. In practice several usually overlap – the 'interweaving of layers' as Perić-Polonijo puts it (1988:161). But there is also the possibility of conflicting but equally tenable classifications, and different scholars highlight different elements (some influential systems are usefully summarised in Jason 1986: 179f, 188f). One account may concentrate on verbal style and form, another on performance or functions, and a category picked out under one of these (the lament, say) might look different under other criteria.

This once again raises the question of why we engage in genre attribution at all. Given the relative, arbitrary and inconsistent character of this process should we, as Jason puts it, 'do without "genre"?' (1986: 187).

That is certainly one possible view. And many scholars are indeed moving away from the earlier preoccupation with genre typologies and the concept of fixed, mutually exclusive and 'pure' types. On the other hand, there *are* recognised conventions and patterns in verbal expression which analysts of verbal art forms rightly wish to study – they are not just imposed by outside scholars. There are also practical reasons why researchers have to face up to decisions about genre classification. These relate to how verbal utterances should be transcribed and represented, specially when – as often – this means presenting oral art forms to a wider or a foreign audience. In compiling an anthology of poetry or a collection of tales, how should they be titled? What principles should be used to group and divide them? Should these be directed to the projected readers' expectations? Or base themselves on content or on function? The answers are not self-evident, even if they are sometimes implicitly assumed by apparently neutral (but actually genre-laden) typographical formats or headings.

Many thus find that it is still illuminating to work with the concept of genre, if in a more open-ended sense than in the past, perhaps recognising the polythetic rather than single nature of any definitions, perhaps also looking to processes of mobilising conventions and resources rather than to fixed entities. For such purposes the criteria just discussed can still provide pointers to the kinds of regularities and continuities found in many forms of verbal expression.

7.4 SOME COMMON GENRE TERMS AND CONTROVERSIES

A huge number of genre-terms have been developed in both popular and scholarly usage, many by now with a quasi-technical status. Whatever your general reaction to the problems of classification, some of these will almost certainly be terms which you will either consider using yourself or meet in others' writings. A selection only is discussed below, as these can illustrate the controversies which can lie behind even the more innocent-sounding words.

A general problem underlying all these terms is that even when scholars endeavour to prescribe standard definitions, these are seldom universally followed. Thus 'myth', by some confined to only certain types of narrative (see below), is often used in popular collections to refer to any or all unwritten verbal forms. The same sometimes applies to 'legends', 'sagas', 'folktale' or even 'epic' – titles of books and articles can be misleading!

(A comprehensive bibliography for this huge area is impossible here, but a few starter – not necessarily systematic – references for specific terms are mentioned below; other general references worth consulting include entries in M. Leach 1949 (useful despite its age), Barnouw 1989 (see esp. under 'Folktale'), Ben-Amos 1976, Bødker 1965 (full list of terms, with further references), Ranke 1977–, and summaries in surveys of folklore or comparative literature such as Dorson 1972a, Brunvand 1986, Chadwick 1932–40, Preminger 1974.)

7.4.1 Myth

There have been many approaches to this emotive term: from philosophers, classical scholars, Jungian analysts, and earlier theorists like Max Müller or Andrew Lang, to the 'functionalist' definitions (myth as social 'charter') or Lévi-Straussian structuralist interpretations more familiar to anthropologists. This extensive history cannot be rehearsed here (for some initial references and examples see Dundes 1984, P. Maranda 1972, Puhvel 1987), but is worth bearing in mind as overtones from these and similar debates attach themselves variously to the term even when it is apparently used as a transparent and unloaded word.

Some attempts have been made to legislate on its usage. One

influential definition was laid down by Bascom. This links into Bascom's classification of 'prose narratives' more generally (see Fig. 7.1):

> *Myths are prose narratives which, in the society in which they are told, are considered to be truthful accounts of what happened in the remote past.* They are accepted on faith; they are taught to be believed; and they can be cited as authority in answer to ignorance, doubt, or disbelief. Myths are the embodiment of dogma; they are usually sacred; and they are often associated with theology and ritual. Their main characters are not usually human beings, but they often have human attributes; they are animals, deities, or culture heroes, whose actions are set in an earlier world, when the earth was different from what it is today, or in another world such as the sky or underworld. Myths account for the origin of the world, of mankind, of death, or for characteristics of birds, animals, geographical features, and the phenomena of nature. They may recount the activities of the deities, their love affairs, their family relationships, their friendships and enmities, their victories and defeats.
>
> (1965a: 4)

FORM	BELIEF	TIME	PLACE	ATTITUDE	PRINCIPAL CHARACTERS
Myth	Fact	Remote past	Different world: other or earlier	Sacred	Non-human
Legend	Fact	Recent past	World of today	Secular or sacred	Human
Folktale	Fiction	Any time	Any place	Secular	Human or non-human

Figure 7.1 Bascom's three forms of prose narratives (*source*: Bascom 1965a: 5)

This definition sums up the commonest (if often unstated) connotations of the term, pointing to its arguably key features. It is not always easily applicable however. In some African cultures the boundary between 'myth' and 'legend' is blurred (Finnegan 1970: 361ff), and the term is also widely used in broader senses. It is easy, but dangerous, to assume that all these features automatically go together, for in practice this is not always so. A story which happens to be about – say – the origin of human beings in some 'other' time, cannot be just labelled 'myth' and thus *assumed* to be well known and the basis for sanctioned beliefs; nor are all ritualistic or authoritative narratives (including many modern so-called 'myths') necessarily about sacred beings or remote time. 'Belief' too is difficult to pin down: what is believed in one sense or context may not be in another, and in any case what is it to 'believe'? This bundle of associations needs to be approached sceptically and in each specific case checked against the ethnographic findings.

Bascom's primary focus is on content – suitable for some purposes but not all – so for some it is unsatisfying as downplaying the function of upholding the social order (for some anthropologists once *the* defining essence of 'myth'), and the cognitive, psychological and symbolic aspects so emphasised by other analysts. It is still influential, however, and illuminating in its encapsulation of so many commonly-held connotations of the term (for further discussions or examples see, besides references above, Abrahams 1985b, Bremmer 1988, M. Jackson 1968, Malinowski 1948, E.K. Maranda 1973, Ray 1980, Röhrich 1984a, Samuel 1988, Samuel and Thompson 1990, Weigle 1982, 1989, Willis 1981; also references and discussion in 2.4, 8.3.3).

7.4.2 Legend, folktale, and other narrative forms

Given the many collections of narratives and the importance of narrative in human culture generally, the proliferation of connected terms is scarcely surprising. A few leading or specially controversial terms are picked out here (for further discussion and references see Scullion 1984, Röhrich 1984a, Finnegan 1970 chap. 13, Dégh in Dorson 1972, Ben-Amos 1989a, Rooth 1975, also for narratology generally 8.3.4 below, and 7.4.1 above on 'myth').

1) *Legend.* Usages in the past often implied a distinction from both 'myth' and 'folktale', again well enunciated in Bascom's schema (1965a: 4–5 – see Fig. 7.1 above) and with much the same features as his treatment of 'myth': widely used and recognised in roughly this sense, but sometimes not fitting detailed ethnographic concepts or practices. Recently the term has taken on new vitality in its application to contemporary and urban legends (Brunvand 1981, D.R. Barnes 1984, Smith 1984, Bennett 1985, Bennett et al. 1987, Bennett and Smith 1988 (esp. Part I), 1989).

2) *Folktale.* This is the third component of many classifications, complementary to 'myth' and 'legend'. Bascom defines folktales as 'prose narratives . . . regarded as fiction', with the further characteristics that:

They are not considered as dogma or history, they may or may not have happened, and they are not to be taken seriously . . . may be set in any time and place . . . . They have been called 'nursery tales' but in many societies they are not restricted to children. They have also been known as 'fairy tales' but this is inappropriate both because narratives about fairies are usually regarded as true, and because fairies do not appear in most folktales. Fairies, ogres, and even deities may appear, but folktales usually recount the adventures of animal or human characters.

(Bascom 1965a: 4)

This delineation is often followed (and if only for this reason worth knowing about), again with similar costs, benefits and puzzles as for the complementary terms. It is equally often used more broadly to denote (1) *any* oral narrative which is not specifically a 'myth' or 'legend', whether fictional or not and whatever the setting, or (2) *all* narratives (including myths and legends) regarded as oral, popular, 'traditional' or told by 'the folk' (a wide and sometimes ambiguous meaning). But whatever its exact referent, the term continues to be popular and over the years has stimulated a huge number of collections and publications (for recent analysis and references see Ben-Amos 1989, also Lüthi 1982).

3) *Other narrative terms.* Among the many other terms are: *saga* (sometimes used as an inclusive term for *all* oral or folk narrative and/or the prose equivalent of epic; sometimes roughly overlapping with legend and/or with the German *Sage*: see Nicolaisen 1988, Whybray 1987: 143ff, Bremmer 1988: 6f, Scullion 1984, Oinas 1978); *Märchen, fairy tale, housetale* (often used more or less interchangeably with 'folktale' and subject to the same ambiguities; perhaps now less popular than in the past, at least in English, but see Bettelheim 1976, Bottigheimer 1986b, Holbek 1987, Zipes 1979, 1983; also Ben-Amos 1989); *fable* (usually defined as a short narrative about animals or plants, with an explicit moral; for references see Carnes 1985); *memorate* and the more or less equivalent *personal narrative* (a focus of increasing interest in keeping with current emphases on individual artistry and experience, see Dégh and Vázsonyi 1974, Stahl and Dorson 1977, Bennett 1984, Personal Narratives Group 1989, Labov 1972: chap. 9, Myerhoff 1980, Samuel and Thompson 1990, Abrahams 1985b).

The broader term *narrative* is now coming back into its own with the increasing interest in analyses cutting through more limited generic divisions and crossing the oral/written boundary (see Bauman

1986, Mitchell 1981, and further discussion and references in 8.3.4, 8.5). Much the same applies to *story* and *fiction* (see Bauman 1986, Abrahams 1985b) where, as with narrative, recent studies on verbal art come into closer conjunction with current work in literary and linguistic theory.

7.4.3 Epic

This influential term was originally based on classical Greek litera-ture (*the* exemplars of epic being Homer's long heroic poems), then extended to arguably similar forms widely found in Eurasia in the past and present and to a lesser extent (though this is debated) elsewhere. The term is usually a noun, denoting – variously – a single self-contained poem; a group or cycle of more, or less, related poems; a poetic tradition. Its adjectival use has broader reference in such phrases as 'epic moments', 'epic tales', 'epic quality', or (as in Olrik 1965) 'epic laws'. The word is also used of written epics, sometimes labelled 'secondary' as against the supposedly 'primary' oral forms – the exact dividing line often unclear. All or any of these usages are well established, though their overlaps and differ-ences can be confusing.

The relatively accepted criteria in the traditional definition of 'a long narrative (oral) poem on heroic subjects' are hard to oper-ationalise in practical terms. How long is 'long', for example? Some expect many thousands of lines, others around one to two thousand, others less again, or – as in some Russian scholarship – groupings of shorter poems (see Honko 1988: 23). This in turn raises the question of how far an epic has to be a single poem. Here again there are differing views, including the category of 'cyclic epics' contrasted with 'unitary' or 'unified' epics (J.W. Johnson 1980: 311).

The 'verse' or 'poetry' criterion poses problems too. Some texts widely accepted as epic contain passages which by most definitions would be classed as prose (see Finnegan 1977: 10). Further, the once-assumed division between 'prose' and 'poetry' is now being rethought (see 7.2.2 above) and music or performance as well as purely textual qualities sometimes considered. Perhaps we need a new definition of the 'poetic' aspects of epic in the context of actual oral delivery. This might mean revising some earlier classifications (see Okpewho 1977:172, 186–7).

There are comparable problems with other elements in the defi-nition. 'Oral' is a slippery word (see 1.3.1), and the line between narrative and other poetic forms, particularly panegyric, sometimes hard to draw. Finally, what exactly is 'heroic'? We may feel we have some intuitive understanding (still based on readings of Homer?) but it is scarcely easy to pin down.

Even the standard definition thus has problems, suggesting that the concept of epic may be essentially polysemous and relative. But to this has to be added further controversies and political overtones. Some date from nineteenth-century evolutionist and Eurocentric models – the assumption that any nation worthy of the name must pass through a heroic stage with an epic to match. Its role in nationalist movements intensified this. There was 'a feeling abroad', as Hatto well puts it, 'that every European nation should have its epic, a feeling so strong that where there was none an epic was, if not invented, nevertheless somehow got together and produced' (Hatto 1980: 18) – a process not without parallels in twentieth-century post-colonial nation-building. Because of this background, even the most innocuous-seeming definition or attribution of 'epic' can be emotive. (Among the huge literature see specially, besides references already cited, Oinas 1978, Koljević 1980, Opland 1986, Foley 1990a; for the controversy over African epic, which illustrates the problems above, see Finnegan 1970: 108–10, with responses or further comments in Biebuyck 1976, Okpewho 1977, 1979, J.W. Johnson 1980, Ben-Amos 1983, Seydou 1982, Opland 1983: 143ff.)

7.4.4 Riddles, proverbs and conversational genres

There is a vast literature on proverbs and riddles. As so often, there are disputes about definition and interpretation, often useful in pointing to features that might otherwise be neglected. (On riddles see Abrahams and Dundes in Dorson 1972a, Finnegan 1970: 426ff, Pepicello and Green 1984, Haring 1985; on proverbs Abrahams in Dorson 1972a, Kuusi 1972, Mieder and Dundes 1981, Mieder 1982, Briggs 1988:101ff.) In recent years there has been some reaction against the compiling of yet more and more lists of proverbs, etc., in favour of more analytic study of their usage, context and interpretation.

Other conversational genres, like word play, greetings and blessings, have attracted less work, and not yet, it seems, an established vocabulary (on jokes, however, see Briggs 1988: 171ff; on conversational genres generally Abrahams 1968b, Tannen 1989, also further discussion or examples in Bauman and Sherzer 1974, Sherzer 1983, Kratz 1989, Finnegan 1969b, 1970: 466f).

7.4.5 Other terms

The terms discussed above have attracted substantial interest and controversy but are illustrative rather than comprehensive. Other relatively established terms too may – or may not – prove useful, if not without their own controversies. Some are briefly listed below (in some cases with further references – random rather than systematic but at least one entry into the voluminous literature); see also general references on p. 146.

Panegyric/praise poetry (Opland 1983, n.d.); *lyric* (Burke 1951, Finnegan 1970: chap. 9, 1977: 13ff, Perić-Polonijo 1988); *lament* (Nketia 1955, Nenola-Kallio 1982, Finnish Folkloristics 1/Studia Fennica 17, 1974, Kaufman 1988, 1990, Urban 1988, Feld 1990); *ballad* (Child 1882–98, Buchan 1972, Webber 1987); *chante-fable* (where prose alternates with verse); *oratory, speech, rhetoric* (Bloch 1975, Braden 1983, Paine 1981, Parkin 1984); *hymn* (Roberts 1989, Finnegan 1970: chap. 7); *sermon* (Rosenberg 1970a, G. L. Davis 1985, Lawless 1987, 1988, Suojanen 1989); *drama* (Schechner 1985, Schechner and Appel 1990, Peacock 1968, Finnegan 1970: chap. 18, Brooks 1989, Turner 1982, Bendix 1989: esp. chap. 6 and references there); *festival, carnival* (Bakhtin 1968, Babcock 1978, Abrahams 1987, Stoeltje 1989) – and many others depending on which of the criteria for classification are followed (categories based on content or function are particularly prolific).

7.4.6 Cross-generic analyses

Some scholars prefer to treat all the genres within a community together rather than separately. This may involve some genre differentiation, but means that all forms can be analysed together and compared or contrasted within the same framework (this may include visual or material as well as primarily verbal forms). As illustrated in Fig. 7.2, this approach can lead to new insights into the relation between local categories, based on the ethnographic evidence, but sometimes of wider comparative significance too (see also Sherzer 1974, 1990, Howell 1986, Briggs 1988, Glassie 1982, Gossen 1974, Harries 1977, Tedlock and Tedlock 1986, Ben-Amos 1987, Feld 1988, Moyo 1986).

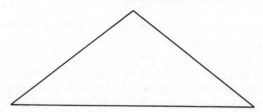

ngére (song)
Priority of melody over text
Text and melody entirely fixed by
   non-human source
Highly structured temporally
Timbre an essential feature
Tone structures are essential

kapérni (speech)
Priority of text over melody
Text constructed by speaker in
   free improvisation
Timbre relatively unimportant
Tone is important

iarén (telling)
Relative priority of
   relatively fixed text
   over melody and
   textual improvisation
Timbre relatively
   unimportant
Tone is important

Figure 7.2 Song, speech and telling compared: genres of Suyá Indians of Brazil (*source*: Seeger 1986: 69; reprinted by permission of Mouton de Gruyter, a division of Walter de Gruyter & Co.)

7.5 CROSS-CUTTING THEMES

As well as the accepted – if shifting – boundaries and genres just discussed, certain other themes have been posited. These are not so much the basis for differentiation as strands running through a number of genres and divisions (some have a specific generic manifestation).

7.5.1 Drama, rhetoric and performance

There is a sense in which *all* forms of verbal expression – indeed all our actions – can be seen as dramatic performance or, similarly, as rhetoric in the sense of the conventions of argumentation running through so much human communication (see Arnold and Bowers 1984, Perelman and Olbrechts-Tyteca 1969, also references in 5.1 and 7.4.5 above). Such viewpoints challenge imposed boundaries between 'art' and 'life' or between otherwise separate genres. Should we really draw a line between fully-fledged 'drama' or 'speech-making' and everyday performances? Are these themes not sometimes as significant as arguably superficial genre-based divisions?

7.5.2 Myth and mythic imagination

The term 'myth' is used not only as a specific genre word but also in a more general sense which indicates the somehow symbolising, cosmic, eternity-laden aspects of human consciousness. Myth is thus opposed to 'history' (in the sense of secular chronological narrative) or, in its adjectival form, contrasted with such concepts as 'worldly', 'literal' or 'temporal'. Sometimes this mythic quality is seen as distinctive to certain forms, but it can equally be presented as permeating, to a greater or lesser extent, many kinds of genres or tellings (for example the 'mythic mode of consciousness' in some South American historical narratives, Hill 1988: 8ff).

7.5.3 Narrative

Narrative can be seen not just a specific genre or work, but as a theme running through many forms, non-verbal as well as verbal. This too can be studied in its own right, irrespective of conventional genre classification (see 2.4.8, 8.3.4). Once again this cross-cutting element can emerge in different genres and media, a mark of conjunction among surface differences.

7.5.4 Other possible schemes

A number of other differentiations also get away from the somewhat realist idea of separate genres, or cut across them. Some arise from wider distinctions in particular cultures (as in the example in Fig. 7.2). Others are more general. Among these are the more, or less, useful distinctions between popular and élite forms, or between fixed and fluid genres. More complicated is Roger Abrahams' account of 'the complex relations of simple forms' (Fig. 7.3). As well as considering the 'structural levels' of the materials and the dramatic structure (1976: 197) he particularly emphasises context in the sense of the level of interaction between performer and audience to draw up four main categories of genres (conversational, play, fictive, and static).

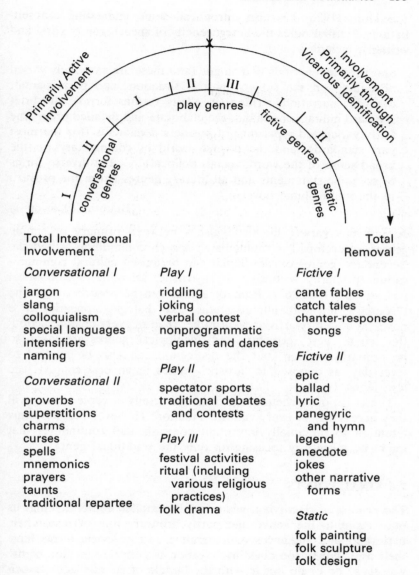

Figure 7.3 The complex relations of simple forms: range of level of inter-action between performer and audience (*source*: Abrahams 1976: 206)

Bakhtin (1986) has also introduced some interesting differentiations. He first notes the heterogeneity of speech genres (oral and written), including

> Short rejoinders of daily dialogue (and these are extremely varied depending on the subject matter, situation, and participants), everyday narration, writing (in all its various forms), the brief standard military command, the elaborate and detailed order, the fairly variegated repertoire of business documents (for the most part standard), and the diverse world of commentary (in the broad sense of the word: social, political) . . . the diverse forms of scientific statements and all literary genres (from the proverb to the multivolume novel).
>
> (Bakhtin 1986: 60–1)

Amidst this variety he distinguishes between primary or simple genres – developed in 'unmediated speech communion' – and the 'secondary' genres of 'developed and organised cultural communication (primarily written) that is artistic, scientific, sociopolitical and so on' (1986: 62). Primary genres can be absorbed into the secondary, but with altered status, like dialogue appearing in a novel 'as a literary-artistic event rather than as everyday interaction' (loc. cit.). These secondary and 'ideological' genres are taken to be primarily written, but the distinction can also be applied to 'everyday' as opposed to 'artistic' genres in an oral context (see also Dorst 1983).

These various schemes are not universally accepted, nor will they necessarily fit every cultural situation. However they do draw attention to potentially important contrasts and continuities that might be missed by focusing on only the traditional genres.

7.6 FINAL POINTS

The process of classifying, whatever the detailed content, brings us once again to the active and partly arbitrary role of researcher, performer and audiences. Comparative and historical terms have their uses, but so too does investigation of cultural specifics, of the way these do or do not fit with the bundle of connotations associated with cross-cultural terms, of local taxonomies, and of developing formations and transformations around existing expectations. And even when we have settled on the particular classifications that best seem to match the needs of the research and the ethnography there may be yet other strands to divide or unite these categories.

The traditional labelling of genres or of other differentiations, whether by ourselves or others, only represents one aspect of reality.

Finally it is not just outsiders or scholars who disagree about use and interpretation; the creators and performers may do so too and themselves be part of the debate. The target, furthermore, is sometimes a moving one: new genres arise, old ones are developed, manipulated, or reinterpreted, and, whether explicitly or imperceptibly, new practices become established under old names. Contrary to what used to be assumed, such changes and continuities are nothing new but a predictable part of human culture.

8 Analysing and comparing texts: style, structure and content

Most accepted methodologies within literary and linguistic study can in principle be applied to oral texts once they are represented in written form. Indeed textual analysis has often been taken as *the* method for studying verbal forms, following the model of text as something bounded and organised, a unit through which the traditional methods of philological and literary scholarship can be extended to unwritten forms. Rather than trying to cover all these methodologies, I have concentrated here on those particularly exploited in analysing *oral* forms (with some brief further discussion in 8.5). I have also mainly left to one side the problematics within the concept of text (on which see 1.4) or its broader sense as 'any coherent complex of signs' (Bakhtin 1986: 103), so the focus here, as in most traditional forms of textual analysis, is primarily on texts-as-verbal.

The presentation is within a vaguely historical order, but methodologies in practice overlap in time and coverage, and 'old' methods take on new twists. Some topics such as typology or narrative could have been treated under several heads, while terms like 'style' and 'structure' can be interpreted in differing senses (here 'style' is mainly taken as lower-level aspects, 'structure' as more the overall form and its constituent divisions). Amidst these continuing overlaps and ambiguities, the categories and ordering here are for convenience not definitive classification.

8.1 TEXTUAL ANALYSIS: PROBLEMS AND OPPORTUNITIES

There are continuing arguments about the value of focusing on verbal texts. Some issues are broadly theoretical and concern such questions as the evaluation of contrasting perspectives for studying oral forms or problems in the concept of 'text'. Others relate to practical questions of access or resources. It may thus be as well not to take it for granted that analysing the verbal text-as-given is the only possible focus, but also to weigh up such questions as the following:

1 Possible alternative or complementary approaches (see chapter 2).

2 Nature of the texts to be studied. This is crucial for the validity of the final analysis, but often not explained – or perhaps thought about – by researchers. Even if few or no details about context, performance or local evaluations initially seem to be available (often the reason for adopting text-based approaches in the first place) some information can sometimes be discovered once the questions are raised; at the least you need to be aware that this affects the nature or authority of the conclusions. The text's source and status need exploring through such questions as whether it is a summary of the 'content' or 'plot' of a longer performance (summarised by whom and in what context?); a word-for-word reproduction of a commonly-performed text (memorised? resulting from composition-in-performance?); first synthesised into a bounded linear text by the collector or writer; an already-crystallised and 'texted' form in the local culture and/or among specific groups; written down in response to some particular set of historical circumstances (for further comments on the status of texts see 1.4, Hanks 1989, Finnegan 1988: 169ff). In practice the units being analysed generally consist of written verbal transcriptions, often translations. So information is also needed about the processes of how these were recorded, dictated, transcribed, translated and represented in writing (see chapters 4,9).

3 Performance properties. Was the text delivered by one or by several performers; by leader with chorus; with frequent verbal repetitions; through music or dance? Such factors can affect its meaning and nature and thus what kind of analysis is feasible.

4 Representativeness of the text(s) being analysed. This at the least includes questions about why *that* text rather than another was selected for transcription, transmission, publication, or analysis. Again the answers affect the conclusions.

5 Number of texts available. Having a large corpus so as to compare many instances of the same theme, genre, etc., rather than trying to deduce rules from just one or two items is always important and for certain methods essential.

6 The language(s). For textual questions linguistic competence has to be taken seriously, specially for any study of stylistics and meaning. Some highly-regarded comparative work on content or structure has been undertaken with little language knowledge or through translations, though even this remains controversial.

The type and feasibility of textual analysis partly depends on the questions above. Certain text-based analyses might, for example, be rewarding for epics or lengthy narratives where there is plenty of 'meat' in the verbal forms themselves, but not for performance-oriented songs or short anecdotes; while if only summaries or translations are available, stylistic or symbolic analysis will be less illuminating than comparisons of content or plot. These issues need consideration early and openly. Textual analyses carry less conviction if they give the impression of tacitly sliding over such questions or of replacing ethnographic enquiry by *post hoc* speculation or introspection.

The comments above focus on the problems. This is both because traditional textual methods may seem deceptively easy – and so sometimes carried out with little prior thought – and because of recent reactions against the earlier dominance of text-based approaches. They have a positive side too however. As it becomes more widely recognised that content, style or structure are not absolute matters – nor perhaps are texts either – so new possibilities open up for the *re*-analysis of existing transcriptions. Attention to new factors, or to a wider range of factors, may reveal previously unrecognised features, as in re-assessments of American Indian narratives as verse (see 7.2.2) and other attempts to re-interpret or amplify the bare text (as in Bowden 1987 on auditory aspects, Pickering 1982 on the historical context). Similar re-analysis is probably in principle possible with any corpus of texts and may become a prominent feature of research in the future. The important counterpoint to the problems, finally, lies in the many methods open to researchers interested in textual analysis, feeding directly into and from a body of highly reputable modern scholarship.

8.2 VARIATION, TYPOLOGY AND COMPARISON

One often-noted feature of verbal forms, both oral and written, is variability: the appearance and re-appearance of similar but non-identical versions of what is in some sense the 'same' plot, motif, theme or whatever. This feature provides the basis for a large number of textual analyses. One prominent strand in this scholarship concerns analysis of variation in terms of content, the focus of this section (structure is treated in 8.3).

8.2.1 Working with variants: some methods and questions

Methods for comparing, analysing or classifying the content of variants have been particularly developed in folklore scholarship (see 2.4.1–2). Some understanding of these methodologies is useful background to any kind of textual analysis for, though nowadays less dominant than in the past, they still influence contemporary studies and reappear in more modern dress. The most common – with some overlapping and mutual influence – can be listed as:

1 Trying to find the origin or the original form (archetype) of a particular narrative by collecting and comparing variants. Versions may come from anywhere in the world, though in practice the sources are mainly Indo-European (examples include Cox's study (1893) of the Cinderella tale, cf. also Rooth 1951, B.H. Smith 1981: 212ff and Dundes 1982).

2 Tracing the detailed historical dispersion of a particular tale or (less often) song, often accompanied by distribution maps (for example Stith Thompson's charting of the spread of the 'star husband' story through North America; see Dundes 1965: 414ff, and Thompson 1946: esp. 428ff).

3 Differentiating and/or studying particular subtypes. This may involve delineating specific ethnic or regional subgenres (sometimes following Von Sydow's concept of 'oikotypes' (1948); see also recent work on urban forms as in Bennett and Smith 1989). 'Redaction analysis' provides techniques for classifying versions into related groups of 'all those variants which resemble each other more than any other variant lying outside the scope of the redaction' (Kuusi 1974: 40): a table is constructed of recurrent traits and their connections (see Kuusi's authoritative analysis 1974).

4 Publication and/or analysis of parallel or variant versions of the 'same' tale, song or rhyme, sometimes with comment on historical or regional contexts but without necessarily drawing conclusions about origins or diffusion. Influential collections include Child's volumes of English and Scottish ballads (1882–98) and the Opies' studies of nursery rhymes and schoolchildren's lore (1951, 1961). There are also studies of particular tales or ballads, etc., ranging

from brief synchronic comparisons to full-scale accounts like Schmitt's treatment of 'The holy greyhound' legend over several centuries (1983) drawing on both structural analysis and comparison of variants (methods which here shade into each other).

5 The comparison and contrasting of versions so as to elucidate meaning in a way not possible by considering single items (Calame-Griaule et al. 1983, also 8.7 below).

Related methods include constructing typologies or indexes based on plots and motifs (8.2.2), the analysis of differing versions within a wider corpus to identify formulaic expressions and recurrent themes (2.4.9 and 8.6.2 below), and narratological work on plot structure (8.3.4).

These methods are not necessarily outdated, as sometimes assumed, for the study of identity and variation still deserves attention. Earlier attempts to deduce *origins* from the study of multivariate versions admittedly proved difficult, perhaps misguided, and the process of identifying and transcribing 'variants' problematic. Even the term 'variant ' is not totally agreed: sometimes broadly interchangeable with 'version', sometimes confined to 'those versions that diverge appreciably from standard forms' (Dundes 1965: 420, see also Dundes 1964b, M. Leach 1949 under 'variant'; also more generally Brunvand 1986: 9, B.H. Smith 1981: 211ff, Cancel 1989: 19). But the issues underlying the comparison of variants still fascinate researchers. Beneath the same-but-different versions *is* there an abiding text or 'basic' version? Few scholars now seek an answer purely in terms of origins, while oral-formulaic and performance scholars, among others, have undermined older answers which assumed a fixed 'original' archetype. But the question does not go away. Amidst the variations or the separate performances *what* is it that remains, and in what sense?

Acceptable answers to such questions depend partly on your theoretical assumptions about language, mind or memory. Is it a matter of searching for some pre-existing or pre-learnt form somehow embedded in people's minds (or in some people's minds); a basic generative structure; emergence in performance within given conventions? *Is* there something 'real' at all behind the variants? If so, should we be searching for verbal text – or for mental image? Or are such questions naive, as Barbara Herrnstein Smith suggests (1981), in presupposing some Platonic ideal or 'essential' story over and above the contingent re-tellings whereas the reality perhaps lies in the act of narrating? Alternatively, is there some basic human concept of 'tale type' shared by human beings irrespective of academic fashions (Georges 1983)?

Some answers are probably empirical and culture-dependent. The relation between variation and stability in texts, together with how this is conceived of and practised, may vary between cultures, genres, historical periods, even perhaps individuals. So the variant renderings, their interrelations, and how to study them become suitable questions not just (as in earlier work) for historical reconstruction, establishing typologies, or textual collecting and editing, but also for direct ethnographic investigation into specificities.

8.2.2 Indexing tale types and motifs

The study of variation has often gone with an interest in classification. This too was a particular preoccupation of folklorists in the past, if only because the huge numbers of collected stories needed means for ordering and retrieval.

The many tale classifications include those based on the great Grimm collection of fairy tales; on the name of the central character; or on specific incidents. The standard system however has come to be Aarne's tale-type index (1910) with revisions and amplifications by Stith Thompson in 1928 and 1961. This concentrates on plots or story-lines, dividing tales into Animal Tales, Ordinary Tales and Jokes, each with its own divisions and sub-divisions, and covers 'the folk-tales of Europe, West Asia, and the lands settled by these peoples' (Aarne and Thompson 1961: 7). Like most such compilations, it has strengths and limitations. The under-representation of certain regions means not just a gap in coverage but the problem that the categories do not always easily accommodate examples from other cultures. Researchers are thus sometimes caught between either having to modify, even reject, the scheme, or force their own material to fit (for discussion see Azzolina 1987: xxixff and, for a supplement on non-European material, Crowley 1973). Another drawback is the limitation to tales (for the relatively sparse typologies of other forms see Azzolina 1987: xxxvii and, for proverbs, Kuusi 1972). Whatever the problems however, this standard system is widely used by researchers and has inspired a huge number of more detailed indexes (see below for examples; for general critique and references see Azzolina 1987: xxxv–xxxvi, also Georges 1983).

Different in scope, but on the same general lines, is Stith Thompson's 'Motif-index', first published in the 1930's, the revised and enlarged 6-vol. edition appearing in 1955–8, with 'motifs' defined as 'narrative elements' in the sense of specific incidents, items, or actors. This index is world-wide and draws on a wide range of folk literature: not just 'folktales' but also 'ballads, myths, fables, mediaeval romances, exempla, fabliaux, jest-books and local legends' (to cite its sub-title), and includes written as well as oral sources. Both the index itself and the schema which it set up have become the authoritative standards (see references and critique in Azzolina 1987: xxiiiff).

The tale type and motif indexes have been particularly influential within folklore. Their original development reflected and reinforced the Finnish 'historical-geographical' method, but they also form the basis of recent work. Dundes argued recently that:

> Appropriate citation of motif and tale type numbers in published research is the hallmark of the professional folklorist while conversely the failure either to know about or properly utilize established motifs and tale types is demonstrated all too often in the writings of amateurs or dilettantes who are wont to write about myth, folktale, legend and ballad.
>
> (Dundes in Azzolina 1987: ix)

Many anthropologists (and folklorists too) query too extensive a reliance on content-based cross-cultural typologies, pointing to the problems of isolating plots or motifs and the constructed nature of indexed versions (Rooth 1979, 1980, B.H. Smith 1981). Gender bias in the compilation and presentation of type- and motif-indexes has also been discussed (Lundell 1986), amid a general trend towards questioning what were once seen as value-free and mechanical indexing techniques. Dissension still continues over basic categories too, for although the Thompson systems mostly swept the board, they are not universally accepted (for some debates and alternative systems see P.P. Waterman 1987, Haring 1982; for earlier but sometimes revived classifications such as Slavic systems based in Arnaudov's work on Bulgarian tales, see Azzolina 1987: xxvii, 10–11).

Despite the controversies, interest in motif and tale classification is still alive, and indexes being compiled in large numbers. They can be consulted to put a particular form in cross-cultural perspective; provide a convenient comparative framework for classifying and indexing; or suggest units for content analysis. Information about the distribution, recurrence or patterning of particular plots need not entail following the classifications uncritically but can build into more detailed and topical questions about interactions between individual creativity and 'traditional' patterns, or form the basis for comparative and historical studies like Lévi-Strauss' treatment of the myth of Oedipus (1963), Stanford's tracing of the 'Ulysses theme' through the ages (1964), and, more recently, French Africanists' analyses of plot and theme in different parts of Africa (Görög et al. 1980, Görög-Karady 1982; see also the 'Cinderella' story in Rooth 1951, Dundes 1982, 'Oedipus' in Edmunds and Dundes 1983, Edmunds 1985, and 'the flood myth' in Dundes 1988). New developments are also perhaps on the horizon through interconnections between index compilers and those interested in structuralist or narratological analyses. Whatever one's theoretical bias, then, these indexes can prove useful at the least as a bibliographical tool and perhaps also as background for comparative analysis and resultant theoretical debate.

(Notable among the indexes are Aarne-Thompson 1961 (the authoritative tale-type index) and Thompson 1955–8 (motif-index), and, among more specialised indexes (not here differentiated between tale-type and motif): Arewa 1967 (Africa), Ashliman 1987 (English-language folktales), Baughman 1966 (English and N. American folktales), Clarke 1958 (West African), Cross 1952 (early Irish), Hodne 1984 (Norwegian), Ikeda 1971 (Japan), Kirtley 1971 (Polynesian), Klipple 1938 (African), Flowers 1952 (West Indies), Haring 1982 (Madagascar), Lambrecht 1967 (Central Africa), MacDonald 1982 (children's books), Thompson and Balys 1958 (India), P.P. Waterman 1987 (Australian Aborigine). The massive *Enzykopládie des Märchens* (Ranke 1977–) uses the Aarne/Thompson categories to compare 'the rich stock of narrative material . . . transmitted orally and through the medium of literature . . . thus illustrating the persistent interrelation between literature and oral tradition' (blurb circulated 1989), their main concentration being on Europe and the countries influenced by 'European culture'. See also Courtés 1982, Goldberg 1984, and Azzolina's annotated bibliography of type- and motif-indexes (1987, a comprehensive survey and discussion, drawn on extensively here), also 2.4.2 above.)

8.3 STRUCTURE AND STRUCTURALIST METHODS

'Structuralism' refers to several approaches within anthropology, literature and folklore, particularly influential in the 1960's and 1970's but still widely used (see 2.4.7). 'Structure' is also, however, referred to in less specialist senses which also need to be considered before moving on to the explicitly 'structuralist' methods drawing on Propp's morphological approach, Lévi-Straussian analyses, and the subsequent extension into narratological study.

8.3.1 Structure as organisational principles within texts

One aspect of any text lies in its inner construction and divisions. 'Structure' is a useful term for this, for though sometimes used more or less interchangeably with 'style' (see 8.4), it directs particular attention to the principles, as Barbara Herrnstein Smith puts it, 'according to which one line (or any other unit, larger or smaller, from a sound to a sentence or a stanza) follows another' (1968: 6; see also Hymes 1981: 42ff, 333ff).

Analysing a text's internal organisation raises a series of questions to investigate. These include: the ordering and development of the text (paratactic, sequential, 'envelope patterns'/'ring structure' (see Foley 1987a: 245ff, Lord 1986a: 53ff) and so on); sub-divisions within the text and how these are achieved (as by songs or dialogues within stories, moves of scene or time, or differing linguistic registers); formulaic runs and patternings; opening and closing formulae; and recurrent patterns for starting and coming to an end. Larger questions arise too: is the basic structure 'prose' or 'verse' and in what sense; if there are 'lines',' verses', or 'stanzas' how are these defined and what is their relation to each other; what are the principles of punctuation, syntax or subdivision with which oral versions have been organised into written transcriptions; how do performance practices (separated in time perhaps) affect questions of artistic unity and the structure of the text; what is the structural interplay within texts between differing modes of performance? There are also questions about the logical and persuasive structure underlying the argument (see Perelman and Olbrechts-Tyteca 1969). All in all such analyses often reveal more systematic, recurrent and artful patterns than appear on the surface.

Such questions sometimes feed into narratological or other distinctive approaches, but can also be pursued almost whatever your theoretical orientation. Their investigation may anyway be needed for the practical reason that they affect how you present your transcriptions as texts. For example where should paragraph, line or stanza divisions come? Where does a 'separate' story or song begin and end? What do the apparent textual unity or sub-divisions conveyed on the printed page represent in the original performance (see also 9.3)?

8.3.2 Morphology and structure

Propp's analysis of the morphology of Russian folktales (English translation 1968) led to a spate of work on both oral and written texts. The main focus is on elucidating the structural rules underlying the form taken by particular genres (usually but not always narrative).

What is meant by 'form' or 'structure' varies however. Propp himself (1968) distinguished a series of 'functions' in the sense of fundamental moves or themes such as absence, violation, pursuit and rescue. A tale is then made up of a sequence of such functions. He also points to recurrent characters (villain, princess, hero . . .), which appear and reappear in different stories. Identifying these narrative regularities behind superficially different stories makes it possible to uncover the basic story 'grammar'. Similar analyses work with the same concept of underlying structure but differ in precise objectives, terminology, or definition of key units. Dundes looks to the sequence of 'motifemes' in North American Indian folktales (1964a), while others have analysed the sequence of related actions (Brémond 1973), recurrent patterns in plot categories (Todorov 1986), patterned image-sets in narrative (Cancel 1989), or, as illustrated in Fig. 8.1 (see p. 168), a set of narratives seen as moving through such rhetorical functions as orientation, evaluation, complicating action, resolution, and coda (Labov 1972: chap. 9, see also 2.4.7).

Another interesting example is Denise Paulme's work on African stories, based on morphological analysis of texts from many parts of the continent (1976 esp. chap 1). She draws attention to

> la nécessité, pour qu'il y ait oeuvre littéraire véritable, d'une intrigue. La seule narration d'événements selon leur suite dans le temps ne suffit pas: un conte est reconnu comme tel par son auditoire dans la mesure où l'accent porte sur la modification qui permet le passage d'une situation à une autre, d'un manque à une situation normale ou le contraire.
>
> (Paulme 1976: 44–5)

African narrations, she concludes, move between 'euphoria' and 'dysphoria' via the 'normal situation' (equilibrium), deterioration (away from equilibrium), lack (disequilibrium), amelioration (removing the lack) and back to the 'normal' situation (see Fig 8.2, p. 169). There are thus six main structural types: ascending (from lack to success), descending (the opposite), cyclical (from one state to the other and back again), spiral (more than one cyclical move),

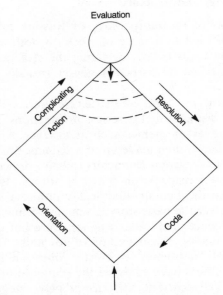

A complete narrative begins with an orientation, proceeds to the complicating action, is suspended at the focus of evaluation before the resolution, concludes with the resolution, and returns the listener to the present time with the coda. The evaluation of the narrative forms a secondary structure which is concentrated in the evaluation section but may be found in various forms throughout the narrative.

Figure 8.1 Labov's representation of narrative syntax (*source*: Labov 1972: 369; copyright 1972 by the University of Pennsylvania Press)

mirror (with two parallel or opposed characters), hourglass (parallel actors plus change of places: for fuller discussion see Paulme 1976, also examples in Babalola 1976, Haring 1982: 23ff, Cancel 1989: 33ff).

Morphological methods are not without controversy. They often take little account of context, audience behaviour, historical development, local meaning, even sometimes the original language: an attraction of this approach in one sense (making it possible to analyse texts without such ethnographic information) but a limitation in others. The familar problems of cross-cultural study arise too. Some analysts confine themselves to a particular genre at a particular point in time, others point to comparative patterns underlying narratives (or, less often, other forms) from many different languages, areas, or historical periods.

Such analyses can be undertaken in an unsystematic, even facile way, and convincing work demands at the least a large corpus of representative texts recorded in some detail. Given this safeguard,

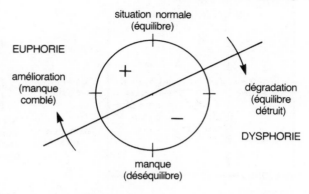

Figure 8.2 Paulme's schema of the morphological structure of African tales (*source*: Paulme 1976: 24; copyright 1976 by Editions Gallimard)

and a proper regard for their scope and limitations, researchers using these methods can justifiably claim to counter previous assumptions about the 'formless' or random nature of oral texts by uncovering hidden rules and interrelationships beneath what might otherwise seem an unpredictable variety of tellings and re-tellings (as Dundes 1964: 17ff pertinently points out for American Indian tales). Classification into different structural types also becomes possible, as do analyses feeding into the comparative study of narrative (see Cancel 1989: esp. chap. 2, and 8.3.4 below).

8.3.3 Lévi-Strauss and structuralist analyses

Somewhat different, but related, methods are used by Lévi-Strauss and his followers (see Lévi-Strauss' classic articles in 1963 (first published 1955) and 1967, his longer analyses (1969–81), and the examples and critiques in E. Leach 1967, 1970a, b; also 2.4.7). Form is still the interest, but this now means the relations between particular themes and/or reference to universal human cognitive processes. The prime focus is again on verbal texts rather than performance, audiences or context, with the texts here usually described as 'myths'. Within these texts or groups of texts the analyst detects the underlying logic, in the form of the transformations, binary oppositions and dialectical relationships which structure them. Formulae or algebraic figures are sometimes used to convey these logical interrelationships, as is the concept of 'mythemes'.

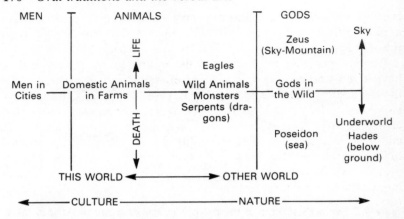

Figure 8.3 The schema of binary oppositions in Lévi-Strauss' analysis of the Oedipus myth, as summarised by Edmund Leach (*source*: Leach 1970b: 71)

These methods usually involve comparing different versions to abstract their basic structure. This may be in relation to the themes or paradoxes in a particular culture or historical period (as in some of Lévi-Strauss' lengthy analyses of South American Indian cultures). Often a yet wider comparative frame is invoked, justified by Lévi-Strauss' view that:

> The mythical value of the myth is preserved even through the worst translation . . . . Its substance does not lie in its style, its original music, or its syntax, but in the *story* it tells.
>
> (1963: 210)

The aims here are to elucidate what is universal: 'bringing to light the hidden logic behind mythic thought' (1978: 507) and discovering the deep structure of the human mind. 'Structural analysis, going beyond the apparent diversity of human societies, claims to be reaching back to common and fundamental properties' (Lévi-Strauss 1973: 475).

This method too has proved both illuminating and controversial. Even scholars who would not follow Lévi-Strauss' methods are sometimes inspired by the broad sweep of his questions or by his attention, in contrast to other methodologies, to cognitive factors, intellectual dialectic and the uses of paradox. And questions raised in Lévi-Strauss' writings can also be combined with other approaches to give comparative perspective or throw new light on ethnographic findings (as in Feld 1982). Others find such analyses too abstract or intellectualist, query the focus on universals, or criticise the lack of culturally-specific contexting (a criticism less applicable to recent field-based works like M. Jackson 1982, Cosentino 1982).

Researchers using these structuralist methods need to ensure they have the resources to deploy them effectively. These would normally need to include a reasonably large body of texts (e.g., many variants of the 'same' myth or whatever, either cross-culturally/ cross-historically or in one culture area); some knowledge of the culture(s) being analysed; and facility for engaging with the kinds of logical relations and paradoxes that typically feature in this approach. Without such a background, the results can be unconvincing. Cosentino well explains the potential problems and their correctives:

> The claims of structuralism are sweeping, and opponents of the methodology are correct to warn against the arbitrary selection of social data and of oral narrative in the anthropologist's creation of 'myth on myth'. Without being grounded in a representative body of oral narratives, and in knowledge of the performing art those pale transcriptions represent, and without being grounded in the particular culture whose forms these narratives embody, an armchair critic can construct and justify nearly any Rube Goldberg model his ingenuity might devise. The corrective to such critical fancy footwork is specificity. The critic must work with a comprehensive body of narratives, and ideally he should derive his model from a particular community whose structures he has experienced and defined. If that sort of rigor is maintained, then the critic may repeat the apology Edmund Leach offered for his analysis of the myth of the Garden of Eden: 'the pattern is there; I did not invent it, I have merely demonstrated that it exists' [Leach 1970: 60].
>
> (Cosentino 1982: 28–9)

8.3.4 Narrative and narratology: an extension of structuralist methods

The structuralist study of narrative, with roots in Proppian morphological analysis, has also developed as an articulate body of literary scholarship in its own right. The aim again is to uncover underlying rules which continue irrespective of the particular content, context or medium. There are arguments about how widely the scope of 'narrative' should be drawn and which questions should be central (see Mitchell 1981), but overall the methods and questions under the head of narratology are ones which many students of oral texts – including oral historians – now take seriously.

Narratological methods include the identification and analysis of such comparative narrative features as: recurrent moves in the structure of the plot (following up the earlier Proppian analyses); stock characters that recur widely in narratives across many different cultures, and how they are treated; ordering and sequences within narratives (whether or not the narrative is presented in the order of the narrated occurrences, and how it might or might not relate to performance or reading times); conventional openings and closings; the 'framing' of narrative; 'meta-narration' (the 'story in the story' as Babcock 1977 has it); 'narrativity' (the degree of *narrative*-ness as opposed to non-narrative in a given narration). There is also interest in the different 'voices' in the narration: the viewpoint of the narrator in various roles; of the characters; the 'narratee' (the one addressed – who may change during the narration, and may or may not be a character); the expected or implied audience; interchanges between first and third person; or the narrator's evocations of yet other voices.

Earlier analyses mostly focused on textual and formal questions. But some narratologists now ask about social context, performance, or the social and cognitive roles of the narrative and its narrator (sometimes including analysing allegory or ethical dilemmas in somewhat Lévi-Straussian mode). The contributions of readers/audiences, neglected in formalist studies, are now more often noticed, sometimes in the context of the heterogeneous and often ideological dialogics involved. This in turn can imply a view of narration as performance, or of narrative structure as emergent in the interaction between performer(s) and audience. A further set of questions which, though still focusing on the text, also lead beyond it, concerns the interaction between fiction and event: a complex interrelation in which it is no longer always assumed that 'events' necessarily come first (cf. Bakhtin 1981, B. H. Smith 1981, Bauman 1986: esp. 5ff, Shuman 1986, Clerk 1990).

As with other structuralist methods, narratological analysis can be conducted in a facile, even mechanical way. Its effective use depends not only on acquaintance with the narratological literature but also on the resources available and their appropriateness for the particular research aims. Questions of a formal textual nature might (arguably) be tackled without extensive ethnographic knowledge, but access to a large corpus of narratives would be essential.

These could be from a particular culture, preferably in full rather than summary form, and come either from one genre or a group of several different genres, not necessarily all verbal. Alternatively narratives could be drawn cross-culturally – a method running the risk of superficiality or ethnocentric misunderstanding, but also, as in Paulme's work (1976), sometimes with rich rewards. Questions relating to context, audience or function, however, are near-impossible to pursue satisfactorily on the basis of texts alone without some detailed knowledge of the culture(s) in which the narratives were composed, told or circulated. (For examples of recent work see – besides those cited above – Cancel 1989, Feld 1989, LeRoy 1985, K. Stewart 1988, Ben-Amos 1982, Siikala 1989, Samuel and Thompson 1990; also 2.4.8.)

8.4 STYLISTIC FEATURES AND PROBLEMS

In the study of texts 'style' is regularly taken as one obvious aspect to investigate, at least in the sense that any genre has its formal patterns (the earlier picture of so-called 'primitive' forms as without art or stylistic conventions would seldom be accepted now). Despite its wide application, however, the concept of style is an elusive one. One approach is that it is simply what makes art artful: the heightened awareness of form that sets certain forms of communication apart. From another viewpoint there are stylistic conventions in any recognised form of human communication ('speech genres' as well as self-consciously 'literary' genres), including patterns which are below the participants' consciousness. Whichever approach is followed, however, 'style' has to be seen as a culturally-defined and relative facet of verbal expression, particular forms of which may be more, or less, explicitly recognised. As such the nature and specific role of 'style' in particular texts perhaps always needs to be investigated rather than just assumed.

In oral art forms performance conventions often play a central role, sometimes as important in genre attribution as the narrowly verbal or content properties. So though most stylistic analyses of texts focus on verbal aspects, this may be only part of the whole picture and will need to be supplemented by consideration of performance features, such as those discussed in 5.3 above. (Of the huge literature on style particularly relevant discussions include Wellek and Warren 1949: chapters 13–15, Sebeok 1960 (esp. Jakobson), Hymes 1961, 1964: Part 6, 1981, Kiparsky 1973, D. Tedlock 1971, 1977, 1983, Briggs 1988: 9ff.)

8.4.1 Some specific stylistic features

There have been various attempts to differentiate the characteristics of oral style, or of oral narrative style. Examples are Olrik's 'epic laws' (1965), formulaic density in oral-formulaic scholarship (see 2.4.9, 6.1.3), and Lüthi's essential laws of the (European) folktale in terms of one-dimensionality, depthlessness and abstraction (1982; see also Lord 1987a, Ong 1982: esp. 33ff and references there). These sometimes provide a stimulus for more detailed analyses (like Cancel 1989) or feed into comparative work. A different, but sometimes complementary, assumption is that style should be investigated in specific genres rather than in generalised or polarising terms (for discussion and references see Finnegan 1977: chap. 4, Ben-Amos 1982).

However, whatever your ultimate position, there are comparative patterns, or (at the least) recurrent questions to be explored. The possible features here are endless, covering every imaginable facet of style and ultimately only discoverable in the light of cultural or generic specificities. The following merely suggests some lines of approach by highlighting questions that previous researchers have found particularly illuminating or controversial: the rest is left to your own perceptiveness.

1 *Special literary language or registers*. An appreciation of complexity and sophistication has now mostly ousted the older view that oral forms are simple, communal, or equally accessible to everyone. In practice they are not always presented in a language everyone understands (on learned and poetic languages see Finnegan 1977: 109ff, 234ff, Best 1923). It is therefore relevant to investigate such questions as: how far are there special registers for specific genres/forms of utterance? What elements and spheres do these differences extend to: the whole language (a totally foreign one perhaps?), vocabulary, grammar, pronunciation, denseness, imagery? How far can all participants understand or control these forms? The style may appear 'natural' to the participants or to those reading the transcriptions – all the more reason for conscious investigation.

2 *Prosody*. Prosody is another obvious feature of style, in some ways easily susceptible to cross-cultural analysis, in others more elusive. One set of problems comes from the apparently simple, but in effect controversial, boundaries between 'prose'/'poetry' and 'speech'/'song' (see 7.2). In addition more is often involved

than metre, the traditional focus of classically trained scholars. Thus such topics as the following may need researching:

Metre, and whether based on quantity, stress, syllable or some other principle

Rhythm more generally

Rhyme, assonance, alliteration

Tonal patterning

Parallelism (see also below)

Performance features (such as patterning through volume, stress, vowel lengthening, phrasing, speed, gesture)

The relation of any or all of the above to music

There can be tricky problems. One is how far apparent prosodic features are deliberately intended or heard, for example in rhyme or tonal patterning (Finnegan 1977: 95ff). Another is the identification and analysis of 'the line', a topic in which there is now a developing literature (for example on 'the intersection and interplay of linguistic, sociolinguistic, and poetic structures, patterns and processes' in the Kuna line in Sherzer and Woodbury 1987: 103ff), and the complex interactions with music (see 5.3.3, 7.2.1). Euphony may be relevant too: indeed even in written forms acoustic qualities can play a part in prosody. Finally, prosodic patterns are not confined to verse but can also be looked for in genres labelled 'prose' (for prosody see further Jakobson 1960: 358ff, Finnegan 1977: 90ff, Okpewho 1990: 119ff; for recent work on metre Junaidu 1988; also on parallelism below).

3 *Repetition and parallelism.* The importance of repetition and – one variant of repetition – of parallelism is often commented on. This sometimes draws on arguments about how far these are particularly characteristic of oral forms, and also sometimes links with controversial suggestions that oral expression may be characterised by particular syntactical forms such as additive and aggregative rather than subordinative or analytic style (as in Ong 1982: 36ff; for general discussion see Jakobson 1960, Finnegan 1977: 90ff, Tannen 1989). Whatever the general conclusions, studies pursuing the patterns of repetition and parallelism usually come up with rich results, again for prose as well as poetic genres. Differing but recurrent forms of parallelism have been distinguished such as direct parallelism, chiasmus (cross-parallelism), and chain parallelism, and can include syntactic, semantic, phonological and musical patterning (see Finnegan 1977: 98ff, Fox 1988, Briggs 1988: 9).

4 *Imagery.* Metaphor, symbolism and allusive language have always

attracted attention in the literary study of style. Oral forms are no exception. Established categories such as simile, metaphor (in its various forms), personification, allegory, and allusive or emotive overtones provide useful starting points. The topic has been widely and variously examined both in analyses of specific texts and in general discussions (for example Basso 1976, Ortony 1979, Fletcher 1964, Finnegan 1977: 112ff, Tannen 1989). Any brief summary would be unrepresentative, but aspects worth noting, either because of the influential literature attached to them or because their significance has only recently been appreciated, include the role of personification in some genres (for example South African panegyric, see Finnegan 1970: chap. 5), floral imagery (see Firth 1990) and the symbolic depth sometimes inherent in names, specially place-names (Basso 1984, 1988, Feld 1990, Pond 1990, Nketia 1955, Finnegan 1970: 470ff). Such features are again specially prominent in poetry, but metaphor, personification and allegory can also be significant in 'prose' forms (M. Jackson 1982, Feld 1989, Cancel 1989: 28ff). It is worth repeating (since sometimes ignored) that it is near-impossible to interpret imagery without knowledge of the social and literary context; relying on translations is also risky. There can be layers of meaning and imagery, thus dangers in assuming a single authoritative interpretation whether of particular images or of the 'fact' of an expression's being 'symbolic' in some agreed sense.

5 *Personal diction and presentation*. This heading is an extension of the earlier ones (the difference being relative only), used here to draw attention to the manipulation and development of stylistic conventions by individual artists. These personal characteristics and activities too – not just collective tradition – can be relevant for stylistic questions.

Some of the questions here coincide with those already discussed, others are sometimes of a lower order. The kinds of terms applied are, for example, 'spare' narrative style, allusive versus 'straightforward' (and/or emotive versus neutral) diction, rhetorical effects, 1st/3rd person, short/long sentences, abstract or impersonal versus concrete/personal presentation, or the use of humour, irony or surprise. Any or all of these can be characteristics of personal, as of generic, style (for examples see Dorson 1960, Bauman 1986, Bennett 1988). A further interesting, if elusive, question is the scope for individual freedom left to the performer within particular genres, and how and in what respects this is exploited (see Abrahams and Foss 1968: 14, Abrahams

1970b, Finnegan 1977: 125ff, and, for Maori women's use of unexpected twists in 'traditional' expression, Orbell 1990).

8.4.2 Need to see the whole style

This discussion has concentrated on verbal aspects of texts – the traditional focus of stylistic analysis. However, a full picture would also take account of structural patterns in the sense of both inner structural principles and the place of the unit(s) being analysed within a wider corpus. Style also needs to be set in its literary and linguistic context, including its relation to the grammatical and other resources offered in the language (see Sherzer 1989), to the intertextual framework of other texts within the same or related genres, and to cross-genre stylistic patterns within a given culture (as for Kuna poetics in Sherzer and Woodbury 1987: 103–39 and Sherzer 1990; for analysis of style across art genres more widely, see 7.4.6).

Finally the point made at the outset cannot be too often repeated: that, though some aspects can certainly be pursued through traditional textual methods, for oral art a full appreciation can only be gained by also considering acoustic, visual and kinetic features as realised in performance; in some cases too this may also need reliance on, or cooperation with, musicological techniques (as in Feld 1982, Seeger 1986). This has many ramifications (on which see also 6.4, 5.3), but is perhaps particularly important to remember for stylistic aspects such as characterisation, irony, humour, or detached comment, often conveyed through performance rather than, as in written forms, through the words alone. For oral poetics, it could be argued, traditional textual analysis centring on the words can capture only a small part of the full stylistic reality.

8.5 RELEVANCE OF LITERARY ANALYSIS AND WRITTEN LITERATURE

Insofar as instances of oral tradition or verbal art are considered forms of literature, they can be approached through any, perhaps all, of the established methods of literary analysis. There is some disagreement on how far this should be taken (Yai, for example, pleads for a literary criticism founded in performance rather than the textual criticism of western scholars, 1989), but in principle the many methods developed within the study of literature are open to those analysing oral texts.

This gives the analyst access to a host of possible approaches, supplementing and extending those discussed earlier. The more traditional methods include analyses in terms of allegorical and symbolic interpretations; the influence of author or genre; the relevance of social and cultural setting or of specific historical processes; meaning in relation to 'real' events or experience; formalist and hermeneutic approaches; or – still an abiding theme – the elucidation of beauty and art as some kind of universal quality (all these, of course, with their own scholarly literatures). There are also the recurrent debates about how far literary texts 'reflect' society or vice versa, or their psychological or class basis. The analysis of oral texts might also benefit from recent developments in the study of literature, both the extending of the canon to include more 'popular' forms, and the approaches summed up in such labels as post-structuralism, semiology, feminism, reception theory, deconstruction or critical theory generally. The developing interest in 'performance', speech act theory, the dialogic relationship between texts and readers or audiences, and the concept of discourse also brings the possibility of considering oral and written forms together. So too does the expanding field of narratology and, in some cases, of 'comparative literature' (still often confined to written genres, but with wider coverage in such periodicals as *New Literary History* or *Comparative Criticism*). The methodologies developed in studies of written literature therefore present a rich resource, and it is unfortunate that designating a form 'oral' has often obscured their possible relevance. (Useful discussions of this huge subject – potentially the whole of literary criticism – can be found in both older (e.g. Wellek and Warren 1949) and more recent works (Williams 1977, R.C. Davis 1986, Fish 1980, Adams 1989, Eagleton 1983, 1984, Rice and Waugh 1989, Jefferson and Robey 1986, Adams and Searle 1986); for interesting applications of insights and methods drawn from literary study see specially B.H. Smith 1978, 1981, Barber and Farias 1989: 13ff, also 8.3.4 on narratology.)

Studies of written literature are relevant for their substance as well as their methodology. One important area is the interaction of written and oral forms. The mutual influences between oral and written literature provide one set of questions, which can sometimes be studied in long historical perspective (Foley 1986, 1987b, Nagy 1989, P. Burke 1978). Such interactions are increasingly viewed as normal rather than strange, often in the form, as Elizabeth Gunner puts it, of a 'three-way dialectic between print, performance and . . . orality' (1989: 55). Similar dialectics have been detected in studies of 'popular literature' or – the term more common among historians – 'popular culture' (P. Burke 1978, Gurevich 1988, Vincent 1989) and in work on the ways written fiction, including novels, 'novelettes' and pamphlets, develop from or build on oral narrative forms (for some African examples see Vavilov 1987, Nikiforova 1987, Cosentino 1978, Obiechina 1973, Andrzejewski et al. 1985, Scheub 1985). The trend is to move away from simplified models of encounters between two 'different' streams (oral and written) to looking at the complex processes by which texts are shaped by a series of influences and constraints. What in the past were regarded as 'syncretic', 'composite' or 'creole' texts are taken as worthy of study in their own right as well as exemplifying the complex dynamics between printed, written and oral media.

The influences do not just go from oral to written. Models from various genres of written literature and the preoccupations of particular groups of intelligentsia often influence oral forms. Some investigation of the local experience and role of written literature is thus essential background for analysing oral texts. This obvious point is often neglected, perhaps still due to romantic views of 'oral' or 'traditional' texts as somehow independent of and impervious to the written tradition.

8.6 SPECIALIST TECHNIQUES: COUNTING, CONTENT AND COMPUTERS

Counting, classification and cross-referencing have long played a part in textual analysis. It is unnecessary to elaborate on all the varying modes of quantification here (though a couple are singled out for further comment below), merely to make the general point that most can equally be applied to oral texts, as in the construction of concordances, identification of recurrent stylistic patterns or the comparison of variants. Many are in fact merely the quantifiable face of methods discussed earlier in this chapter. But it is also interesting – and so elaborated further below – that developments in computing are now opening up new possibilities in textual analysis.

8.6.1 'Content analysis'

This high-sounding term, particularly used in the context of the mass media, often covers little more than the familiar methods for analysing theme, motif, plot, style, etc., with the additional implication of quantification and generalisation. In practice some kind of content analysis, if not necessarily under that title, is implied in most of the methods discussed earlier in this chapter (for references specifically related to oral verbal forms see Dundes 1962, Colby 1973, P. Maranda 1967, and, especially, Jason et al. 1977). General discussions of the methodological strengths and limitations of analysing 'content' may be worth consulting, since most are in principle equally applicable to oral forms (Pool 1959, Weber 1985, Krippendorff 1989).

8.6.2 Formulaic analysis

Methods for identifying and counting formulae and formulaic elements are well developed within oral-formulaic scholarship, with standard conventions for indicating these by various forms of underlining. A large number of arguably 'oral' texts from most areas of the world, particularly classical, Anglo-Saxon and mediaeval European, have been annotated and analysed, with greater or lesser degrees of quantification. As well as throwing light on the structure of the text, this method has also been used to draw comparisons with other similar texts, and sometimes for evidence as to whether the text was originally orally composed (higher density of formulae perhaps arguing for oral composition) and how far it was 'traditional'. There are controversies here, such as the delimitation of the 'formula' as the basis for quantification or conclusions, and the representativeness of the passages being analysed, which leading oral-formulaic scholars now often consider explicitly, sometimes also relating their textual analyses to questions about context or audience (for references see 2.4.9 and 6.1.3).

Effective use of formulaic methods needs not only acquaintance with the extensive oral-formulaic literature but also, perhaps even more than with other textual methods, a large corpus of texts. Without this there is no solid basis for identifying what is formulaic, let alone for generalisation or comparison. Computers can now sometimes assist in such analysis (see below) but do not of themselves avoid the controversies.

8.6.3 Computers

Although computing is more a speedier way of carrying out certain analyses than a separate method, recent developments in electronic technology are worth attention in that they are both making computers more accessible and opening up new questions. Established computer methods in the study of oral forms include formulaic

Jalah reče,/zasede đogata; — With "By Allah" she mounted her horse;

790 Đogatu se/konju zamoljila: — 790 She implored the white horse:

"Davur, đogo,/krilo sokolovo! — "Hail, whitey, falcon's wing!

Četa ti je/o zanatu bila; — Raiding has been your work;

Vazda je Mujo/četom četovao. — Ever has Mujo raided.

Vodi mene/do grada Kajniđe! — Lead me to the city of Kajniđa!

795 Ne znam đadu/ka Kajniđi gradu." — 795 I know not the road to the city of Kajniđa."

Hajvan beše,/zborit' ne mogaše, — It was a beast and could not talk,

Tek mu svašta/šturak umijaše. — But the steed knew many things.

Ode gljedat'/redom po planini. — He looked over the mountains

Uze đadu/ka Kajniđi gradu, — And took the road to the city of Kajniđa,

800 Pa silježe/planinama redom, — 800 And crossed one range after another,

Pa ga eto/strmom niz planinu, — Until lo he rushed down the mountain,

I kad polju/slježe kajnićkome, — And when he descended to the plain of Kajniđa,

Kome stati/polje pogljedati, — Were anyone to look out over the plain,

Figure 8.4 Example of oral-formulaic analysis from Albert Lord's *The Singer of Tales* (1960: 46): repeated phrases definitely classifiable as 'formulae' underlined; probable formulaic expressions marked with broken underlining (reprinted by permission of Harvard University Press, copyright 1960 by the President and Fellows of Harvard College)

analysis (Goody and Duly 1981), the comparison of variants (Rosenberg and Smith 1974), assessing a multiplicity of factors in genre classification (Perić-Polonijo 1988), metrical patterns (Foley 1978, see also Foley 1981), and the structural analysis of myths (P. Maranda 1967, 1971, 301ff, 1972: 151–61). Recent technological advances take computers well beyond crude quantification, however, so electronic aids can now be considered for almost any method of analysis which involves the ordering or interrelation of different factors in a corpus of material, and new applications are constantly being devised (on computers in literary analysis see Abercrombie 1984 and on new developments on computers in the humanities, including the use of 'hypertext' in literary theory, the periodicals *Literary and Linguistic Computing* and *Computers in Literature*; also Krupat 1982: 332ff, Fischer n.d.). Computer text-production and analysis also add further to current reconsiderations of the older concept of 'text' as something fixed and permanent (Bolter 1989).

Current developments in micro-computing also create opportunities for bringing together textual and performance aspects. The possibilities are illustrated by the techniques developed in the linguistic anthropology laboratory at the University of Texas at Austin:

> It is now possible, with relatively inexpensive equipment, to digitise sound that has been tape-recorded and to display that sound as a composite wave form on the computer screen. The form can then be analysed and manipulated, with different stretches of sound being juxtaposed and compared. The sound can then be resynthesised and played out through an external speaker. The researcher is able to perform such tasks as measuring line lengths and pauses, and comparing the wave forms of distinct segments. Somewhat more expensive equipment allows the researcher to perform pitch extraction and to study the form and structures responsible for timbral characteristics. An exciting aspect of this work has been the integration of sound analysis with the relational database study of texts. Researchers can, for example, call up on the computer screen a map, determine the locations on the map where certain speech styles occur, then call up a wave form representation of one instance of the style and play it back and hear it.
>
> (Urban 1989)

These and the other techniques that will no doubt be formulated over the coming years are likely to lead to important developments in making visible and manipulable certain stylistic and structural attributes which were previously relatively inaccessible to analysis.

Electronic assistance can thus be invaluable in certain cases, saving the need for lengthy manual drudgery and sometimes elucidating quite unexpected patterns. Such methods are only as valid as the approaches for which they are used, however, for if the original aims are confused or controversial, no amount of computation can cure the problems. (This section confines itself to textual analysis; on computers in anthropology generally see BICA (Bulletin of Information on Computing and Anthropology, University of Kent), Fischer n.d.)

8.7 THE QUEST FOR 'MEANING'

A concern with meaning perhaps underlies all analysis of oral texts. But this 'meaning' tends to be differently defined, or assumed, according to where you start. For some it is to be looked for in societal functions, for others in psychological significance, cultural roles, the act of performance, the effect on the audience, ideological import, or the conditions for meaning (rather than the 'meaning' itself) – and so on. This section does not attempt to summarise these many approaches to meaning (possible strategies can be gleaned from the theoretical perspectives in chapter 2), far less open up wider debates about 'meaning' in social anthropology generally (see Basso and Selby 1976). It merely indicates some down-to-earth points that are rather easy to overlook and which need to be brought together with the related and partly overlapping question of role or function (see 6.3).

First, there may several meanings, little though this comes through in the dogmatic tone of many research reports. So where differing meanings are proposed, whether by different authors (as in the contrasting interpretations of Cinderella collected in Dundes 1982 and in similar 'Casebooks' in the same series) or by the same analyst (Maranda 1973, 1971: 292–324), it should not be assumed that just *one* of these must be 'correct'. Hymes puts it well:

> In the study of written literatures the work of interpretation is never complete. Major texts are regarded, not as closed, but as open to new insight and understanding. The case should be the same for aboriginal literatures.
>
> (Hymes in Maranda 1971: 50)

Differing meanings may also need to be sought out ethnographically. Here too there can be a series of varying answers: the composer's (intended?) meaning; that (or those) of the reader(s) or the audience(s), or of particular groups or individuals within the audience; in cognitive terms only (the traditional focus of 'meaning') or also taking in emotive and sensual meanings. If you are considering meanings over time, there are yet further 'interested parties', to use the terminology in Holbek's useful, if perhaps only partial, checklist (see Fig. 8.5). Some texts too are multi-layered, intentionally framed to carry different meanings for different individuals or groups (see Cosentino 1988, Pond 1990), or the locale for cultural negotiations or debates (Barber and Farias 1989). Further there may be an explicit or implicit indigenous poetic criticism (see 6.4)

1. The people who created the earliest versions of the tales.
2. Those who transmitted them down through the centuries.
3. The narrators from whom the tales were recorded.
4. Their customary audiences.
5. The collectors.
6. The editors.
7. The secondary audiences, i.e., the reading public and those who have heard the stories read aloud from (or retold on the basis of) printed versions.
8. The interpreters themselves.

Figure 8.5 Holbek's list of 'interested parties' (*source*: Holbek 1987: 191)

or local assessments of published texts and their analysis (as in Feld's illuminating consultations, 1987) – all worth exploring. Given the likely multiplicity of meanings, it is important to be clear about which and whose 'meaning' is being described or investigated and how far, if at all, these interact and change.

It becomes even more complicated where the same text is repeated on different occasions and among different participants. This common situation means the analyst has to consider yet other meanings created among the many parties involved. Meanings may be less stable than texts, so that going outside the 'basic' text may be necessary – a procedure in any case encouraged by recent work on intertextuality.

A second point is the trend in folklore and anthropology towards more interest in subjective meaning. This is partly related to the interest in artistry but also links with reactions against earlier over-emphasis on outsiders' categories. These recent interests have found expression in a number of conferences and reports explicitly on 'meaning' (see Honko 1984 (introducing a special issue on meaning) and the papers in the *Journal of Folklore Research* 20, 2/3, 1983 and 22, 1, 1985, specially Dégh's introduction 1983 and Calame-Griaule et al. 1983; also Honko 1985a, Holbek 1982, 1983: 156ff, and 1987: esp. 187ff, Dundes 1978: 38ff, and the French studies reported in the *Journal of Folklore Research* 1983, 20, 2/3: 145–246 and Görög-Karady and Seydou 1982).

Scholars are now increasingly taking account of interactional and negotiated aspects of meaning: its 'dialogic' nature (to adopt Bakhtin's terminology, 1981, 1986). It is of course an old point that meaning is neither self-standing nor permanent but developed by and between the participants within a communicative situation, and perhaps beyond it, but interpretations on these lines are now particularly explicit and influential. Although in one sense the elicitation of meaning starts from the text, such analyses often go beyond it in seeing meaning as emergent – thus once again highlighting the significance of performance and of an action view of communication. (For examples of this general trend, more explicitly developed in some cases than in others, see Bauman 1977a, 1989a, B.H. Smith 1981: 230–1 (on the multiplicity of functions arising from 'narrative transactions' between teller and audience), Schieffelin 1985, Feld 1987, 1989, Briggs 1988.)

Indeed, irrespective of the particular approach taken up, the analysis of meaning almost inevitably leads outside the 'text proper' (insofar as this is something clearly distinct at all) to context, performance, control, and what people actually do. This raises yet again the question of whether 'meaning' can really be envisaged as something 'in' the text itself.

9 Texts in process: translation, transcription and presentation

Texts look final and unproblematic on the printed page. But each results from a cumulative series of choices by researcher, editor or collector. Such decisions, often unacknowledged, need to be brought into the open. In discussing such decisions, this chapter could be taken as in one sense about the 'post-field' stage (complementing chapter 3), but in another it describes processes which take place throughout any research which involves handling or interpreting texts in any form.

The main phases of text processing are:

1 Recording and collecting.
2 Transcribing and representing in writing.
3 Translating (where appropriate).
4 Wider circulation, publication, or deposit.

The treatment here begins with translation as, although this often comes later, it raises the basic issues particularly sharply. Recording and collecting were covered earlier (chapters 3 and 4) so will only be referred to indirectly; but they too affect the result in parallel ways to the other phases. Indeed the processes are interdependent and similar issues arise throughout, so the sections below need to be read together. They can also only be fully appreciated with some reference to the related ethical and political issues, taken up in the next chapter.

9.1 TRANSLATING

Translation is a common stage in the research process, but is often not thought about directly. For although 'cultural translation' is commonly said to lie at the heart of anthropology, anthropologists do not always approach the translation of verbal texts with much awareness of the literature on translation developed in other disciplines. But the problems of translating are both of interest in themselves and also raise fundamental issues for the processing of oral texts.

9.1.1   What is translation?

This question is worth pondering. It is almost a truism that translation from one language to another is in a way impossible, summed up in such varying terms as *traddutore traditore*, its comparison to a 'stewed strawberry' (Brower 1959: 173), or Quine's 'indeterminacy' of translation (1960). But students of oral texts often have to engage in it and it is as well to be aware of both problems and possible strategies.

There are different viewpoints on translation (see Graham 1989, Schulte et al. 1987, Okpewho 1990: 11ff, and, for a philosophical treatment, Feleppa 1988), but one key question consistently turns on *what* it is that is being translated. This again depends on views about the nature of language and communication, and their relation to 'reality' and to human thought or action. To put these extremely schematically, views about translating – and indeed about other phases of text processing – partly depend on whether language is primarily regarded as representing:

1 Direct correspondence with 'reality', essentially consisting of denotative factual statements.
2 Meanings or thoughts in people's minds: basically an intellectual and cognitive model. The thoughts may be conceived as representing things in the real world (as above) through a system of coding and encoding, but ideas of connotation or metaphor may also come in.
3 A form of expressiveness: a model rejecting the idea that factual and cognitive concerns make up the whole of language, and taking some account of cultural context and of aesthetic, stylistic and personally expressive elements.
4 A form of social action and experience: close to the previous sense but particularly emphasising such concepts as linguistic performance, 'speech acts' or 'meaning-as-use' (Feleppa 1988: 99 see also 2.4.10).

The aim of translation depends on which model is assumed – or is being highlighted for the moment, for these perhaps represent complementary rather than exclusive aspects of communication.

Thus translation in terms of factual content will differ from one emphasising the speaker's ideas ('Tain't what a man sez, but wot he means that the traducer has got to bring out' – quoted in Brower 1959:118); while a view of language as expression suggests that the translator should somehow try to replicate the poetics.

The difficulties of translation in terms of the first two models (factual/descriptive and thoughts/meanings) are extreme enough. There are more problems still if you take the third or fourth seriously, as students of *oral* forms are now inclined to do. Language as expression or as action means attention to context, including performance, non-verbal accompaniments, and audience interactions. But how can these be translated? And what can be done with ambiguous and allusive poetry (like the Boran poems in Baxter 1986), or with levels of meaning for different categories of hearers? A translation of 'content' alone cannot represent that text's full import.

Whichever the decision there will be costs and benefits. Some are already widely discussed among translators; others, further elaborated below, are of specific relevance to the translator of oral or supposedly oral texts.

9.1.2 Can translation be 'accurate'?

'Literal' rather than 'free' translation is often taken as the ideal. But this is not really a clear single-factor opposition since translation involves multiple decisions about models of meaning, delimitation of units, purposes, audiences, and so on. There is no such thing as a neutral 'literal' or 'exact' rendering – or not unless one accepts an extreme denotative model of language (as in some machine translation).

There is obviously a place for translations of a simple word-for-word kind: useful for initial learning, as an *aide-memoire*, for certain linguistic analyses, or merely to convey one kind of summary of verbal content. The traditional advice remains sensible – to translate every vernacular word or text, however roughly, before leaving the field and forgetting. But it has the danger too of rushing into translating before understanding the context or connotations, and perhaps starting from a model of language which may not really be your final assessment.

There can also be differing aims. Much translation implies trying to somehow convey the original to foreign listeners/readers. So-called 'literal' renderings often have the unstated premise that the key units are words or follow a basically correspondence model of meaning. This is common in translations of oral narratives ('myths', 'folktales', etc.), which seldom include explicit discussion of the decisions involved or consider the effects on readers who may experience the wording very differently from how it sounds to the *translator's* inner ear. Thus Andrzejewski well directs attention to the 'emotional bias' underlying certain 'literal translations which always give the impression of the supposed "primitive" level of the original' (1965: 99). Even a knowledgeable and well-disposed writer, he points out, can provide a translation like:

> 'The young woman threw the pestle on the ground; she took a stone; she chased the bird, saying: "It is making me noise". The little bird went. She has pounded. The *mbombo* is finished. She takes up; enters into the house.'

(1965: 99)

Such 'literal' translations, he continues,

> bear no relation to any linguistic reality: the structural character-istics of the sentence cannot be meaningfully transposed from one language to another, and it is no more sensible to attempt to do this with an African language than it would be to introduce the concept of grammatical gender into a translation from French. What could be the purpose of producing this kind of anti-English? Why did the writer not turn the conventions of narrative style in this African language into its equivalent in English, as he would surely have tried to do if he were working with French or Classical Greek. The reader can only be confirmed in his probable view that African oral literature is very inferior stuff.

(1965: 99–100)

Not all attempted translations are so extreme, but in the case of translations from supposedly 'primitive' peoples a surprising number are.

Other attempts aim to be faithful in different ways: 'free-er' if just words or cognitive content are considered, but more directly representing the occasion, poetic form, or 'feeling' of the original. These too have problems. Literary models in the target language may be (implicitly) assumed, but even at the time – and certainly if they go out of fashion among potential readers – may convey misleading impressions. Dell Hymes argues that closer renderings of words and structure sometimes give a better representation than

the florid and padded version offered by some translators (Hymes
1981: 39); similarly with certain 'translations' inspired by or 'after
the manner of' their originals. Some re-creations become new works
of art in their own right. Among these might be the English writings
of the Nigerian Amos Tutuola – usually said to derive from oral
traditional forms – or the way in which, as Yai explains

> African oral poetry translations, particularly the praise tradition,
> [are] visible if not audible in the poetry of Césaire. . . . Similarly,
> the poems of Miguel Angel Asturias. . . . are inspired by Guate-
> mala oral poetry.
>
> (1989: 68)

This may seem at or beyond the margins of 'translation'. But this
is the point. Translation is not an absolute process, and differs
according to aim and interpretation. No one of its manifestations,
not even the often-assumed word-for-word 'correspondence' model,
is self-evidently the most 'accurate' one and translators have to
make up their own minds about appropriate models for their own
purposes.

But if in one sense translation is impossible, at best relative and
disputable, the duty remains not to be *unfaithful* to the original in
whatever respects are being focused on – and up to a point in other
respects too. The responsible translator must fulfil obligations such
as a reasonable command of both original and target language (or
at least make it clear if not), ideally including knowledge not just
of vocabulary but of grammatical and syntactical structures, of differing registers, and of language usage generally. Some translations
are plain incorrect whatever model of language one takes. Claiming
to be 'literal' is not enough – the question is 'literal' or 'accurate'
in what sense, with what purpose, and with what degree of
competence.

9.1.3 What is left out in translation? . . . And in *written* translation?

Some familiar answers on what cannot be translated include: the
poetics ('poetry' in Robert Frost's definition being 'what is lost
in translation'); humour; puns; a play between different linguistic
registers or vocabulary; stylistic qualities ('prose' as well as
'poetry'); multi-levels of meaning, perhaps directed to different
audiences; connotations; imagery; and culturally specific allusion.

These well-known problems apply to oral as much as to written
forms, further compounded if the original culture is little known or

obscured by emotive stereotypes. How you deal with them will, as with all translators, partly depend on your model of language and the elements you are trying to reproduce.

What leads to even greater difficulty, however, is that with oral forms *two* translation processes have to be undertaken: not only from one language to another, but also from an oral to a written mode. This raises issues which run through all stages of text processing.

The problem is least pressing for a correspondence or cognitive model of language, and if the units for translating are seen primarily in terms of content or plot. But if performance and expressive qualities are taken seriously – as more and more scholars of oral forms are now doing – there are real problems. As Scheub writes of Xhosa narration:

> How does one effectively translate the verbal and non-verbal elements of such a tradition to the written word? . . . It is impossible to consider the verbal elements of the performance in isolation from the non-verbal, yet there is no useful way of transferring the non-verbal elements to paper. The superficial plot seems the easiest of tasks for the translator, yet a dynamic translation of the plot might obscure the underlying structures which give logic and meaning to the work . . .
>
> [The Xhosa narrator] will leave gaps in the plot from time to time, which are filled in by the audience. To find an artistically pleasing means of filling in those gaps for an alien reader without interfering with the subtle balance being created by the artist in other regards is another special translation problem.
>
> (Scheub 1971: 31)

Similarly Fine (1984) comments on problems of translating from a source medium (performance) which represents aural (linguistic and paralinguistic), visual (kinesic, artifactual, proxemic) and perhaps tactile elements, to a receptor medium (writing) with a more limited channel capacity. These non-verbal channels of the original are regularly lost in written translations.

The specific performance features not captured in writing naturally vary according to culture, language, genre, and even individual performer. But *some* such elements will always be missing. Particularly frequent ones include:

1 Characterisation. Oral narrative is sometimes assumed to contain only crude (if any) development of individual personality. But

both characterisation and inner feelings can be conveyed through performance: near-impossible to represent directly in written translation.

2 Atmosphere, emotion, tension, irony, differing voices, detached 'meta' reflection on a primary narration. In *written* versions these are conveyed through words, in oral performance through delivery arts and interactions between performer and audience – thus usually missing in written translation.

3 Significance of repetition. In written versions repetition looks redundant (and is often eliminated). But, as Tedlock points out (1985a: 116), what is dull in writing can be electric in performance: as with music, the phrases may never be delivered the same way twice.

4 Onomatopoeic words. Whether these should be 'translated' or left in the original language is a moot point – either way their effectiveness is diminished in writing.

5 The artistic/poetic qualities of a particular genre where, as often, the generic conventions include more than the purely verbal.

These elements are near-impossible to transfer – trans-late – into the narrow channel capacity of print. If a written translation is necessary (it often is) then it can be helpful to at least comment on these limitations or supplement the written word by other means (for suggested strategies in transcriptions and publications see 9.2, 9.3).

Some question whether written translations should be used to represent oral performances at all. Hymes *performed* his translation of a Chinookan text, emphasising that some re-creative element is unavoidable, the issue simply being its character 'in terms of fidelity, insight, and taste' (Hymes 1975a: 356) while Yai urges the following 'methodological steps' for rendering oral poetry:

1 The translator must first be immersed in the culture of the source language. No attempt to translate with the aid of special dictionaries can help in oral translation, as the putative translator must have 'lived' oral performances in the source culture.

2 The second step is the search for viable and orally acceptable equivalent forms in the target language.

3 Extensive experimentation in oral rendition is required, with a written text as an optional visual aid.

4 The performance is nonmediated.

(1989: 68)

He eliminates the aim of a final rendition in writing, going on to add that if the original performance allowed improvisation then it should similarly be open to the translator-performer to 'add "lines" of his/her own making to the "text" which is never closed, once he/she is inspired by the mood or the muse of the genre' (Yai 1989: 69).

Such a position may seem extreme, and perhaps raises practical as well as theoretical problems. But it indicates the kinds of issues that translators of oral forms need to face.

9.1.4 The interest of translation

Anthropologists of all people will recognise that translating is a social, not just technical, activity and that the conventions and values surrounding the process of translation will affect not only the translator but also any assistants, in some cases the original performers too, and certainly eventual readers or hearers. Some ethnographic investigation may be pertinent here. Do translated texts circulate locally and if so, how do they influence local views about translation? If nothing else, there will almost certainly be biblical translations; but in fact there are usually many more written translations around – both manuscript and print – than researchers dominated by models of 'pure' oral tradition often realise. Are there conventions about verbal equivalences between languages which affect people's offered translations? Is there a tradition of retaining certain vernacular terms in translations? Furthermore, since translation between languages is not engaged in solely by academic researchers nor confined to western languages, it is worth remembering that many cultures contain multi-lingual speakers who may already be experienced interpreters, reflect self-consciously on language and its translation, or work with terms or usages common to several languages (see Hill 1986, J.E. Jackson 1983: esp. chap. 9, Le Page and Tabouret-Keller 1985, Finnegan 1988: 46ff). Local conventions and expectations are part of the subject matter, and need to be considered seriously.

For this reason too it is interesting to give some thought to the main purposes and likely audiences for the translations. Though these audiences will doubtless be multiple (whether intentionally or not), it can be helpful to distinguish between different possible targets: there is no such thing as an all-purpose translation. Is the aim a selective *aide-memoire* of certain features for your own use; a translation for specialist colleagues; a version for specific categories of other readers (if so what are *their* likely expectations and background?); an attempt to transfer meaning into a comparable genre or indicate the poetics of the original for a wider readership; a re-creation of a work of art in the new language? The potential audiences will have prior assumptions both about what translation is and about the nature of what is being translated. These may be misleading and unhelpful but will still have an effect. It is also worth considering what demands should be put on the readers: should they be expected to 'work at' the translation to get some grip on unfamiliar terms or structures (one aim, for example, in Sherzer 1990) or cope with annotated texts so as to reach some understanding of performance? Or is the aim a blander version in some comparable genre in the target language? Translation can be regarded as a kind of transaction between different media and between different participants – *all* of which ideally should be considered.

Translating, furthermore, is also worth reflecting on in its own right. It has attracted relatively little explicit debate among anthropologists compared to the extensive discussion among philosophers and linguists. Theorists of translation are now, however, looking for down-to-earth descriptions of the processes of translating to supplement speculative or prescriptive comments about how it *ought* to be. Since, as Schulte argues, 'Translators do not engage in the mere transplantation of words; they always transfer situations from one culture to another' (1987: 2), translation theory needs interdisciplinary input from social and cultural, not just from linguistic, scholarship. Anthropologists and other translators of oral material can provide ethnographically-based insights into how 'translation' and interpretation are actually carried out – and at the local (not just metropolitan) level. They can also comment on their strategies for coping with the problems, above all the issues arising from the *oral* features of the originals. At the very least anthropologists will contribute if they reflect self-consciously on the decisions they are taking as they translate, and make these clear to themselves, to their collaborators and to their readers.

9.2 TRANSCRIPTION AND REPRESENTATION

Transcription is a common stage in processing texts, normally in the form of transforming audio-recordings into written words. Similar issues arise as for translating – of which in a sense transcribing is one form.

9.2.1 Basic issues in transcribing

Contrary to what is often implicitly assumed, 'equivalence' between spoken and written texts is neither a self-evident nor a culture-free matter. For this reason if no other the process of transcribing is a problematic one and models of what this consists of – whether held by the researcher or by other participants – will almost certainly affect the final result.

The challenges of transcribing from a totally-unwritten language seldom arise nowadays. But writing conventions are themselves part of the subject, so it is important to explore not only your own expectations but also local perceptions of the relation between written and spoken language. This may mean investigating such questions as: what, if any, printed texts of local forms are used in schools; do songs circulate in writing and what is their status; are there arguments about differing spellings, 'standard' forms or written formats; how far is language a political issue? Further, it is essential to be aware that anyone assisting in your transcriptions, local or not, will have their own experiences and assumptions. These may or may not be fully shared by others but will certainly be culturally-defined rather than neutral.

Transcribing will also be affected by your own assumptions about the nature of 'a text' and about the relation between written words and performance which transcriptions in some sense represent. This relation is neither 'natural' nor transparent, although our (European) folk conventions commonly picture it as so. Two powerful assumptions are worth scrutinising. First there is the idea of a 'correct' super-existent text, somehow existing 'out there' in its own right, of which the spoken words are merely the secondary reflection – a model lying behind many transcriptions. Even if this fits written texts, can it apply to orally performed genres? Second is the powerful model of a single-line text, as in the lines of a printed book. Here *one* voice speaks at a time; others are at best diversions from the 'real' story or song. But the multiplicity of many oral performances, with several simultaneous or overlapping speakers, may also need representing – or, if not, this needs recognising explicitly. Further 'interruptions' or 'digressions' – as they seem to transcribers preoccupied with the 'basic' text – may be crucial for the performance (well-exemplified in Cosentino 1980). Musical scores with their scope for representing differing but simultaneous voices may provide better models than prose text-pages.

The choices of media or occasion for initial recording (see chapters 3 and 4) also have knock-on effects on the kind of transcription you end up with. These are worth reviewing again, if only as a reminder of how the source being transcribed has already been shaped by earlier decisions.

A final (perhaps prior) question concerns your aim. How far – if indeed at all – do you need transcriptions and for what? If you merely want some acquaintance with content, a summary and index might be adequate, while if your main interest is performance, the disadvantages of freezing these into a written text may turn out too high and you might better work with the original recordings. Some researchers make a fetish of transcribing everything word-for-word (an alibi for postponing analysis?) but there is little point if this is not appropriate to your purposes.

9.2.2 Some practical problems

It might seem obvious that the aim should be accuracy: as Dorson puts it, the text 'comes from the lips of a speaker or singer and is set down with word for word exactness by a collector' (1964: 1). Certainly one should avoid trying to 'correct' or 'improve'. But, as with translating, there are different ways of being 'accurate', depending once again on such questions as what is being transcribed, for whom, why, and the theory of language or communication that lies behind it. The researcher's aims also shape what details are conveyed, and the format and status of the resulting document. Because of this multiplicity of choices, no two researchers will transcribe a tape in the same way, perhaps not even the same transcriber on different occasions.

It is thus not feasible to prescribe general rules about what should or should not appear in a transcription. Here is one list however (adapted from Ives 1980: 94ff, Preston 1982: 309ff) to indicate the kinds of issues that have to be faced:

1 Leave out 'uh's' and other hesitation phenomena including false starts and fill-ins like 'you know', or 'I mean'.
2 Repair false starts and corrections (unless these, or an unusual pause, seem significant for content).
3 Omit interviewer responses like 'I see', 'yeah'.
4 Use standard spellings, not dialect or pretend dialect.
5 Do not use 'eye' spelling ('enuff' for 'enough', 'wuz' for 'was').
6 Use punctuation as for normal written prose, without over-reliance on under-lining or exclamation marks.

7 Subject to the provisos above, do not correct or interpret: put down what the speaker actually said, not what you thought he meant.

Such a list demonstrates how contentious transcribing can be. The touchstone must of course be your purpose in transcribing.

If the aim is factual content, then including hesitation phenomena or non-'standard' pronunciations might indeed not be worth the time. But even transcribing just for 'content' is not simple, for the 'message' may be conveyed as much by non-verbal as verbal signals. There will also still be questions to be sorted out over punctuation, sentence or paragraph divisions, overall structure or constituent units, and perhaps emotive issues over 'standard' spellings and readers' susceptibilities, together with some quite practical problems over level and content of the transcription. Ives illustrates (1980: 99) how an apparently problem-free factual statement can be transcribed in different ways. A 'full' transcription would be:

> J. I don't know, I don't know that I ever had a a tougher job a tougher job handed me. But the uh the uh two of us, him and me, him and me together, we – on that unjeezily job, all winter we was man and man about.

Including all this may seem unnecessarily pedantic or literal-minded, as well as burdensome for the transcriber, and an alternative which conveys the sense could be:

> J. I don't know that I was ever given a tougher job, but he and I worked man and man about on it all winter.

Does this omit too much? Ives' own suggestion represents the original grammar, word order, and idiosyncratic 'unjeezily':

> J. I don't know that I ever had a tougher job handed me. But the two of us, him and me together on that unjeezily job, all winter we was man and man about.

On such decisions, you will have to exercise your own judgement – and be conscious of having done so.

There are also other purposes in transcribing. Hesitation phenomena might be precisely the subject to be researched, in studies of conversational interactions for example (as in Schegloff 1982). Or the aim might be to capture poetics as well as content, not easy to transfer into writing. As well as theoretical issues over equivalences (see 9.1) there are some direct problems. One is deciding whether to transcribe 'as verse' or 'prose' – the answer not always being clear-cut (see 7.2.2). If it *is* transcribed as verse, decisions about line and verse demarcation will have to be considered and (as in Berndt 1952: 62 or Sherzer and Woodbury 1987: 103ff) made clear to potential readers. Similar questions arise about larger units (see 9.3.2) and about representing the relation if any between musical and verbal features (see 7.2.1). Sometimes utterances like sobs, shouts, yodels, which may not look like 'words', are essential to the genre. Other details yet again might be needed for analysing, say, generic conventions, oral composition techniques, play between differing linguistic registers, comparison between different speakers, audience interaction, and so on.

Where *performance* is a specific focus further questions have to be faced – indeed they are not really avoidable if your interests include poetics, style and generic conventions at all. Should transcription always be accompanied by notes on non-verbal and delivery aspects? Should you try to incorporate such information in the transcript itself? Should written representation be avoided altogether on the grounds that translating a multi-channel medium to the limiting format of print distorts it so seriously (while purporting to represent it) that it is best not attempted? It could be argued that for studies of performance and poetics the analyst should be working not from secondary transcriptions but from the tape itself – or indeed from the performance itself of which the tape is only a representation.

Once again one has to face the problem that transcription, like translation, is inevitably a value-laden and disputed process. Cultural assumptions about the 'equivalences' between audio-record and written document, or between specific elements within these, affect what you and others 'hear', and thus the nature of the interpretation and transcription.

There are no definitive answers. However since much communication in the world today does use the written word and transcribed texts are an expected part of both the scholarly and popular tradition, you will probably, like others, find yourself engaging in transcription at some point. Various strategies have been developed to try to address the difficulties. An added written commentary can, depending on your purposes, be an essential supplement – scarcely a glamorous or innovative medium, but a long-established mode for filling out the bareness of written transcription. So too can be a series of supplementary systems within or associated with written transcriptions: these are discussed later (9.3), but briefly include: musical notation and scores; dance notation; special typographical techniques; and visual records. Finally, it is true that some problems have no satisfactory solutions. But it is at least a mark of intellectual honesty to convey some idea of what is missing, what the points at issue might be, and the rationale for your decisions.

9.2.3 Implications for dictated texts and use of others' transcripts

Dictated texts raise many of the same issues, whether they are being written down directly from dictation or 'tidied up' after earlier transcription. Similar decisions as for transcribing from tape may need to be made.

If you are using texts transcribed by others, it is important to reflect on how the transcriptions came to be as they are. Oral-derived texts are sometimes presented as authoritative, but without knowing the transcribing strategies it is dangerous to accept this at face value. They are not simple 'primary' data. Even if it is impossible to uncover the original transcription processes, it is still worth considering critically the kind of factors that might have been in play and taking existing transcriptions not as definitive reports but as provisional versions, themselves open to re-analysis. The same caution might equally be needed when you come back to your own transcriptions at a later stage.

9.3 THE PRESENTATION AND DISSEMINATION OF TEXTS AND PERFORMANCES

After transcribing and where appropriate translating, the texts may be presented or distributed in some relatively finalised form. This may be just for the researcher's own analysis, but also quite likely for further circulation among academic colleagues and/or the original performers, if not also for publication or archive deposit.

Whatever the final form(s), this phase is, once again, not merely mechanical. There are questions to be asked about medium and format as well as about purposes and audiences. Though the issues here are not broadly different from those for translating and transcribing – processes which overlap with that of 'final' presentation – some specific points can be explored further here. Again it is important to relate this stage in the processing back to the earlier ones: the resulting presentation can only be as sound (and as ethical) as those.

9.3.1 Audiences, purposes and formats

The published book for specialist colleagues is often *the* prime model for presenting the products of research, and this is likely to continue given institutional arrangements in the world of academe. But, quite apart from political or ethical reasons for considering other possibilities, developments in the technologies of text processing and audio-video representation are creating new opportunities both for the presentation of texts and for information retrieval and distribution in new forms. This opens up new questions about the representation and distribution of oral-derived texts and performances.

Some questions are familiar. In preparing versions of texts which are in any sense to be regarded as 'final' or in publishing to wider audiences, it is worth going back over such questions as:

What elements in the originals are the texts or other representations intended to convey?
Should writing be used as the sole medium (or at all), and in what form?
What should be done about music?
How much additional commentary is needed?
What categories should be used?
How will the intended (or unintended) audience interpret the format and presentation?

There are no single answers to such questions. The point is to ask them – and before not after publication. The final choices will depend on circumstances and purposes, but the following comments gather together some of the commoner problems and strategies.

9.3.2 In what units and with what labels?

Scholars have often found it easiest to present texts following the conventions and genres of their own culture. Up to a point this is unavoidable but how far to go and with what rationale, has to be decided:

Titles: oral forms do not always have titles in the same way as written works, so you may have to decide how far to follow written conventions here.

Attribution of authorship: again a normal expectation for written compositions, but sometimes more complex or multiple for oral forms. There are intellectual and ethical obligations to give due credit to the originators of the material but perhaps also to comment on such complexities.

Format as prose or poetry: recurrent problems arise about how and whether to demarcate prose/poetry, and, following that, lines, verses or paragraphs (see 7.2.2 and 9.2.2).

Larger units: printed formats often implicitly assign a text to a particular category, often building on such models as the literary genres and concepts familiar from our own culture ('poem', 'narrative', 'song cycle', 'epic', etc.). This can be controversial. For example can the fluid and in a sense endless Yoruba *oríkì* praises (Barber 1989) be reasonably represented as bounded texts? Should stories told on differing occasions but about the same protagonists be presented together, and if so in what format? What is one song, what a series of songs, what a 'song cycle'? Should 'floating' ideas be systematised into integrated narratives? How closely linked do performances have to be for a text to be presented as, say, an 'epic' or 'epic cycle'? Texts once published can become fixed within such categories, making it hard to question them later.

Which texts?   When several comparable or (in some sense) identical texts have been transcribed or recorded, should *all* be published; the 'best' (and in what sense); a 'representative' selection; the researcher's favourites; those fitting particular audiences or stereotypes? Factors often considered include the research circumstances and aims; degree of variation, 'textness' or fixity; local evaluations; researchers' assessment of either the 'best' or the most 'typical' texts; likely audiences. There are also questions of how fair it is to present a single text – with the connotations of independence or authoritativeness that that implies – either out of the context of its wider canon, or based on only one rendering of what was, perhaps, an often-told tale or genre (on such issues, see Feld 1987, also Andrzejewski 1985: 39–40).

In all such cases the basis of your decisions needs clarifying, if only because a text once published tends to become frozen as *the* unquestionable form.

9.3.3 What media?

A range of media can be considered, including different ones for different purposes, or a mixture. Practicalities, cost and existing institutional arrangements and ideologies may be constraints, but it is useful at least to think about some of the possibilities and their implications.

1) *Print and print-related media*

Despite its drawbacks printed text remains an expected and widely-distributed medium, together with certain visual and graphic forms (like photographs or maps) that are commonly associated with print formats. It is true that traditional publishers tend to be unwilling to print collections of texts as such, specially in non-European languages. But there are also now additional or alternative options like microfilm/fiche; video or audio-discs, tapes or cassettes; electronic communication; more modest formats using camera-ready copy or desk-top publishing; finally, local publishers are sometimes more interested than their grander counterparts in small-scale and inexpensive distribution. One way or another, hard-copy printed texts will continue to circulate, with the problems and opportunities that this implies.

In such cases it is worth considering including some straight-forward statement of the principles used to transfer performance into printed text and of what is omitted. Egudu and Nwoga's printed translations of 'Igbo traditional verse', for example, aim at texts accessible to those used to reading conventions but are prefaced by a description of performance conventions. Their honest and well-argued rationale is worth quoting:

> Because the performer is in contact with his audience, he is capable of interjecting references to individuals without confusing the audience as to the trend of the main material. He is able to shift from one situation of thought to another, indicating that he is doing so by a mere change of facial expression or gesture of the hand or body. Moreover, and this is significant, except for narration, the oral situation calls for succinct statements rather than for long logical discussion. The performer is therefore expected to show expertise, not in the building up of a complicated sequence of thought, but in the variety of expressions with which he can state, expand and deepen a single statement. When this fails the result is uninteresting tautology. When it succeeds it is a marvellous exposition of imaginative wealth.

In writing these verses down, therefore, there has been the need to cut out from the transcriptions those interjected passages which were the outcome of interplay between the performer and individuals in the audience and keep to the main line of thought. Even so, the cumulative rather than the progressive development of the oral performance has had to be preserved so as not to falsify the material.

(1973: 3–4)

As will already be clear, transforming spoken *words* into written texts presents problems enough. Performance qualities raise more difficulties still, for features like music, gesture or dance transfer poorly into print-based texts. Some argue that performances should only be presented and circulated through audio or video recordings or by new live renderings. However, there are some possible strategies for trying to convey at least some performance elements directly through relatively traditional print- or graphic-based media.

One is musical transcription. If there are musical as well as verbal qualities, both should ideally figure in textual representations. Some scholars present both verbal texts and musical scores using western-type notation or alternative formats (e.g. Kaufman 1988, Feld 1982) sometimes supplementing these with audio-recordings. Others feel unqualified to undertake this but have collaborated with musicologists to provide notated scores or at least some commentary on the musical characteristics of the texts (see Innes (1974) with King, Firth (1990) with McLean; on problems of musical transcription and notation – a subject in its own right – see Merriam 1964: esp. 57ff, Stone 1982: 32–3).

Visual records in the form of drawings, diagrams or photographs can supplement verbal transcriptions, particularly effectively in conveying an impression of immediacy and individual personality. Sequential dynamics can be represented through a series of photographs, as in Scheub on Xhosa story-telling (1977a) or Sándor's photographs illustrating the 'dramaturgy of tale-telling' (1967; see also Cancel 1989, Calame-Griaule 1982, 1985, and on photographs generally 3.3.3).

Gestures and movement constitute another aspect of performance, sometimes in the stylised and highly developed form that might lead to their being defined as dance. Attempts at capturing these by photographs (see above) or by such notations as the Laban system or the kinesic symbols developed by Birdwhistell (1970) are sometimes used in otherwise print-based presentation and circulation (for further details see Fine 1984: esp. 118ff).

Easier access to differing typographical representation is now increasingly possible with technological developments in text-processing. This has been exploited by some scholars to represent certain elements of performance. Much of this arises directly from work on American Indian texts – once printed as prose narratives but now sometimes re-presented as verse (see 7.2.2) – which has led to continuing discussion about presentation. There is scope for innovation here. As Hymes puts it:

> The format for presenting narrative texts in terms of their verse structure has to be invented, just as the conventions for presenting the texts of the Bible in terms of verses, and Shakespeare in terms of scenes, have had to be invented.
>
> (Hymes 1987: 20)

There have been a number of such 'inventions'. These have been taken furthest by writers associated with the journal *Alcheringa/Ethnopoetics* who have developed avant-garde approaches to typographical representation, emphasising the transfer of performance qualities in oral poetry in the broadest sense – recorded from living traditions, ancient texts with oral roots, and modern experiments in oral poetry. They aim to present 'performable scripts (meant to be read aloud rather than silently), experiments in typography, diagrams, and insert disc recordings' (Editorial, *Alcheringa* new series 2, 1, 1975). Their systems build on existing linguistic or musical conventions to indicate such features as timing (pauses, lengthening syllables, etc.); volume; intensity or stress in speaking; tonal contours; other actions such as gestures and audience reactions.

The following examples illustrates some of these formats. First an extract from Sherzer's account of his presentation of Kuna texts:

> Lines . . . end with a period. Long pauses without falling pitch are transcribed as blank spaces between words within lines. Short, interlinear pauses are represented with a comma . . .
>
> Other expressive devices represented in the text are lengthening of sounds (indicated by doubling of letters), loud speech (indicated by capital letters), decreasing volume (indicated by > placed before the stretch of speech in question), stretched-out, syllabic pronunciation (indicated by dashes between syllables), vibrating voice (indicated by dashes between letters), slowing of

tempo (indicated by stretching out of letters and words), faster tempo (indicated by a dotted underline under the words which are spoken faster), rising pitch (indicated by é placed before the stretch of speech in question), falling pitch (indicated by è placed before the stretch of speech in question), a whole line higher in pitch (indicated by ê placed before the line), and part of a line higher in pitch (indicated by raising the words of higher pitch).

(Sherzer 1990: 29)

Second is the system used in transcribing a Baptist sermon which alternates between chant (transcribed with indented lines) and sequences of lines in relative repose (Fig. 9.1).

Figure 9.1 Excerpt and key from Titon's transcription of the Rev. Sherfey's sermon (*source*: Sherfey 1977: 21, 11; copyright 1977 by the Editorial Boston University Trustees)

He wants us to live for him.

That's why we need the helmet of salvation. Brother I tell you praise God that if you got the helmet of salvation   it'll protect you; now Christ is that helmet. Amen; you can't have   you can't have that helmet if you're just bein a Baptist. Amen. You can't have that helmet on just bein a Methodist. You can't have that helmet on just goin down to the river and be baptized. But you got to be borned again in the spirit of God. Jesus made it so plain to ol Nicodemus one time

    a man my friend   +hah+
    was a ruler, one that was HEIGHTY and MIGHTY;
    BUT YET JESUS SAID "NICODEMUS YE MUST BE borned again."
    Brother that's what's the matter with the world today.
    They dined the churches; they dined and they danced and they left God out of it.
    Honey we must be borned again. We must have the spirit of God in our life.
    You say "Preacher we'll get that when we get to heaven."
    Honey you get it HERE.
    Praise God; listen neighbor;
    I want to say this brother; we're going to a WEDdin after a while.

You don't wait til you get to the weddin to get DRESSed;
+hah+
**praise God you're DRESSED BEFORE YOU GO TO THE
WEDDIN. +HAH+**
Hallelujah. +hah+
Why if you women wait for your husbands come +hah+
or your boyfriend come to pick you up +hah+
**and then you have to go get DRESSed you'd be LATE
for him. +hah+**
And the SAME WAY WITH YOU + HAH+
**THAT ARE CHURCH MEMBERS THAT ARE NOT RIGHT
WITH GOD. +HAH+**
**WHEN JESUS COMES YOU'RE GOIN TO BE LATE
+HAH+**
for the gatherin in the sky.

Key
Full left margin, sequence of lines: period of repose.
Indented margin, sequence of lines: period of chant.
New line (chanted sections only): pause about ⅓ second.
Double-space between words (repose sections only): pause about
½ second.
Return to full left margin; read without pause as continuation of
prior line.
Period(.): terminal intonation fall.
Semicolon: syntactical imposition by transcriber.
Standard (roman) type: ordinary volume and intonation of dramatic
and projected speech (e.g., public speaking, stage acting).
Boldface type: increased volume and expanded intonation range.
BOLDFACE CAPS: greatly increased volume and expanded inton-
ation range.
Italic type, in brackets: stage direction; tone of voice.
*:pounds rostrum.
=:claps hands.
+hah+:loud expulsion of breath that punctuates the chant.

Similar systems have been used for longer collections, particularly
in Tedlock's influential work on Zuni narrative poetry (1972) which
comes with directions about how to read it aloud (Fig 9.2, see also
1983, Seitel 1980, Briggs 1985, Fine 1984: esp. chapter 7).
    Such formats are controversial and relatively infrequent. Some
find them too 'strange' for ordinary reading expectations. They are

She went out and
went down to Water's End.

●

On she went until
she came to the bank
and washed her clothes.

Pause at least half a second each time a new line begins at the left-hand margin, and at least two seconds for each dot separating lines. Do not pause within lines (even at the end of a sentence) or for indented lines.

Up on the hills
HE SAW A HERD OF
DEER.
The ^{girl} would sit ^{wor}king.

Use a soft voice for words in small type and a loud one for words in capitals.

Chant split lines, with an interval of about three half-tones between levels.

O— — — — —n he went.

Hold vowels followed by dashes for about two seconds.

KERSPLASHHHHHH

Hold repeated consonants for about two seconds.

aaaaaaAAAAAAH

Produce a crescendo when a repeated vowel changes from lower case to capitals.

ta^la_a_a_a

Produce a glissando for ascending or descending vowels

(gently) Now come with me.

Tones of voice, audience responses, gestures, etc., are indicated by italics.

Note: In the songs, the pauses, loudness, lengthened sounds, glissandi, and the pronunciation of Zuni words are as indicated above. The beat follows the stresses and pauses in the words. The contour of the melody is indicated by the ups and downs of each song line; the reader may determine the exact pitches according to his own ear.

Further Note: The reader should not attempt mechanical accuracy to the point where it interferes with the flow of performance.

Figure 9.2 'Guide to Reading Aloud', prefacing Tedlock's translations of Zuni narrative poetry (*source*: Tedlock 1972: xxxiii)

also time-consuming and expensive to produce – though with new text-processing technologies now perhaps becoming less so. There are the arguments too over whether written text should be used at all rather than actual performances or at least audio tapes: such points however have equally been made *by* proponents of new typographical presentations, who emphasise live performance and often include audio-recordings with their transcripts. Finally, though some acoustic qualities can be indicated, even the most innovative typographies are limited in conveying visual elements. This set of arguments will no doubt continue.

Printed presentation can thus include graphical and musical re-presentations, or be supplemented by audio or perhaps video recordings. The traditional focus of most publishers has been on words but they do increasingly accommodate photographs and occasionally audio-tapes or discs as optional extras. These enhancements may become easier in the future as new developments bring down the price of such 'extras'.

A final point is that it may also be productive to investigate local experiences of printed publications, for these may affect both the reception of printed texts and perhaps (in a hidden way) how it has been formulated. Though such expectations used to be ignored as marginal or non-existent, there is now – and has been for many years – wide circulation of 'vernacular' literature in 'developing' countries (among the relatively few discussions of this important subject see Sherzer 1990: chap. 1, Huebner 1986, Ben-Amos 1978, Bloch 1989).

2) *Audio and video presentations*

These seem – and are – an excellent means of presenting oral performance. But despite much lip service to their value, audio recordings are less widely circulated than one might suppose. Video or film too are still rather rare as forms of research dissemination (and in some circles devalued) and seldom closely keyed to print-based circulation. However, there are significant counter-examples in the older – and extensive – ethnomusicology collections on records, such as Hugh Tracey's Music of Africa Series, some commercial recordings, and recent audio recordings linked to written scholarly analyses (like Calame-Griaule's film on Tuareg story-telling, or Feld's annotated 'Kaluli weeping and song' record 1985 which complements his other published work). Since film and visual representation are growth areas within anthropology, these media may become increasingly important as alternative or complementary media for the circulation of oral art forms (for references and discussion see 3.3.3).

Although anyone contemplating much reliance on audio or video distribution will eventually need to consult current specialist sources, many issues mirror those for print-based presentation. Audio and video media are not necessarily more transparent than verbal text, so here too it is worth considering the processes of handling and shaping that lie behind the 'final' product. Decisions about what, where and how to record will already have affected what is included (just the lead performer, say, rather than the group, or – an issue for audio too – story-teller rather than audience or ambience; similarly with decisions on where to start or end, or how to treat 'interruptions'). Editing and selection will similarly have come in, perhaps even more sweepingly, for many film- and record-makers are accustomed to drastic editing and cutting. Parallel issues arise as for translation, complicated by yet further questions about how to handle, say, voice-over translations as against dubbing or sub-titles. Though it is more difficult than with print-based publication to explain the rationale for such decisions within the medium itself, some strategies can be explored for making this clear, perhaps in accompanying print, as on record sleeves, or introductory statements or credits in films.

Once again, it may well be relevant to consider local expectations and conventions about the nature, format and distribution of such media. Films and audio recordings are, after all, now a common element of many cultures throughout the world.

3) *Live performances and renderings*

This form of distributing and publicising oral 'texts' is mostly kept invisible in the scholarly world, so not much can be said about its frequency or conventions. But some scholars certainly advocate or practise it (see Yai 1989, Hymes 1975b and the 'ethnopoetic' emphasis on performable texts to be read aloud), and both academic and amateur researchers may in fact give many such renderings, formal or informal. Such performances may be important in supplementing other media. It has been well argued (Luykx 1989) that it is only those with experience of comparable performances who can effectively 'read' their attempted representations in other media. So even innovative typographical experiments may primarily function only as aide-memoires indicating some, but only some, of the elements of the original performance which could be equally – or better? – represented through another performance.

This begs yet again the familiar question of just what if anything is the 'essential text', what a (more, or less) faithful rendering of it, what a re-creation. Live performance as a medium for dissemination raises in a direct form issues that need to be considered throughout all the stages of processing texts. It can certainly not be assumed to be self-evidently less faithful than other media.

9.3.4 Deposit of records

Whether or not the results of research are published in some form, there is still a question about what should happen to unpublished material, or to the originals of recorded items.

Many but not all researchers deposit data in the form of texts and recorded items. The possible destinations range from small personal or local collections to larger university, regional or national archives. Some, like the folklore collections in Ireland, Finland or parts of Eastern Europe, are very extensive, partly because one of the main purposes of folklore research used to be to contribute to national archives – accessible to researchers and thus one form of publication. There are also specialist regional, subject or organisational collections. Traditional deposits were mainly of manuscripts but these have now sometimes been extended to sound and visual archives. There are also specialist audio or video collections like the National Sound Archive and the Royal Anthropological Institute's Film and Photo Libraries in Britain, or the Archive of Folk Song in the Library of Congress in America.

The usual arguments for deposit are that this provides for the security, storage and preservation of records and makes them more widely accessible; it may also have been a condition of funding or research permission. Possible counter-arguments include the sensitivity of some material; the danger of regarding deposit as itself the end result, so 'fossilising' the material; or the researcher's modesty. Preparing material for deposit can also be time-consuming. Some archives require release forms from performers, and proper documentation from the researcher: no light task if not organised early or if your system is incompatible with the archive's (most researchers will anyway want to provide systematic documentation of some kind).

The specific circumstances will also be relevant. Can the archive in fact guarantee effective security and storage. There are technical questions about preservation of paper, film, photos or tapes – perishable commodities if not treated properly – and perhaps duplicate copies should also be deposited elsewhere. An institution's future prospects may also need investigation; there have been cases of collections being later dispersed or lost on the break-up of their original home.

Accessibility raises other questions. Accessible to whom and where? Should it be a small specialist or local archive (and local to whom?) rather than a national or metropolitan institution? And since access needs to be actual rather than theoretical, will the material just be locked away? Does the organising and filing system make for easy retrieval – and for tapes as well as written records? How open will it be to the users you are intending (these may not just be the 'world of scholarship' but additionally or alternatively other participants in the research – or their grandchildren in the future)? What is the institution's policy and practice in publicising its holdings?

It is usually taken for granted that researchers have the obligation to make their data open at least to other interested scholars, and this should presumably apply to oral not just written sources. But this has to be balanced against rights and responsibilities to other parties. Those who provided the material in the first place have rights; formal releases (see 4.3.3) may even be needed for the material to be deposited and/or consulted at all. Tapes or transcripts may be sensitive, dangerous, or embarrassing, and those with rights in the material may wish their names not to be used or hold that certain items should not be on general release, should be restricted to certain groups, or only be open after a period of years. Alternatively the original performers and/or the researcher on their behalf may (perhaps should?) feel strongly that the authors' names and their consequent rights over their compositions *should be* part of the record and used in any subsequent citation.

Those who own or control archives have their own interests and obligations to consider too. These may include scholarly research, fostering national identity, or representing a particular political or cultural ideology or the interests of some particular group. This is likely to affect the uses of what is deposited, particularly if the institution draws on its holdings actively through publications, film shows, or exhibitions. For this and other reasons it may also need to be made clear what *kind* of use can be made of the material: only consulted in situ; borrowed; copied; usable for analysis or edited publication by other scholars; exploited commercially? And who retains what rights in what items or should be consulted for further permissions? Such concerns cannot just be brushed aside and appropriate conditions may need to be laid down about access and use.

Sometimes it has been a condition of funding or access that the results be deposited in a particular place or be accessible to certain parties. In such cases there may seem little room for manoeuvre, but it might still be possible to negotiate over conditions for access and exploitation and/or to arrange duplicate deposit.

Another choice is simply not to deposit such items. This decision too needs considering in the light of the various obligations and rights involved. An alternative or additional option is to return originals or copies to the initial performers and/or their associates, or make them available in some other form to interested colleagues. In these cases too similar intellectual and ethical issues might need to be faced (for further comment on deposit etc. see Ives 1980: 102ff, Toelken 1979: 304ff, P. Thompson 1988: chap. 8, Henige 1982: chap. 7).

9.4 CONCLUSION

The apparently separate phases in the processing of texts in practice overlap and perhaps none is ever really complete for it is possible to go back over earlier decisions, ending up with alternative versions. This kind of revision may indeed be desirable, not just to 'improve' your texts but because different versions are appropriate for different purposes. Gven the human decisions which mould it at every stage, there is no such thing as one correct and immutable version.

So a concluding checklist for reconsidering the aims and assumptions likely to have affected your own or others' decisions throughout the various stages of text processing might be:

1 Why are the texts being recorded?
2 What is assumed to be their nature?
3 How important are contextual, paralinguistic and non-verbal elements of the texts assumed to be: by the researcher; by other participants in the research; by the performers and/or their audiences; by potential readers?
4 What audience(s) and purpose(s) are envisaged for each phase: transcription, translation, publication or deposit?
5 What are the locally recognised conventions and experience about translation, transcription, publication, etc., and their implications?

6 For whose benefit are the texts being processed (there may be several answers)?

These questions are worth reviewing at all stages, for handling texts is a social process, and their control is in its way one kind of power. So although how this works out in practice will vary, some sensitivity is needed to the wider issues, above all if the researcher is in a dominant position in regard to those being studied. Some consequences are quite likely innocuous, others perhaps less so (for further comments on ethical implications see 10.4). For these reasons, as well as for the standards of good scholarship, it is worth trying to be clear about the rationale for the decisions and selections that have inevitably been made during the recording, transcribing, translating or distributing of texts.

10 Ethics

There used to be little discussion of the ethics of research, with fieldworkers just expected to get on with it. Nowadays we are more aware of moral and political issues, and no serious student within the human sciences – whatever the particular theoretical orientation – can now afford to ignore the ethical dimension. This applies in research on oral traditions and the verbal arts too, for oral forms are the creations of human beings, part of their social, political and artistic activities rather than (as once assumed) a-social products of some impersonal Tradition. Further, collecting and analysing these creations are inescapably human processes too, with all that means for social controversies and responsibilities. Moral dilemmas are perhaps particularly pressing in field-based studies, but there are also issues long after any field phase is completed, some of them also applicable to work with archive sources.

Certain moral questions have already been touched on earlier, but some wider consideration is also needed: the subject of this concluding chapter. Very general issues are only touched on lightly here, since they are widely discussed in the scholarly literature, but their particular application to the study of oral forms needs some special comment. Some questions are the subject of hot dispute or depend so intimately on particular social and personal circumstances that it is impossible to generalise. But there is also some emerging consensus about certain principles which can and should form the framework for research. (For discussion of ethics within anthropology or social science generally see Akeroyd in Ellen 1984, also Beals 1969, Kidder and Judd 1986: chapter 18, Bulmer 1982, J.A. Barnes 1977, Georges and Jones 1980, J.M. Johnson 1975, Wax and Castell 1979, H.S. Becker 1979, Kimmel 1988, Fetterman 1989: chapter 7; for discussions focusing on folklore or oral art forms, Jackson 1987: chapter 16, Goldstein 1964, Jansen 1983. Statements by professional associations include American Anthropological Association 1973, Association of Social Anthropologists of the Commonwealth 1987, Society for Applied Anthropology (in Bernard 1988: 458–9), British Sociological Association 1982/9.)

10.1 AIMS AND ATTITUDES

Research that involves other human beings – as all research in this area does either directly or indirectly – can never be a merely mechanical activity for, whether the researcher is aware of this or not, it inevitably has repercussions for those other human beings.

This can raise problems to which there are no simple solutions. It may be impossible to foresee all the likely human and moral dilemmas or ultimately satisfy all the different interests within a pluralist world. However, trying to be clear about the underlying reasons for the research is at least one preliminary step in clarifying your position. These are therefore worth considering first.

10.1.1 Purposes of research

So – why do we do research? It is illuminating to reflect on the different (if overlapping) aims of research in oral traditions or verbal art forms. Any simplified summary takes scant account of people's complicated motivations but a schematic list makes a convenient starting point for focusing on some recurrent moral implications:

1 Advancing knowledge for its own sake (as for any subject).
2 The recording, celebration, or better understanding of particular forms which (like some of those discussed in this volume) are regarded as not widely enough known or under threat of dying out.
3 The conservation or protection of such cases or of the 'lore of the folk' generally.
4 The documentation and dissemination of particular forms in order to assist some specific end, for example developing national or group identity or providing vernacular reading material for schools.
5 Research explicitly or indirectly commissioned or paid for by some particular sponsor, for a variety of purposes.
6 Indirect (perhaps secondary) motivations like enhancing the researcher's career, fulfilling peer group expectations, organising teaching projects.

The first aim – advancing knowledge – may seem to raise few problems. But there are consequential questions: for *whom* is this knowledge intended; how will it be published; will there be feed-back to those who have been studied; did they consent to being studied in the first place (perhaps they do not share the ideal of advancing knowledge or prefer their affairs to remain unknown); will this knowledge be held in some central metropolitan power (perhaps overseas) with little or no local access; who (if anyone) will benefit from it? There is not necessarily anything immoral about advancing knowledge, but these questions certainly arise – and not just in principle for some are already being asked. Jansen gives an example:

> Few who attended the IXth International Congress of Anthropo-logical and Ethnological Sciences held in Chicago in September 1973 will ever forget the flying teams of angry young African anthropologists who ran from session to session to deliver appro-priately modified versions of a message that went something like this: 'You, sir or madam, spent fifteen months studying my vil-lage, published two books about "your" (spare the mark!) people, and never sent us so much as a copy of either book or helped us in any way to profit from what you learned.'
>
> Had there been young Eskimo, or Oglala, or South Pacific, or Chicano (or whatever) anthropologists in any noticeable numbers at this polysyllabically entitled congress, they could undoubtedly have formed similar flying teams to deliver the same angry message.
>
> (Jansen 1983: 533)

In own-culture research also, feedback to, and collaboration with, the subjects of the research (who may – or may not – belong to different sectors of society from the researcher) can raise parallel issues.

It can in any case be naive to assume that the search for knowl-edge is necessarily an unsullied pursuit free of disputatious moral issues. Anne Akeroyd rightly points out that 'knowledge is not only a source of enlightenment but also of power and property and . . . entails the power both to harm and to benefit those studied' (1984: 134). Indeed some radical social scientists argue that all research is exploitative: the researcher holds the reins of power, and no code of ethics, however carefully followed, can change this (see Kidder and Judd 1986: 455). Others seek some kind of balance between possibly conflicting obligations. One dominant duty for social scientists is often held to be to discover and reveal the facts – *even* where participants would prefer these to remain concealed, in some cases concealed from themselves. Some researchers seem to feel that critical revelation of local practices may be ethically acceptable in one's own society, but has problems in other cultures, specially those in a disadvantaged position. There are counter-arguments too: that it can be patronising not to apply in other cultures the academic standards one expects in one's own, that one cannot always tell beforehand which knowledge *will* prove acceptable or uncongenial, and that there may be hidden (or contending) interpretations whose revelations some local groups themselves might welcome.

Preservation of folk or traditional material for future generations is also often regarded as an unquestionable imperative for researchers as well as governments and other organisations. The recent UNESCO declaration on 'the safeguarding of folklore', for instance (defined as 'the totality of tradition-based creations of a cultural community' or, alternatively, as 'traditional and popular culture', Honko 1989a: 8), includes stirring words about safeguarding and conserving this part of 'the universal heritage of humanity' so as to promote 'better understanding of cultural diversity and world views, especially those not reflected in dominant cultures' (op. cit.: 7, 9). This morally-based position would no doubt be shared by many researchers. It is often further reinforced by the value many attach to works of the human imagination or of our past, and the desire to document or celebrate them. This has been an important theme in the study of oral forms. Since they are ephemeral in the sense that written records are not, there is often felt to be a particular need to preserve them in some more permanent form before they vanish.

In one way this kind of research obligation seems incontrovertible. It raises questions too, however, not least because concepts like 'tradition' and 'folk' are often emotive and politically-loaded. The earlier assumptions that oral forms were 'dying out' and needed salvaging are nowadays queried for both intellectual reasons and for impliedly freezing supposed 'older' forms as if in a museum. There is also the romanticising tone sometimes inherent in such aims – as if only the 'old' or 'traditional' items from earlier generations are worth attention, rather than individuals who enact and represent the continuing voices of the present. The basis for selection can have evaluative overtones too. If the main motive is 'preservation' this usually means some but not other genres, some but not other groups, the focus being on those labelled as the 'traditional' or 'authentic' voice of the past. A researcher may in effect be not only accepting but giving active currency to limited or contested evaluations (by government, church, competing interest groups, scholarly élites, or whoever) at the expense of others.

A common assumption is that the documenting of oral traditions or verbal arts is to everyone's interest and that those involved will be proud to have as much recorded as possible. This harmonious model does not always accord with the facts. There can be disagreements among different participants or groups about the nature, validity or ranking of particular forms and/or of those who practise them, and power relations as well as aesthetic expression may be a real part of the scene. The question of *which* views or *which* forms should be given dominance can have ethical, not just methodological, dimensions. Such dilemmas can be painful – but sometimes bring one closer to an appreciation of real life than earlier models picturing collective agreement about everything classifiable under 'tradition' and similar terms.

Research explicitly sponsored by someone else can raise further dilemmas. The sponsors' aims may or may not overlap with your own (or with all or any of those discussed earlier), and sometimes the hidden agenda as well as the overt statements may need considering. It may (or may not) prove difficult to satisfy simultaneously obligations to colleagues and subjects as well as to paymasters. Research findings and prospects furthermore often turn out different from what was expected. If you have undertaken to pursue certain questions or come back with specific material (recording an epic, say, or making a film of a typical story-telling session), you may feel obligated to deliver the goods as promised – but this may turn out to need some conscious or, more likely, implicit, manipulation of the empirical data. There may also be ethical conflicts over confidentiality, ownership of material, and constraints on publication.

Conflicting obligations, while perhaps never totally avoidable, can be somewhat mitigated if they are anticipated and perhaps made explicit in the initial application or contract. As Bruce Jackson sums it up:

> Money rarely comes free. A good rule of thumb is: Before you take someone else's money for work you want to do, know exactly what that money is buying and decide if you're really willing to pay the price.

(Jackson 1987: 278)

A final point is that all research is in a sense sponsored. Financial support may be relatively easy to recognise and take account of. But there is also indirect moral, political and intellectual sponsoring: by an academic institution, research council, colleagues, members of your peer group, gatekeepers, particular groups among those you are studying – indeed almost anyone who plays a significant role in the research process. These sponsors too have expectations and interests which you may or may not completely share and which may conflict with other obligations. Because such sponsorship is less visible than for overtly commissioned or funded research, these conflicts are less often recognised – and thus the more worth thinking about.

10.1.2 Attitudes and values

There are no simple solutions to such dilemmas. One's basic approach to the research and its participants does however form one touchstone against which some of these dilemmas can be judged.

It is in part a matter of values. If you take the research and those implicated in it seriously you will presumably wish to engage in the proper linguistic, empirical and theoretical preparation and uphold the professional standards of methodology and analysis that reflect this seriousness. At a more specific level, the particular choices from among the many possible theoretical approaches also have implications. Some approaches very popular in the past are now criticised for moral and political (not just academic) reasons, for example for implicitly perpetuating a now-outdated image of 'the primitive' and thus supporting colonial or neo-colonial ideologies. Other theoretical viewpoints have, variously, been criticised for downplaying human creativity, ignoring (or alternatively exaggerating) power relations, overstressing tradition – criticisms which sometimes have moral, not just intellectual, foundations. Each researcher will probably evaluate these aspects differently. But it is worth being alive to the possible ethical overtones of differing theoretical approaches for they are likely to affect the type of methods, treatment of collaborators, and final interpretation and publication of the results.

The researcher's personal attitude to those being studied is also relevant. One pattern is common enough to warrant comment – that of treating people as automata or 'samples' rather than as full human beings. Hamish Hamilton's precept in the Preface to Goldstein's classic *A Guide for Field Workers in Folklore* could be attacked as a little romantic and outdated in its expression, but is still worth pondering:

> The collector-folklorist should never, in the heat of the chase, forget his humanist role. He is helping to interpret man to man – his beliefs, glories, dreams, darknesses. If he adopts a patronizing attitude to what he is studying, he may well blind himself to its real nature. And if he treats his informants purely as sources of information, to be taken up and discarded as occasion demands, he is in grave danger of losing more than their friendship . . . . If ever an academic collector is tempted to proceed on the assumption that he 'knows' more about folklore than his informants do, he'd be well advised to remember the wise words of A.N. Whitehead: 'The self-confidence of learned people is the comic tragedy of civilization'.
>
> (Goldstein 1964: xi)

The point is more than just warmth and 'rapport' in field-collecting, useful – and sometimes facile – as this can be. What it implies is a respect for the full human qualities of those 'on' whom you are researching. And, specially in archive research, this can include authors and performers you have never met.

10.2 RESPONSIBILITIES TO PARTICIPANTS IN THE RESEARCH

Whatever your aims there will be certain obligations to those in one way or another participating in the research – and given the many different roles for such participation, potentially conflicting obligations. Akeroyd reminds us of the many parties to the research enterprise whose rights and interests researchers have to try to reconcile:

> Informants and other research participants (citizens); gate-keepers; sponsors and funders; themselves; colleagues; their own and host governments; their universities or employers; and the public(s). Moral and ethical decisions occur at all stages of research, from the selection of topic, area or population, sponsor and source of funding, to publication of findings and disposal of data.
>
> (1984: 137)

Participants therefore range from those treated as research 'subjects' at the one end, to academic colleagues or financial sponsors at the other. This is essentially a continuum rather than (as once assumed) a matter of clear-cut distinctions, but some rough categories are given below as a way of highlighting some further ethical issues.

First however, a point about terminology. Remembering that what is involved are human people and their creations is more important than detailed verbal usage. But it is worth being sensitive to certain terms, particularly in field-based study, for even if they do not reflect your own attitude, applying them to those you are studying can cause offence or give the wrong message.

There is no single uncontentious word to describe those being studied and/or assisting in the research in various roles. The main terms over the years include: informants; subjects; respondents/interviewees; sample; performers; participants; consultants; collaborators; citizens; voices; friends/ourselves. Also, for particular genres (though also sometimes used more widely): narrators; story-tellers; poets; singers; bards (these terms often prefixed by the adjective 'folk'); tradition-bearers or traditors.

You will presumably exercise your own judgement about the appropriateness of such terms. The following comments, though not comprehensive, can illustrate the kinds of issues worth considering.

Informants: once a popular term, with its own methodological and sometimes rather depersonalising connotations; still used but now with more caution (see critique in Jansen 1983: esp. 534, 538). Similar overtones can apply to *interviewees, respondents* and, even more, *sample*.

Subjects: as Kimmel (1988: 37) points out the term has pejorative implications, being associated both with political inferiors and, in the context of medical research, with cadavers.

Citizens: has the merit of drawing attention to people's rights and duties as fellow human beings but the problem of not distinguishing their research role (see Barnes 1979: 14ff, Akeroyd 1984: 134).

Participants: now often favoured because of its implications of equality, but once again rather general; people participate in many *different* roles. Those being studied are not necessarily actively or intentionally participating in the research, as is perhaps implied. A merit of the term however may be precisely that it does highlight the need to specify roles more exactly, rather than, as with some other terms, projecting a passive and homogeneous, even impersonal, picture of the contribution of those being studied. Similar problems and advantages to some extent apply to *colleagues, collaborators*, and *consultants*.

Voices: this is sometimes used to imply that different people (and peoples) have different views and cultural riches, all to be taken seriously. It cannot replace the more personal and concrete nouns above, but the basic point implied accords with values held by many recent researchers.

Other apparently technical terms, while appearing neutral, may also reflect and reinforce certain attitudes to the research and hence to its potential participants. Looking for 'tradition bearers', say, or 'folk poets' can over-value categories like the old or the non-literate while assuming that others have nothing of weight to contribute ('folk' is in any case a loaded word, see 1.3.5). Your own personal characteristics or assumptions too, projected onto terms like 'bard' or 'story-teller', might blind you to the possible contribution of, say, women, younger men, players of electric guitars, etc. Using particular labels to locate or, alternatively, screen out certain types of participants as irrelevant may have moral not just methodological implications.

Terminological problems may vanish as you get into the ethnographic detail for then more specific terms can be used. This is probably the ideal situation, for it is no longer a question of some general category subordinate to the researcher's project, but a matter of human beings (attached, no doubt, to particular roles or groups) whose beliefs, actions or products are being interpreted by the researcher with their active collaboration.

10.2.1 Those participating as 'informants', 'interviewees' 'performers', etc.

Although basic attitudes matter more than terminology or general rules, some practical comments can elucidate possible conflicts. It should not need to be said that basic human courtesies apply here as elsewhere (e.g., not being late, offhand or insulting), but the zeal for recording and the assumption that everyone shares this can sometimes lead to their neglect: recording media easily impose their own tyrannies. The usual professional codes for social research apply: ensuring, as appropriate, some explanation of the research aims and of the likely destination and rights involved in any recordings (plus a means of contact if needed); avoidance of unfulfillable promises; care over payments, in particular any hint of bribery or coercion. This last is a difficult area, for sometimes people *want* to be persuaded to perform and some pressure may be an accepted local convention.

Such points are unexceptionable, if not always easy to interpret where local conventions are different from one's own. More difficult is where there are conflicts between individuals or groups about their own rights or the evaluations and definitions of the material. It is easy to say you should not get committed to either side. But this may not be avoidable or even ultimately acceptable, the more so given the commitment of many fieldworkers to the group they are studying and perhaps promoting.

The over-riding advice is normally that participants should above all be treated with dignity as human beings and not exploited by the researcher – easier said than done. Participants' wishes may not fit the researcher's: they may want only their 'best' performances recorded (whereas you may want typical and ordinary exponents too), specify certain genres as the only ones worth studying, or insist on festive rather than everyday accoutrements. Taking the definitions and values of one group may not accord with your own critical investigations; but these, if published, may make the original participants feel their views devalued. Such problems may sometimes (but only sometimes) be partially surmounted by fuller explanations about aims.

The comments above have – like most discussions – focused on those taking a relatively active role but said little about those who are subjects of research in a more passive way, the subjects for example of more or less covert observation or generalised about as co-members of the group or culture studied. You may also need to consider what obligations, if any, you have to such people.

10.2.2 Assistants and co-workers

This category is less discussed in the literature (for some comments see Akeroyd 1984: 140). In the study of oral arts and traditions, however, it is common for people to take such roles as research assistants, transcribers, interpreters, technical assistants in recording, assistants in archives. Though sometimes regarded as distinct these shade into the previous category – indeed any distinctions may themselves be the subject of dispute. Many of the same obligations thus apply, though there may also be additional ones, such as that of proper remuneration. The question of giving credit and due acknowledgement – and in some cases co-authorship of later scholarly publications – also needs considering.

10.2.3 Colleagues and other researchers

This might seem the least contentious category. But there are still questions: how far do you share your data or records (see 10.3.2 on intellectual property rights – some things may not be yours to share); what access should be given to other research participants; who should decide on this (for some examples see Jackson 1987: 274ff); how should the division of labour within any kind of collaborative research be arranged, and rights over publication or commercial exploitation be distributed; can the ethic of open-ness of knowledge be reconciled with one's own personal rights; how far should *dis*agreements or differing commitments be brought into the open; is there conflict between intellectual duties to scholarly colleagues and those to the subjects of the research? Where the research is outside your own culture, particular attention may also need to be paid to the interests of local scholars cooperating in or following up the research.

Finally, the whole concept of 'colleague' is increasingly being opened up in the modern study of oral arts and traditions. It can extend not only to fellow academics in the older scholarly mould, but also to all those participants who are themselves fellow interpreters and analysers of what is being studied, above all in the sphere of oral traditions and formulations.

10.2.4 Sponsors, governments, officials

As discussed earlier, conflicting obligations may arise here too (not necessarily so). Again, while there are no general solutions, it can be helpful to try to get clear for oneself, both beforehand but also as they emerge in the course of the research and its aftermath, just what these obligations are.

10.2.5 Follow-up

The later phases of research still carry obligations to many interested parties, not just to yourself or your academic colleagues as is sometimes assumed. The older model by which one 'left the field', typically a far-away colonial country, is now being replaced by continuing interaction rendering these obligations more evident. Many of the relevant issues are already implicit in the discussion above, but some points deserve additional emphasis.

There are clearly responsibilities to academic colleagues to explain the findings, methods, and limitations of your research, not suppress the facts (unless other binding obligations make this essential), and make the results available with reasonable speed. This is straightforward, though not always easy, particularly when time-consuming processing of texts is needed or when interpretations and conflicts are not easily resolvable.

Less recognised is the responsibility to keep explicit and implicit undertakings to participants in the research, particularly those at the local level. Sometimes this may mean further explanation of the findings or purposes, specially if any aspects were covert. Different kinds of communication, publication and deposit may need considering, including local and/or 'popular', not just specialist academic, channels, and audio, video and personal communication as well as the written word. The broadcast media too may have a serious part to play (on their responsibilities see O'Neill 1978).

In addition drafts sometimes need checking back before publication, not just for factual details but also for interpretations (these may be genuinely contentious) and the elucidation of any rights in the material. Transcripts of texts can be a sensitive matter (see 10.4 below), and material acceptable during oral delivery may look obscene or offensive when in written non-contextualised form. Discussion with the original authors may not solve the dilemmas, but will at least point up the difficulties.

Similarly there are problems about the selection and presentation of items for publication, etc.: which tapes should be deposited or which songs printed; whose criteria used to govern the choice? Local consultation will not necessarily resolve the issues, but the originators may have a view and the right to enter into the dialogue (for interesting disussion of such points see Feld 1987).

Many would now hold that the research process should no longer be a top–down activity setting academic researchers apart from the 'subjects' they study, but a matter of interaction and dialogue between cooperating (if sometimes disagreeing) participants who in one sense are all parties to and collaborators in, the process and aims of research. The perfect balance between all these responsibilities is no doubt impossible to achieve, and it should not be presumed that *only* thinking of one's responsibilities to the subjects studied is always wholly satisfactory either. Perhaps the best that can be done is to try to face the difficulties explicitly.

10.3 OWNERSHIP, CONFIDENTIALITY AND REMUNERATION

The discussion is not complete without some reference to these particularly knotty – and related – points.

10.3.1 Confidentiality, anonymity and privacy

The main issues here are no different from the familiar ones of all social research. The guiding principle – widely agreed, if seldom simple to apply – is usually taken to be to safeguard participants from harm or embarrassment due to the divulging of confidential, personal or dangerous information learned from the research (see Kidder and Judd 1986: 500ff; Akeroyd 1984: 147, 151; Jansen 1984: 536). In addition some specific points are worth mentioning.

Some oral forms are secret, or restricted to particular exponents or audiences in terms of, say, age, gender or status. This raises problems about confidentiality in publication or archive deposit. Should such genres be given wider publicity either for the sake of truth generally or quite specifically to reach a wider audience (including present or future generations of the culture being studied)? Or confined to more limited categories of audiences as some of the original proponents might have wished or assumed? Asking for explicit permission may be one strategy, but this will not necesssarily solve questions about whose interests should prevail.

The use of anonymity or pseudonyms to conceal identity and thus safeguard confidentiality and invasion of privacy is one established practice in social research, but also attracts controversy (compare Akeroyd and Davis in Ellen 1984: 151–2 and 317–18 respectively; also Finnegan 1989: 346–7). An additional twist here is the earlier assumption that oral material is 'traditional' and thus without named authors. This view is now less common and by now most researchers feel an obligation to supply the names of those whose performances they recorded, not only in their own field notes but also in their publications. In such cases anonymity or pseudonyms might appear, as Bruce Jackson rightly argues, 'very close to plagiarism' (1987: 271, see also 10.3.2 below).

10.3.2 Intellectual property rights

In research on oral forms, this issue often takes precedence over questions of confidentiality, the more so that specific artistic works and their ownership may be involved. This aspect often needs direct attention, together with the related ethical, commercial and legal issues (for general discussion and references see Akeroyd 1984: 150, Jackson 1987: 259ff, Wallis and Malm 1984).

Here again the general principle is agreed (if hard to interpret): to give credit where it is due. There is still sometimes the hidden assumption that the researcher somehow owns the people and the material collected, a position rationalised by earlier notions about lack of individual creativity in oral arts and tradition and the sometimes dominant position of researchers (and their recording technology) in other cultures. But as Bruce Jackson again puts it in characteristically forceful style, 'Who owns the folklore? Not you or me, that's for sure' (1987: 259).

In practice this is often a complex problem. There may well be a number of different (and often shared) rights involved – not that this absolves the researcher from at least thinking about such issues as the following:

1 *Attribution of authorship in publications* (for specific items within a publication and perhaps co-authorship as a whole). In the past the author's name was quite often not given, though the academic's always was. Nowadays this would be regarded as unacceptable.

2 *Rights in spoken or recorded words and sounds* (audio and video recordings as well as written transcriptions, and interview materials as well as performances). A series of issues arise here, the more pressingly because there are sometimes commercial implications. Who owns these? Who has the right to reproduce them? Need copyright be cleared for further reproduction? How are the rights shared between researcher and interviewee (for some incisive comments on this in the case of interviews see Henige 1982: 113ff)? The answers are not always evident, but it can by now be presumed that few researchers could feel happy about commercial records or radio broadcasts being made from performances obtained in research without clearance from, or advantage to, the original performers. On the other hand, obtaining permissions from individuals in remote areas is sometimes genuinely hard. Perhaps researchers need to be aware of this in advance and ensure not only full documentation of any recordings but also some channel (perhaps themselves) through which later contacts or payments can be made.

3 *Formal and legal sanctions.* Because researchers are now more

sensitive to such issues than in the past some have adopted a system of obtaining permission from research participants, often in the form of explicit waivers or releases – not that these necesssarily solve all the problems (see 4.3.3). In some cases there is now some legal protection through copyright laws. These vary in different countries and need to be consulted in detail, but it is interesting to note the gradual extension of concepts of intellectual property from written forms to audio and video compositions and recordings. There are genuine difficulties in the case of sounds and images and still problems about application, particularly in the case of cross-cultural exploitation of material in the 'public' or the 'traditional' domain, which the World Intellectual Property Organization (WIPO) and other international organisations are endeavouring to address (see Wallis and Malm 1984: esp. chap. 6). This is a set of issues that will continue to raise problems.

4 *Rights of* all *participants in the research*. The rights of assistants, interpreters, local collaborators, local sponsors, audiences, etc., may also need to be remembered (and investigated), not just those of the performers. It may also be pertinent to think about your own rights.

5 *Remuneration*. This is another complex and much-discussed area (see Goldstein 1964: chap. 9, B. Jackson 1987: 267ff). There can be no definitive rules, but relevant points are the importance of taking account of local conventions (particularly those relating to payment or other recognition for performance), the possibility that freelance performers may need and expect recompense for their time, and that rewards and expectations do not necessarily always take a monetary or an immediate form. It cannot be assumed that payment at the time necessarily means transfer of all rights over recorded or other materials.

6 *Research income*. It is true that academic books bring little direct financial gain to set against expenses or to share with others. But there may be indirect gains to the researcher, and consequently the question of whether and how far royalties from books or other outlets should be shared with or given to other participants in the research and/or used for the general benefit of those being studied (see discussion of pros and cons in B. Jackson 1987: 267ff).

The question of rights is usually thought about after recording, but may also need to be considered in advance. Making recordings without the participants' knowledge is dubious practice – participants in this context meaning performer(s), organisers, perhaps audience and others with rights of ownership or control. Audio recordings are easy to make surreptitiously, and local conventions may regard this as acceptable. But the technology does not excuse taking liberties or over-riding people's rights in the eventual recording or its use; nor does it solve the problem that rights and responsibilities may be shared, so that what is acceptable or known to one category (say, the organisers of an event) may not be so to others (like specific performers). Other recording media perhaps raise fewer issues, but the question of who holds which rights even in, say, dictated or specially written texts, may need investigation – not always the immediate person you are dealing with. There is also the complex question of whether those with rights in such material may not also have the right to know that it is being recorded, or to be consulted about its ultimate destination.

10.4 ETHICAL AND POLITICAL ISSUES IN TEXT PROCESSING

There are also some specific issues relating to the handling of texts. The social rather than mechanical nature of this process (the theme of chapter 9) means that those involved inevitably make a series of decisions. These often carry moral and political implications.

Translating is one obvious example. Decisions about aims and style, or *which* version to translate, what language or which kind of linguistic register to translate into, or in what context it will be presented are not mechanical ones. Many questions arise here. Is translating a 'local' text into a western language a form of neo-colonialism? What if such translations start being accepted and circulated as literary works in their own right? Whose kind of English should be used ('BBC' English; some 'comparable' English dialect; 'West African' English)? Where there are differing values and expectations, whose should be paramount? Should translators avoid downgrading the acoustic and non-verbal overtones by refusing to transfer oral performances into purely verbal and written translations at all?

Settling such questions is not a merely neutral matter for as illustrated earlier (9.1.2) it is easy to start from stereotypes of foreign speech, and import these, perhaps unconsciously, into the translations. Dennis Tedlock pictures readers' reactions to translations of American Indian narratives:

[They] will soon wonder whether the original style of these narratives was as choppy and clumsy as that of most English translations . . . [and] end by agreeing with La Farge, who said,
'The literary value of a great deal of primitive literature, whether
myths or tales, is nil'.

(1971: 114)

Lefevere aptly refers to the 'ideological underpinnings' (1986: 44)
of decisions implicit in translating, reminding us that translation
involves 'power as well as language' (loc. cit.) and can have negative
as well as positive implications. Comments initially made about
Biblical translation can be applied more widely too:

There is a direct connection between politics and translation. In
discussing cultural diffusion, our political perspective is the liberal
one that welcomes the freewheeling open forum of ideas: I see
translation as the only hope for a truly *democratic* 'global village'.
But translation or near-translation are just as easily instruments
of obfuscation and propaganda.

(Glassgold 1987: 20–1)

Decisions in transcribing similarly have wider implications, specially
if the transcriptions are disseminated elsewhere (which they may
be even if this is not originally intended). Again the form used may
convey unintentionally derogatory images. Transferring a spoken to
a written medium gives rise to some intractable problems here
for conventions expected of *written* formulations differ from those
assumed for oral communication. Thus spoken forms transcribed
into writing can look 'illiterate' and consequently be both offensive
to the speakers and give a misleading impression of their intelligence or verbal skill (one reason for the common advice to omit
'uh's' and false starts). In the past this may have seemed less of a
hazard for researchers working in largely non-literate and remote
areas, where local readers were unlikely to come across the transcriptions; but the same principle applies, and in any case, where
is truly remote now? Whatever the final strategy the transcriber's
decisions and their rationale are best made explicit. One partial
solution is to highlight the spoken basis, as in the phrasing in some
release forms: 'Any reader should bear in mind that he is reading
a transcript of my spoken, not my written word and that the tape,
not the transcript, is the primary document' (Ives 1980: 111).

Spelling creates similar problems. Given the accepted conventions
about orthography in written communication, non-standard spell-

ings can convey an unjustified impression of the speakers as uneducated and incapable of following accepted rules. Clearly there is a dilemma here, for conventional orthography may not convey the pronunciation, texture or non-verbal elements of the original oral performance. But if these *are* to be represented in non-'standard' ways this needs to be done with care and explicitly justified. If re-spelling is used, then why not other changes? And why is it felt necessary to re-spell *some* regional pronunciations but not others? The problem has political, not just intellectual, overtones, if it is true, as sometimes suggested, that special spellings are more common in transcriptions from groups already thought of as marginal, despised or romanticised (Preston's survey of articles in the *American Journal of Folklore* in the 1970's suggested that researchers found it 'more necessary to respell the speech of Blacks and Appalachians than that of others', 1982: 305). Even with the best of motives, special presentations – even perhaps the typographical devices described on p.204ff – can be misunderstood. This is compounded where there are already political sensitivities or if there is the temptation (or even motive?) to introduce a 'folk' or 'primitive' aura through the presentation. Unless there are compelling reasons to the contrary it is worth considering the principles behind Ives' uncompromising advice:

> Don't write 'wa'p' when you know the informant would probably spell it 'warp' for example, or 'jest' for 'just', and don't leave off final 'g's (write 'going,' not 'goin'). Transcribed dialect always contains within it an element of condescension, and you will never have to apologize for or 'explain' the use of standard spelling.
>
> (1980: 98)

Even that does not wholly settle the matter for linguistic expression commonly has political overtones. If so, whose versions of disputed spellings, interpretations or definitions should be taken? Among several participants, whose voices should appear in the transcription (remembering that what is transcribed often becomes fixed as *the* version)? And if there are implicitly competing views about the 'reality' or value of differing media whose view should prevail and why?

Even in the apparently innocuous process of transcribing, then, there are obligations to a series of parties, including (but not necessarily confined to) those of the original authors of the texts. Fulfilling these obligations is not always straightforward. It is however at the least incumbent on researchers to make clear what principles have been used and why, for the results are likely to have consequences not just for themselves but also for several other rightly interested parties (for some strategies to deal with the problems, while making the transcriber's own position admirably clear, see Bauman 1986: ix–x, Briggs 1988: 55ff, Sherzer 1990, also discussion in Jansen 1983).

The aim and form of wider dissemination also needs considering (see 10.2.5 above, also 9.3.1 and on issues concerning deposit and access, 9.3.4). The ethos of research is moving away from the model of outside researchers 'doing research on' or 'collecting from' some particular people and themselves somehow owning the results, to that of a collaborative venture in which the outcome is of wider interest than just for specialist 'researchers' and their colleagues. So alternative or additional modes of dissemination beyond the traditional media of specialist books, Ph. D. theses and learned articles may need considering. These might include more popular publications (including anthologies) directed largely to non-specialist readers and/or amateur researchers; modestly-produced and circulated booklets, including those for school use, perhaps in collaboration with local publishers and institutions; jointly authored works in various media; making materials available for use in local arts centres or museums (the latter increasingly relevant with expanding museological interests in multi-sensory experiences); illustrated lectures to various audiences; oral communication and performances (not the traditional medium for researchers, perhaps, but in the case of oral art surely not to be disregarded); broadcasts, films and other forms of audio-visual presentation; and various mixtures of these. Researchers nowadays can look further than the traditional academic mode and audience, and consider different possibilities and audiences for the presentation of the products of their research.

But if wider publication and a sharing of the fruits of knowledge is an obligation to be taken seriously, there are still the problems of potentially competing claims to control and ownership. Who should have the last say on form or content and who owns the results? Yet again we need to remind ourselves that handling texts is never purely routine but one important – and sensitive – sphere in which the researcher, as selector, formulator, translator, transcriber or presenter, is exercising power.

10.5 CONCLUSION

The possible implications seem endless, perhaps as if research is so problem-laden that it is not worth the intellectual or ethical cost. This would surely be too extreme. Certainly we need to try to follow the principles of established good practice and be more sensitive than in the past to dilemmas within research. Certainly too problems will arise on which only those intimately concerned will be in a position to make informed and considerate judgements as human beings, not just as researchers.

In the last analysis however the researcher's duty surely must include (overwhelmingly some would argue) carrying through the quest with all due competence and an ultimate responsibility for how he or she finally formulates it. It would be insulting to all concerned to aim otherwise. But the search for understanding and for tackling the kinds of questions about human expression and performance raised in the first chapter and throughout this book, can perhaps be effectively pursued only by combining this imperative to seek after truth with some awareness of our joint debts to others. This combination is now coming to be seen as a necessary part of a researcher's competence.

Two themes of this book have been that looking just to words on their own is too narrow, and that we need to be a touch cynical about taking words at their face value. Nevertheless expression through words is surely still to be regarded as among the greatest of human gifts. The background, indeed, to why it remains our value-drenched obligation to be concerned for the terms and the methods we use here, is that it is so often through verbal expression that as human beings we somehow get a handle on our experience of ourselves and of the world; and such experiences are themselves in turn formulated and struggled for and transcended by our collaborative deployment of words. Their use and study must, correspondingly, be valued as a profoundly human endeavour: an endeavour that is to our good fortune, and not just by necessity, shared with others.

References

Aarne, A.A. and Thompson, S. (1961) *The Types of the Folk-Tale: a Classification and Bibliography*, 2nd revision, Helsinki: Folklore Fellows Communications 75, 184.

Abercrombie, J.R. (1984) *Computer Programs for Literary Analysis*, Philadelphia: University of Pennsylvania Press.

Abrahams, R.D. (1968a) 'Introductory remarks to a rhetorical theory of folklore', *Journal of American Folklore* 81: 43–58.

Abrahams, R.D. (1968b) 'A rhetoric of everyday life: traditional conversational genres', *Southern Folklore Quarterly* 32: 44–59.

Abrahams, R.D. (1970a) *Deep Down in the Jungle: Negro Narrative Folklore from the Streets of Philadelphia*, 2nd ed., Philadelphia: Aldine.

Abrahams, R.D. (1970b) *A Singer and Her Songs: Almeda Riddle's Book of Ballads*, Baton Rouge: Louisiana State University Press.

Abrahams, R.D. (1970c) 'A performance-centered approach to gossip', *Man* 5: 290–301.

Abrahams, R.D. (1972) 'Folklore and literature as performance', *Journal of Folklore Institute* 9: 75–94.

Abrahams, R.D. (1976) 'The complex relations of simple forms', in Ben-Amos 1976, first published in 1969 in *Genre* 2: 2.

Abrahams, R.D. (1981a) 'Shouting match at the border: the folklore of display events', in Bauman and Abrahams.

Abrahams, R.D. (1981b) 'In and out of performance', in *Narodna Umjetnost* [Belgrade]: 69–78.

Abrahams, R.D. (1983) 'Interpreting folklore ethnographically and sociologically', in Dorson.

Abrahams, R.D. (1985a) 'A note on neck-riddles in the West Indies as they comment on emergent genre theory', *Journal of American Folklore* 98, 387: 85–94.

Abrahams, R.D. (1985b) 'Our native notions of story', *New York Folklore* 11, 1/4: 37–47.

Abrahams, R.D. (1987) 'An American vocabulary of celebrations', in Falassi, A. (ed.) *Time Out of Mind: Essays on the Festival*, Albuquerque: University of New Mexico Press.

Abrahams, R.D. and Foss, G. (1968) *Anglo-American Folksong Style*, Englewood Cliffs: Prentice-Hall.

Abu-Lughod, L. (1986) *Veiled Sentiments: Honor and Poetry in a Bedouin Society*, Berkeley: University of California Press.

Adams, H. and Searle, L. (eds) (1986) *Critical Theory since 1965*, Tallahassee: Florida State University Press.

Adams, H. (1989) 'Literary criticism', in Barnouw: vol. 2: 444–7.

Agar, M.H. (1980) *The Professional Stranger: an Informal Introduction to Ethnography*, New York and London: Academic Press.

Aitken, A.J., Bailey, R.W. and Hamilton-Smith, N. (eds) (1973) *The Computer and Literary Studies*, Edinburgh: Edinburgh University Press.

Akeroyd, A.V. (1984) 'Ethics in relation to informants, the profession and governments', in Ellen.

Albrecht, M.C. (1954) 'The relationship of literature and society', *American Journal of Sociology* 59: 425–36.

Alexiou, M. and Lambropoulos, V. (eds) (1985) *The Text and its Margins: Post-Structuralist Approaches to Twentieth-Century Greek Literature*, New York: Pella Publishing Company.

Algarin, J.P. (1982) *Japanese Folk Literature: a Core Collection and Reference Guide*, London: Bowker.

Almqvist, B., Ó Catháin, S. and Ó Héalaí, P. (eds) (1987) *The Heroic Process: Form, Function and Fantasy in Folk Epic*, Dun Laoghaire: Glendale.

American Anthropological Association (1973) *Professional Ethics: Statements and Procedures of the American Anthropological Association*, Washington D.C.: American Anthropological Association.

American Folklore Society (1987) *Folklore and Feminism*, Special Issue, *Journal of American Folklore* 100, 398: 387–588.

Andrzejewski, B.W. (1965) 'Emotional bias in the translation and presentation of African oral art', *Sierra Leone Language* Review 4: 95–102.

Andrzejewski, B.W. (1967) 'The art of the miniature in Somali poetry', *African Language Review* 6: 5–16.

Andrzejewski, B.W. (1981) 'The poem as message: verbatim memorization in Somali oral poetry', in Ryan.

Andrzejewski, B.W. (1985) 'Oral literature', in Andrzejewski et al.

Andrzejewski, B.W. and Innes, G. (1975) 'Reflections on African oral literature', *African Languages* 1: 1–57.

Andrzejewski, B.W. and Lewis, I.M. (1964) *Somali Poetry: An Introduction*, Oxford: Clarendon Press.

Andrzejweski, B.W., Pilaszewicz, S. and Tyloch, W. (eds) (1985) *Literatures in African Languages: Theoretical Issues and Sample Surveys*, Cambridge: Cambridge University Press, and Warszawa: Wiedza Powszechna.

Arewa, E.O. (1967) *A Classification of the Folktales of the Northern East African Cattle Area by Types*, doctoral dissertation, University of California, Berkeley.

Arnold, C.C. and Bowers, J.W. (1984) *Handbook of Rhetorical and Communication Theory*, Boston: Allyn and Bacon.

Ashliman, D.L. (1987) *A Guide to Folktales in the English Language. Based on the Aarne-Thompson Classification System*, New York: Greenwood Press.

Association of Social Anthropologists of the Commonwealth (1987) *Ethical*

Guidelines for Good Practice, London: Association of Social Anthropologists.

Atkinson, P. (1990) *The Ethnographic Imagination: Textual Constructions of Reality*, London: Routledge.

Attridge, D., Bennington, G. and Young, R. (eds) (1987) *Post-Structuralism and the Question of History*, Cambridge: Cambridge University Press.

d'Azevedo, W. (1958) 'A structural approach to esthetics: toward a definition of art in anthropology', *American Anthropologist* 60: 702–14.

Azzolina, D.S. (1987) *Tale Type- and Motif-Indexes: an Annotated Bibliography*, New York and London: Garland Folklore Bibliographies, 12.

Babalola, A. (1976) 'The morphology of Yoruba tales of tortoise', in Pentikäinen and Juurikka.

Babcock, B.A. (1977) 'The story in the story: metanarration in folk narrative', in Bauman 1977a.

Babcock, B.A. (ed) (1978) *The Reversible World: Symbolic Inversion in Art and Society*, Ithaca : Cornell University Press.

Babcock-Abrahams, B. (1974) 'The novel and the carnival world', *Modern Language Notes* 89: 911–37.

Babcock-Abrahams, B. (1975) '"A tolerated margin of mess": the trickster and his tales reconsidered', *Journal of Folklore* Institute 11: 147–86.

Baddeley, A.D. (1976) *The Psychology of Memory*, New York: Basic Books.

Bahrick, H.F. (1987) 'Functional and cognitive memory theory: an overview of some key issues', in Gorfein and Hoffman.

Bakhtin, M.M. (1968) *Rabelais and his World*, Eng. trans., Cambridge Mass: MIT Press.

Bakhtin, M.M. (1981) *The Dialogic Imagination: Four Essays*, Eng. trans., ed. M. Holquist, Austin: University of Texas Press.

Bakhtin, M.M. (1986) *Speech Genres and Other Late Essays*, Eng. trans., ed. C. Emerson and M. Holquist, Austin: University of Texas Press.

Barber, K. (1987) 'Popular arts in Africa' and 'Response', Special Issue on African popular arts, *African Studies Review* 30, 3: 1–78, 105–32.

Barber, K. (1989) 'Interpreting oríkì as history and as literature', in Barber and Farias.

Barber K. and Farias, P.F. de M. (eds) (1989) *Discourse and its Disguises: the Interpretation of African Oral Texts*, Birmingham: Centre of West African Studies, Birmingham University African Studies Series 1.

Barnard, A. and Good, A. (1984) *Research Practices in the Study of Kinship*, ASA Research Methods in Social Anthropology 2, London: Academic Press.

Barnes, D.R. (1984) 'Interpreting urban legends', *Arv* 40: 67–78.

Barnes, J.A. (1977) *The Ethics of Inquiry in Social Science: Three Lectures*, Delhi: Oxford University Press.

Barnes, J.A. (1979) *Who Should Know What? Social Science, Privacy and Ethics*, Harmondsworth: Penguin.

Barnouw, E. (ed.) (1989) *International Encyclopedia of Communications*, 4 vols, New York and Oxford: Oxford University Press.

Barthes, R. (1975) 'An introduction to the structural analysis of narrative', *New Literary History* 6: 237–72.

Barthes, R. (1977) *Image Music Text*, New York: Hill & Wang.

Bartlett, F.C. (1932) *Remembering: a Study in Experimental and Social Psychology*, Cambridge: Cambridge University Press.

Bascom, W.R. (1955) 'Verbal art', *Journal of American Folklore* 68: 245–52.

Bascom, W.R. (1965a) 'The forms of folklore: prose narratives', *Journal of American Folklore* 78: 3–20.

Bascom, W.R. (1965b) 'Four functions of folklore', in Dundes.

Bascom, W.R. (ed.) (1977) *Frontiers of Folklore*. Boulder: Westview Press, for American Association for the Advancement of Science (AAAS Selected Symposium 5).

Basso, E.B (1985) *A Musical View of the Universe: Kalapalo Myth and Ritual Performance*, Philadelphia: University of Pennsylvania Press.

Basso, K.H. (1974) 'The ethnography of writing', in Bauman and Sherzer.

Basso, K.H. (1976) ' "Wise words" of the Western Apache: metaphor and semantic theory', in Basso and Selby.

Basso, K.H. (1984) ' "Stalking with stories": names, places, and moral narratives among the Western Apache', in Bruner.

Basso, K.H. (1988) ' "Speaking with names": language and landscape among the Western Apache', *Cultural Anthropology* 3, 2: 99–130.

Basso, K.H. and Selby, H.A. (eds) (1976) *Meaning in Anthropology*, Albuquerque: University of New Mexico Press.

Bateson, G. (1958) *Naven: A Survey of the Problems Suggested by a Composite Picture of the Culture of a New Guinea Tribe Drawn from Three Points of View*, 2nd ed., Stanford: Stanford University Press.

Battaglia, D. (1990) *On the Bones of the Serpent: Person, Memory and Mortality in Sabarl Island Society*, Chicago and London: Chicago University Press.

Baughman, E.W. (1966) *Type and Motif-Index of the Folktales of England and North America*, The Hague: Mouton.

Baum, W.K. (1977) *Transcribing and Editing Oral History*, Nashville: American Association for State and Local History.

Bauman, R. (1977a) *Verbal Art as Performance*, Rowley, Mass: Newbury House.

Bauman, R. (1977b) 'Settlement patterns on the frontiers of folklore', in Bascom.

Bauman, R. (1983) 'The field study of folklore in context', in Dorson.

Bauman, R. (1986) *Story, Performance, and Event: Contextual Studies of Oral Narrative*, Cambridge: Cambridge University Press.

Bauman, R. (1989a) 'Performance', in Barnouw vol. 3: 262–6.

Bauman, R. (1989b) 'American folklore studies and social transformation: a performance-centered perspective', *Text and Performance Quarterly* 9, 3: 175–84.

Bauman, R. (1989c) 'Folklore', in Barnouw vol. 2: 177–81.

Bauman, R. (n.d.) 'Contextualisation, tradition, and the dialogue of genres: Icelandic legends of the Kraftaskáld', in Duranti and Goodwin.

Bauman, R. and Abrahams, R.D. (eds) (1981) *'And Other Neighborly Names': Social Process and Cultural Image in Texas Folklore*, Austin: University of Texas Press.

Bauman, R. and Briggs, C.L. (1990) 'Poetics and performance as critical perspectives on language and social life', *Annual Review of Anthropology* 19: 59–88.

Bauman, R., Irvine, J.T., and Philips, S.U. (1987) *Performance, Speech Community, and Genre*, Chicago: Center for Psychosocial Studies, Working Paper 11.

Bauman, R. and Sherzer, J. (eds) (1974) *Explorations in the Ethnography of Speaking*, London: Cambridge University Press (2nd edition 1989).

Bäuml, F.H. (1984) 'Medieval texts and the two theories of oral-formulaic composition: a proposal for a third theory', *New Literary History* 16: 31–49.

Bausinger, H. (1968) *Formen der 'Volkspoesie'*, Berlin: Schmidt.

Bausinger, H. (1987) *Märchen, Phantasie und Wirklichkeit*, Frankfurt: Dipa-Verlag.

Baxter, P.T.W. (1986) 'Giraffes and poetry: some observations on giraffe hunting among the Boran', *Paideuma* 32: 45–63.

Beals, R.L. (1969) *Politics of Social Research. An Inquiry into the Ethics and Responsibilities of Social Scientists*, Chicago: Aldine.

Becker, A.L. (1979) 'Text-building, epistemology, and aesthetics in Javanese shadow theatre', in Becker and Yengoyan.

Becker, A.L. and Yengoyan, A.A. (eds) (1979) *The Imagination of Reality*, Norwood N.J.: Ablex.

Becker, H.S. (1974) 'Photography and sociology', *Studies in the Anthropology of Visual Communication* 5: 3–26.

Becker, H.S. (1979) 'Problems in the publication of field studies', in Bynner and Stribley.

Becker, H.S. (ed.) (1981) *Exploring Society Photographically*, Chicago: Northwestern University Press.

Becker, H.S. (1984) *Art Worlds*, Berkeley and London: University of California Press.

Béhague, G.H. (1989) 'Music performance', in Barnouw 1989: vol. 3: 114–6.

Beissinger, M.H. (1988) 'Text and music in Romanian oral epic', *Oral Tradition* 3, 3: 294–314.

Belmont, N. (1983) 'Myth and folklore in connection with AT403 and 713', *Journal of Folklore Research* 20: 185–96.

Benjamin, W. (1969) 'The storyteller', in Benjamin, W. and Arendt, H. (ed.) *Illuminations*, New York: Schocken Books.

Ben-Amos, D. (1972) 'Toward a definition of folklore in context', in Paredes and Bauman.

Ben-Amos, D. (ed.) (1976) *Folklore Genres*, Austin and London: University of Texas Press.

Ben-Amos, D. (1978) 'The modern local historian in Africa', in Dorson.

Ben-Amos, D. (1982) 'Foreword' in Lüthi.

Ben-Amos, D. (1983) 'Introduction', Special Issue on epic and panegyric poetry, *Research in African Literatures* 14: 277–82.

Ben-Amos, D. (1984) 'The seven strands of *tradition*: varieties in its meaning in American folklore studies', *Journal of Folklore Research* 21, 2/3: 97–131.

Ben-Amos, D. (ed.) (1987) *African Art and Literature*, Special Issue, *Word and Image* 3, 3.

Ben-Amos, D. (1989) 'Folktale', in Barnouw, vol 2: 181–7.

Ben-Amos, D. and Goldstein, K.S. (eds) (1975) *Folklore: Performance and Communication*, The Hague: Mouton.

Benamou, M. and Caramello, C. (eds) (1977) *Performance in Postmodern Culture*, Madison and Milwaukee: Coda Press and Center for Twentieth Century Studies.

Bendix, R. (1989) *Backstage Domains: Playing 'William Tell' in Two Swiss Communities*, Bern: Peter Lang.

Bennett, G. (1984) 'Women's personal experience stories of encounters with the supernatural: truth as an aspect of storytelling', *Arv* 40: 79–87.

Bennett, G. (1985) 'What's "modern" about the modern legend?', *Fabula* 26: 219–29.

Bennett, G. (1988) 'Legend: performance and truth', in Bennett and Smith.

Bennett, G. (1989) ' "And I turned round to her and said . . . ": a preliminary analysis of shape and structure in women's storytelling', *Folklore* 100: 167–83.

Bennett, G. (1990) ' "And . . . ": controlling the argument, controlling the audience', *Fabula* 31: 208–16.

Bennett, G., Smith, P., and Widdowson, J.D.A. (1987) *Perspectives on Contemporary Legend II*, Sheffield: Sheffield Academic Press.

Bennett, G. and Smith P. (eds) (1988) *Monsters with Iron Teeth*, Perspectives on Contemporary Legend III, Sheffield: Sheffield Academic Press.

Bennett, G. and Smith P. (eds) (1989) *The Questing Beast*, Perspectives on Contemporary Legend IV, Sheffield: Sheffield Academic Press.

Bernard, H.R. (1988) *Research Methods in Cultural Anthropology*, Newbury Park: Sage.

Berndt, R. M. (1952) *Djanggawul. An Aboriginal Religious Cult of North-Eastern Arnhem Land*, London: Routledge.

Berry, J. (1961) *Spoken Art in West Africa*, London: School of Oriental and African Studies, University of London.

Best, E. (1923) *The Maori School of Learning*, Wellington: Dominion Museum Monograph 6.

Bettelheim, B. (1976) *The Uses of Enchantment: The Meaning and Importance of Fairy Tales*, New York: Knopf.

Biebuyck, D.P. (1976) 'The African heroic epic', *Journal of the Folklore Institute* 13: 5–36.

Biebuyck, D. (1978) 'The African heroic epic', in Oinas.

Bigsby, C.W.E. (ed.) (1976) *Approaches to Popular Culture*, London: Arnold.

Birdwhistell, R.L. (1970) *Kinesics and Context: Essays on Body Motion Communication*, Philadelphia: University of Pennsylvania Press.

Blackburn, S.H. (1988) *Singing of Birth and Death: Texts in Performance*, Philadelphia: University of Pennsylvania Press.

Blacking, J. (1967) *Venda Children's Songs: a Study in Ethnomusicological Analysis*, Johannesburg: Witwatersrand University Press.

Blacking, J. (1973) 'Fieldwork in African music', *Review of Ethnology*, 3, 23: 177–84.

Blacking, J. (ed.) (1977) *The Anthropology of the Body*, New York and London: Academic Press.

Blacking, J. and Kealiinohomoku, J.W. (eds) (1979) *The Performing Arts: Music and Dance*, The Hague: Mouton.

Blakely, T.D. (1990) *Hemba Visual Communication and Space*, Lanham: University Press of America.

Blakely, T.D. and P.A.R. (eds) (1989) *Directory of Visual Anthropology*, American Anthropological Association.

Bloch, M. (ed) (1975) *Political Language and Oratory in Traditional Society*, London: Academic Press.

Bloch, M. (1989) 'Literacy and enlightenment', in Schousboe and Larsen.

Bocock, R. and Thompson, K. (eds) (1985) *Religion and Ideology*, Manchester: Manchester University Press.

Bødker, L. (1965) *Folk Literature (Germanic)*, Copenhagen: Rosenkilde and Bagger.

Bohannan, L. (1966) 'Shakespeare in the bush', *Natural History* 75, 7: 28–33.

Bolter, J.D. (1989) 'Beyond word processing: the computer as a new writing space', in DeMaria and Kitzinger.

Bornat, J. (1989) 'Oral history as a social movement: reminiscence and older people', *Oral History*, 17: 16–24.

Bottigheimer, R.B. (1986a) 'Silenced women in the Grimms' Tales: the fit between fairy tales and society in their historical context', in Bottigheimer 1986b.

Bottigheimer, R.B. (ed.) (1986b) *Fairy Tales and Society: Illusion, Allusion, and Paradigm*, Philadephia: University of Pennsylvania Press.

Bottomore, T. (1984) *The Frankfurt School*, Chichester: Horwood.

Boullata, I.J. (ed.) (1989) *Arabic Oral Traditions*, Special Issue, *Oral Tradition* 4, 1/2.

Bourdieu, P. (1984) *Distinction: A Social Critique of the Judgement of Taste*, English trans., London: Routledge & Kegan Paul.

Bowden, B. (1982) *Performed Literature: Words and Music by Bob Dylan*, Bloomington: Indiana University Press.

Bowden, Betsy (1987) *Chaucer Aloud: the Varieties of Textual Interpretation*, Philadelphia: University of Pennsylvania Press.

Braden, W.W. (1983) *The Oral Tradition in the South*, Baton Rouge and London, Louisiana State University Press.

Brandon-Sweeney, B. (1972/73) 'Kinesics and its interpretation', *Folklore Annual of the University Folklore Association*, 4/5: 3–51.

Bremmer, J.N. (ed.) (1988) *Interpretations of Greek Mythology*, London: Croom Helm.

Brémond, C. (1973) *Logique du récit*, Paris: Editions du Seuil.

Brenneis, D.L. and Myers F.R. (eds) (1984) *Dangerous Words: Language and Politics in the Pacific*, New York and London: New York University Press.

Brenner, L. (1989) ' "Religious" discourses in and about Africa', in Barber and Farias.

Briggs, C.L. (1985) 'Treasure tales and pedagogical discourse in *Mexicano* New Mexico', *Journal of American Folklore* 98: 287–314.

Briggs, C.L. (1986) *Learning How to Ask: a Sociolinguistic Appraisal of the Role of the Interview in Social Science Research*, Cambridge: Cambridge University Press.

Briggs, C.L. (1988) *Competence in Performance: the Creativity of Tradition in Mexicano Verbal Art*, Philadelphia: University of Pennsylvania Press.

Bright, W. (1979) 'A Karok myth in "measured verse": the translation of a performance', *Journal of California and Great Basin Anthropology* 1: 117–23.

British Sociological Association (1982/89) Code of Practice, reprinted in *Network* 43, Jan. 1989: 4–5.

Bronner, S.J. (1986) *American Folklore Studies: an Intellectual History*, Lawrence Kan.: University Press of Kansas.

Brooks, C.A. (1989) *Duro Ladipo and the Moremi Legend: The Socio-Historical Development of the Yoruba Music Drama and its Political Ramifications*, doctoral dissertation, University of Texas at Austin.

Brower, R.A. (ed.) (1959) *On Translation*, Cambridge: Harvard University Press.

Bruner, E.M. (ed.) (1984) *Text, Play, and Story: The Construction and Reconstruction of Self and Society*, Washington: American Ethnological Society.

Brunvand, J.H. (1976) *Folklore: a Study and Research Guide*, New York: St Martin's Press.

Brunvand, J.H. (1981) *The Vanishing Hitchhiker: American Urban Legends and their Meanings*, New York: Norton.

Brunvand, J.H. (1986) *The Study of American Folklore. An Introduction*, 3rd edition, New York and London: Norton.

Buchan, D. (1972) *The Ballad and the Folk*, London: Routledge & Kegan Paul.

Bulmer, M. (ed.) (1982) *Social Research Ethics: An Examination of the Merits of Covert Participant Observation*, London: Macmillan.

Burgess, R.G. (ed.) (1982) *Field Research: a Sourcebook and Field Manual*, London: George Allen and Unwin.

Burke, K. (1951) 'Three definitions', *The Kenyon Review* 13, 2: 173–92.

Burke, K. (1966) *Language as Symbolic Action: Essays on Life, Literature, and Method*, Berkeley: University of California Press.

Burke, P. (1978) *Popular Culture in Early Modern Europe*, London: Temple Smith.

Burns, A.F. (1983) *An Epoch of Miracles, Oral Literature of the Yucatec Maya*, Austin: University of Texas Press.

Burton, R.F. (1865) *Wit and Wisdom from West Africa: or, a Book of Proverbial Philosophy, Idioms, Enigmas, and Laconisms*, London.

Bynner, J. and Stribley, K.M. (eds) (1979) *Social Research: Principles and Procedures*, London: Longman.

Calame-Griaule, G. (1965) *Ethnologie et Langage. La Parole chez les Dogon*, Paris: Gallimard.

Calame-Griaule, G. (1977) 'Pour une étude des gestes narratifs', in ibid. (ed.) *Langage et Cultures Africaines*, Paris: Maspéro.

Calame-Griaule, G. (1982) 'Ce qui donne du goût aux contes', *Littérature* 45: 45–60.

Calame-Griaule, G. (1985) 'La gestuelle des conteurs: état d'une recherche', in Gentili and Paioni.

Calame-Griaule, G., Görög, V., Platiel, S., Rey-Hulman, D. and Seydou, C. (1980) *Histoires D'enfants Terribles*, Paris: Maisonneuve et Larose.

Calame-Griaule, G. Görög-Karady, V., Platiel, S., Rey-Hulman, D. and Seydou, C. (1983) 'The variability of meaning and the meaning of variability', *Journal of Folklore Research* 20: 153–70.

Campbell, J. (1959–68) *The Masks of God*, 4 vols, New York: Viking.

Cancel, R. (1986) 'Broadcasting oral traditions: the "logic" of narrative variants – the problem of "message" ', *African Studies Review* 29, 1: 60–70.

Cancel, R. (1989) *Allegorical Speculation in an Oral Society: the Tabwa Narrative Tradition*, Berkeley: University of California Press.

Carnes, P. (1985) *Fable Scholarship. An Annotated Bibliography*, New York and London: Garland.

Carrier, J. and A. (1990) 'Every picture tells a story: visual alternatives to oral tradition in Ponam Society', in Finnegan and Orbell.

Cassirer, E. (1946) *Language and Myth*, English trans., London: Constable.

Chadwick, H.M. and N.K. (1932–40) *The Growth of Literature*, 3 vols, Cambridge: Cambridge University Press.

Chadwick N.K. (1939) 'The distribution of oral literature in the Old World', *Journal of the Royal Anthropological Institute* 69: 77–94.

Chafe, W. and Tannen, D. (1987) 'The relation between written and spoken language', *Annual Review of Anthropology* 16: 383–407.

Chatelain, H. (1894) *Folk-Tales of Angola*, Boston and New York: Memoir of the American Folk-Lore Society, 1.

Chatman, S.B. (1978) *Story and Discourse: Narrative Structure in Fiction and Film*, Ithaca: Cornell University Press.

Child, F.J. (1882–98) *The English and Scottish Popular Ballads*, Boston: Houghton Mifflin.

Chimombo, S. (1988) *Malawian Oral Literature: the Aesthetics of Indigenous Arts*, Zomba: Centre for Social Research and Department of English, University of Malawi, sponsored by Harold Macmillan Trust, London.

Chinweizu, O.J. and Madubuike, I. (1983) *Toward the Decolonization of African Literature*, Washington D.C.: Howard University Press.

Clarke, K.W. (1958) *A Motif-Index of the Folktales of Culture-Area V, West Africa*, doctoral dissertation, Indiana University.

Clerk, C. (1990) '"That isn't really a pig": spirit traditions in the Southern Cook Islands', in Finnegan and Orbell.

Clifford, J. and Marcus G.E. (eds) (1986) *Writing Culture: the Poetics and Politics of Ethnography*, Berkeley: University of California Press.

Cocchiara, G. (1981) *The History of Folklore in Europe*, English trans., Philadelphia: Institute for the Study of Human Issues.

Cohen, D.W. (1989) 'The undefining of oral tradition', *Ethnohistory* 36, 1: 9–18.

Colby, B. (1973) 'Analytical procedures in eidochronic study', *Journal of American Folklore* 86: 14–24.

Collier, J. (1986) *Visual Anthropology: Photography as a Research Method*, 2nd edition, Albuquerque: University of New Mexico Press.

Collins, R., Curran, J., Garnham, N., Scannell, P., Schlesinger, P. and Sparks, C. (eds) (1986) *Media, Culture and Society: a Critical Reader*, London: Sage.

Computers in Literature (1990–) Biennial newsletter, Oxford: Oxford University Computing Service.

Connerton, P. (1989) *How Societies Remember*, Cambridge: Cambridge University Press.

Cope, T. (ed.) (1968) *Izibongo. Zulu Praise-Poems*, Oxford: Clarendon Press.

Coplan, D. (1986) 'Performance, self-definition, and social experience in the oral poetry of Sotho migrant mineworkers', *African Studies Review* 29, 1: 29–40.

Cosbey, R.C. (1978) 'The psychodrama of the interview arena', in Rosenberg.

Cosentino, D.J. (1978) 'An experiment in inducing the novel among the Hausa', *Research in African Literatures* 9: 19–30.

Cosentino, D.J. (1980) 'Lele Gbomba and the style of Mende baroque', *African Arts*, 13: 54–5, 75–8.

Cosentino, D.J. (1982) *Defiant Maids and Stubborn Farmers: Tradition and Invention in Mende Story Performance*, Cambridge: Cambridge University Press.

Cosentino, D.J. (1987) 'Omnes cultura tres partes divisa est?', *African Studies Review* 30, 3: 85–90.

Cosentino, D.J. (1988) 'Image, parody, and debate: levels in Mende narrative performance', *Journal of Folklore Research* 25, 1–2: 17–34.

Coupez, A and Kamanzi, T. (1962) *Récits Historiques Rwanda*, Tervuren: Musée Royal de l'Afrique Centrale, Annales (sciences humaines) 43.

Courtés, J. (1982) 'Motif et type dans la tradition folklorique, problèmes de typologie', *Littérature* 45: 114–27.

Cox, M.R. (1893) *Cinderella*, London: David Nutt.

Coyle, M. et al. (1990) *Encyclopaedia of Literature and Criticism*, London: Routledge.

Cross, T.P. (1952) *Motif-Index of Early Irish Literature*, Bloomington: Indiana University Press.

Crowley, D.J. (1973) *Extra-European Folktale Areas of the World: a Tabular Analysis*, Bloomington Indiana: Folklore Students Association, Preprint Series, 1, 1.

Crystal, D. (1987) *The Cambridge Encyclopedia of Language*, Cambridge: Cambridge University Press.

Culler, J. (1975) *Structuralist Poetics: Structuralism, Linguistics and the Study of Literature*, Ithaca: Cornell University Press.

Culler, J. (1981) *The Pursuit of Signs: Semiotics, Literature, Deconstruction*, Ithaca: Cornell University Press.

Culler, J. (1982) *On Deconstruction: Theory and Criticism after Structuralism*, Ithaca: Cornell University Press.

Culley, R.C. (1967) *Oral Formulaic Language in the Biblical Psalms*, Toronto: University of Toronto Press.

Davis, G.L. (1985) *I Got the Word in Me and I Can Sing It, You Know: a Study of the Performed African-American Sermon*, Philadelphia: University of Pennsylvania Press.

Davis, R.C. (ed.) (1986) *Contemporary Literary Criticism: Modernism through Poststructuralism*, New York and London: Longman.

Dégh, L. (1983) 'Foreword: a quest for meaning', *Journal of Folklore Research* 20: 145–50.

Dégh, L and Vázsonyi, A. (1974) 'The memorate and the proto-memorate', *Journal of American Folklore* 87: 225–39.

Dégh, L. and Vázsonyi, A. (1976) 'Legend and belief', in Ben-Amos.

DeMaria, R. and Kitzinger, R. (eds) (1989) *Transformations of the Word*, Special Issue, *Language and Communication* 9, 2/3.

Deng, F.M. (1973) *The Dinka and their Songs*, Oxford: Clarendon Press.

Derive, J. (1975) *Collecte et traduction des littératures orales. Un exemple négro-africain: les contes ngbaka-ma'bo de R.C.A.*, Paris: Société d'études linguistiques et anthropologiques de France.

Derrida, J. (1978) *Writing and Difference*, English trans., London: Routledge and Kegan Paul.

Descola, P. (1989) Head-shrinkers versus shrinks: Jivaroan dream analyses, *Man* 24: 439–50.

Dieckmann, H. (1986) *Twice-Told Tales: the Psychological Use of Fairy Tales*, Wilmette Illinois: Chiron.

Dissanayake, E. (1988) *What is Art for?*, Seattle and London: University of Washington Press.

Dorson, R.M. (1960) 'Oral styles of American folk narrators', in Sebeok.

Dorson, R.M. (1964) *Buying the Wind. Regional Folklore in the United States*, Chicago: University of Chicago Press.

Dorson, R.M. (1968) *The British Folklorists: a History*, Chicago: Chicago University Press.

Dorson, R.M. (ed.) (1972a) *Folklore and Folklife, an Introduction*, Chicago: Chicago University Press.

Dorson, R.M. (ed.) (1972b) *African Folklore,* Bloomington: Indiana University Press.

Dorson, R.M. (ed.) (1978) *Folklore in the Modern World*, The Hague and Paris: Mouton.

Dorson, R.M. (ed.) (1983) *Handbook of American Folklore*, Bloomington: Indiana University Press.

Dorst, J.D. (1983) 'Neck-riddle as a dialogue of genres: applying Bakhtin's genre theory', *Journal of American Folklore* 96, 382: 413–33.

Dubrow, H. (1982) *Genre*, London and New York: Methuen.

Dumézil, G. (1970) *The Destiny of the Warrior*, English trans., Chicago: University of Chicago Press.

Dumézil, G. (1973) *The Destiny of a King*, English trans., Chicago: University of Chicago Press.

Dumézil, G. (1983) *The Stakes of the Warrior*, English trans., Berkeley: University of California Press.

Dumézil, G. (1986) *The Plight of a Sorcerer*, English trans., Berkeley: University of California Press.

Dumézil, G. (1988) *Mitra-Varuna: An Essay on Two Indo-European Representations of Sovereignty*, English trans., New York, Zone Books.

Dunaway, D.K. and Baum, W.K. (eds) (1984) *Oral History: an Interdisciplinary Anthology*, Nashville, Tennessee: American Association for State and Local History, and Oral History Association.

Dundes, A. (1962) 'Trends in content analysis: a review article', *Midwest Folklore* 12: 31–8.

Dundes, A. (1964a) *The Morphology of North American Indian Folktales*, Helsinki: Folklore Fellows Communications 195.

Dundes, A. (1964b) 'Texture, text, and context', *Southern Folklore Quarterly* 28: 251–65, also in Dundes 1978 and 1980.

Dundes, A. (ed.) (1965) *The Study of Folklore*, Englewood Cliffs: Prentice-Hall.

Dundes, A. (1969) 'The devolutionary premise in folklore theory', *Journal of Folklore Institute* 6, 1: 5–19.

Dundes, A. (1976) 'Structuralism and folklore', *Studia Fennica* 20: 75–93, also in Dundes 1978.

Dundes, A. (1977) 'Who are the folk?' in Bascom, also in Dundes 1978 and 1980.

Dundes, A. (1978) *Essays in Folkloristics*, Meerut: Folklore Institute.

Dundes, A. (1980) *Interpreting Folklore*, Bloomington: Indiana University Press.

Dundes, A. (ed.) (1982) *Cinderella, a Folklore Casebook*, New York and London: Garland.

Dundes, A. (ed) (1984) *Sacred Narrative: Readings in the Theory of Myth*, Berkeley and London: University of California Press.

Dundes, A. (1985) 'Nationalistic inferiority complexes and the fabrication of fakelore: a reconsideration of Ossian, the *Kinder- und Hausmärchen*, the *Kalevala*, and Paul Bunyon', *Journal of Folklore Research* 22: 5–18.

Dundes, A. (1987) *Parsing through Customs: Essays by a Freudian Folklorist*, Madison: University of Wisconsin Press.

Dundes, A. (ed.) (1988) *The Flood Myth*, Berkeley: University of California Press.

Dundes. A. (n.d.) *International Folkloristics*, Oxford: Blackwell.

Dunn, G. (1980) *Fellowship of Song. Popular Singing Traditions in East Suffolk*, London: Croom Helm.

Duranti, A. and Goodwin, C. (eds) (n.d.) *Rethinking Context*, Cambridge: Cambridge University Press (in press).

Eagleton, T. (1976) *Marxism and Literary Criticism*, London: Methuen.

Eagleton, T. (1983) *Literary Theory: an Introduction*, Oxford: Blackwell.

Eagleton, T. (1984) *The Function of Criticism*, London: Verso.

Eagleton, T. (1989) 'Structuralism', in Barnouw, vol. 4: 183–5.

Edmonson, M.S. (1971) *Lore. An Introduction to the Science of Folklore and Literature*, New York: Holt, Rinehart & Winston.

Edmunds, L. (1985) *Oedipus: the Ancient Legend and its Later Analogues*, Baltimore and London: Johns Hopkins University Press.

Edmunds, L. and Dundes, A. (eds) (1983) *Oedipus: a Folklore Casebook*, New York and London: Garland.

Edwards, C.L. (1983) 'The Parry-Lord theory meets operational structuralism', *Journal of American Folklore*, 96: 151–69.

Egudu, R. and Nwoga, D. (comp. and trans.) (1973) *Igbo Traditional Verse*, London, Ibadan and Nairobi: Heinemann.

Ellen, R.F. (ed.) (1984) *Ethnographic Research: a Guide to General Conduct*, ASA Research Methods in Social Anthropology, 1, London: Academic Press.

Emeneau, M.B. (1966) 'Style and meaning in an oral literature', *Language* 42: 323–45.

Fabian, J. (1978) 'Popular culture in Africa: findings and conjectures', *Africa* 48: 315–34.

Feld, S. (1982) *Sound and Sentiment: Birds, Weeping, Poetics, and Song in Kaluli Expression*, Philadelphia: University of Pennsylvania Press (new edition 1990).

Feld, S. (1985) *Kaluli Weeping and Song*, 12″ stereo disc with notes (English and German) and musical transcriptions, Kassel: Barenreiter (Musicaphon/Music of Oceania, BM 30 SL 2702).

Feld, S. (1987) 'Dialogic editing: intepreting how Kaluli read *Sound and Sentiment*', *Cultural Anthropology* 2, 2: 190–210.

Feld, S. (1988) 'Aesthetics as iconicity of style, or "Lift-up over-Sounding": getting into the Kaluli groove', *Yearbook for Traditional Music* 20: 74–113.

Feld, S. (1989) 'Narrative and allegory in Papua New Guinea: aka dogs are not animals', unpub. paper.

Feld, S. (1990) 'Wept thoughts: the voicing of Kaluli memories', in Finnegan and Orbell.

Feleppa, R. (1988) *Convention, Translation, and Understanding: Philosophical Problems in the Comparative Study of Culture*, Albany: State University of New York Press.

Fetterman, D.M. (1989) *Ethnography: Step by Step*, Newbury Park, Sage. Applied Social Research Methods Series, 17.

Fine, E.C. (1983) 'In defense of literary dialect', *Journal of American Folklore* 96: 323–30.

Fine, E.C. (1984) *The Folklore Text: from Performance to Print*, Bloomington: Indiana University Press.

Finnegan, R. (1967) *Limba Stories and Story-Telling*, Oxford: Clarendon Press.

Finnegan, R. (1969a) 'Attitudes to the study of oral literature in British social anthropology', *Man* 4: 59–69.

Finnegan, R. (1969b) 'How to do things with words: performative utterances among the Limba of Sierra Leone', *Man* 4: 537–52.

Finnegan, R. (1970) *Oral Literature in Africa*, Oxford: Clarendon Press.

Finnegan, R. (1976) 'What is oral literature anyway? Comments in the light of some African and other comparative evidence', in Stolz and Shannon.

Finnegan, R. (1977) *Oral Poetry: its Nature, Significance and Social Context*, Cambridge: Cambridge University Press (2nd edition, Bloomington: Indiana University Press, 1991).

Finnegan, R. (ed.) (1978) *The Penguin Book of Oral Poetry*, London: Allen Lane (also published as *A World Treasury of Oral Poetry*, Bloomington: Indiana University Press).

Finnegan, R. (1982) *'Short Time to Stay'. Comments on Time, Literature and Oral Performance*, Bloomington: Hans Wolff Memorial Lecture, African Studies Program, Indiana University.

Finnegan, R. (1988) *Literacy and Orality: Studies in the Technology of Communication*, Oxford: Blackwell.

Finnegan, R. (1989a) *The Hidden Musicians: Music-Making in an English Town*, Cambridge: Cambridge University Press.

Finnegan, R. (1989b) 'Communication and technology', *Language and Communication* 9: 107–27.

Finnegan, R. (1990) 'What is orality – if anything?' *Byzantine and Modern Greek Studies* 14: 130–49.

Finnegan, R. (1991) 'Tradition, but what tradition and tradition for whom?' *Oral Tradition* 6.

Finnegan, R. and Orbell, M. (eds) (1990) *Oral Tradition in the South Pacific*, Special Issue, *Oral Tradition* 5, 2/3.

Firth, R. (1990) *Tikopia Songs*, Cambridge: Cambridge University Press.

Fischer, J.L. (1959) 'Meter in Eastern Carolinian oral literature', *Journal of American Folklore* 72: 47–52.

Fischer, J.L. (1963) 'The sociopsychological analysis of folktales', *Current Anthropology* 4: 235–95.

Fischer, M. (n.d.) *Social Anthropology and Computing Techniques*, ASA Research Methods in Social Anthropology, London: Routledge (forthcoming).

Fish, S. (1980) *Is there a Text in this Class? The Authority of Interpretive Communities*, Cambridge, Mass: Harvard University Press.

Fletcher, A.J.S. (1964) *Allegory: the Theory of a Symbolic Mode*, Ithaca: Cornell University Press.

Flowers, H.L. (1952) *A Classification of the Folktale of the West Indies by Types and Motifs*, doctoral dissertation, Indiana University.

Foley, J.M. (1978) 'A computer analysis of metrical patterns in *Beowulf*', *Computers and the Humanities* 12: 71–80.

Foley, J.M. (1981) 'Editing oral texts: theory and practice', *Yearbook of the Society for Textual Studies* 1: 75–94.

Foley, J.M. (1985) *Oral-Formulaic Theory and Research: an Introduction and Annotated Bibliography*, New York and London: Garland Folklore Bibliographies 6.

Foley, J.M. (ed.) (1986) *Oral Tradition in Literature: Interpretation in Context*, Columbia: University of Missouri Press.

Foley, J.M. (1987a) 'Formula in Yugoslav and comparative folk epic: structure and function', in Almqvist et al.

Foley, J.M. (ed.) (1987b) *Comparative Research on Oral Traditions: a Memorial for Milman Parry*, Columbus Ohio: Slavica.

Foley, J.M. (1988a) *The Theory of Oral Composition: History and Methodology*, Bloomington and Indianapolis: Indiana University Press.

Foley, J.M. (1988b) 'Toward an oral aesthetics: a response to Jesse Gellrich', *Philological Quarterly* 67: 475–80.

Foley, J.M. (1990a) *Traditional Oral Epic: The Odyssey, Beowulf, and the Serbo-Croatian Return Song*, Berkeley and London: University of California Press.

Foley, J.M. (ed.) (1990b) *Oral-Formulaic Theory: a Folklore Casebook*, New York: Garland.

Forrest, John (1988) *Lord, I'm coming Home: Everyday Aesthetics in Tidewater North Carolina*, Ithaca and London: Cornell University Press.

Foucault, M. (1972) *The Archaeology of Knowledge*, English trans., London: Tavistock.

Fowler, A. (1982) *Kinds of Literature: an Introduction to the Theory of Genres and Modes*, Cambridge Mass: Harvard University Press.

Fox, J. (1987) 'The creator gods: Romantic Nationalism and the en-gender-ment of women in folklore', *Journal of American Folklore* 100: 563–72.

Fox, J.J. (ed.) (1988) *To Speak in Pairs: Essays on the Ritual Languages of Eastern Indonesia*, Cambridge: Cambridge University Press.

Fox, W.S. (1980) 'Folklore and fakelore: some sociological considerations', *Journal of the Folklore Institute* 17: 244–61.

Furniss, G. (1989) 'Typification and evaluation: a dynamic process in rhetoric', in Barber and Farias.

Gailey, G. (1989) 'The nature of tradition', *Folklore* 100: 143–61.

Geertz, C. (1975) *The Interpretation of Cultures: Selected Essays*, London: Hutchinson.

Genette, G. (1980) *Narrative Discourse: an Essay in Method*, Eng. trans., Ithaca: Cornell University Press.

Gentili, B. and Paioni, G. (eds) (1985) *Oralità: Cultura, Letteratura, Discorso*, Roma: Ateneo.

Georges, R.A. (1969) 'Toward an understanding of storytelling events', *Journal of American Folklore* 82: 313–28.

Georges, R.A. (1976) 'From folktale research to the study of narrating', in Pentikäinen and Juurikka.

Georges, R.A. (1980) 'Toward a resolution of the text/context controversy', *Western Folklore* 39: 34–40.

Georges, R.A. (1983) 'The universality of the tale-type as concept and construct', *Western Folklore* 42: 21–28.

Georges, R.A. (1986a) 'The folklorist as comparatist', *Western Folklore* 45: 1–20.

Georges, R.A. (1986b) 'The pervasiveness in contemporary folklore studies of assumptions, concepts, and constructs usually associated with the historic-geographic method', *Journal of Folklore Research* 23, 2/3: 87–103.

Georges, R.A. and Jones, M.O. (1980) *People Studying People: The Human Element in Fieldwork*, Berkeley and London: University of California Press.

Giglioli, P.P. (ed.) (1972) *Language and Social Context*, Harmondsworth: Penguin.

Glassgold, P. (1987) 'Translation: culture's driving wedge', in Schulte and Kratz: 18–21.

Glassie, H. (1982) *Passing the Time in Ballymenone: Culture and History of an Ulster Community*, Philadelphia: Pennsylvania University Press.

Glassie, H., Ives, E.D. and Szwed, J.F. (1970) *Folksongs and their Makers*, Bowling Green: Bowling Green University Popular Press.

Godzich, W. and Kittay, J. (1987) *The Emergence of Prose: an Essay in Prosaics*, Minneapolis: University of Minnesota Press.

Goffman, E. (1971) *Relations in Public: Microstudies of the Public Order*, London: Allen Lane.

Goffman, E. (1974) *Frame Analysis: an Essay on the Organization of Experience*, New York: Harper & Row.

Goldberg, C. (1984) 'The historic-geographic method: past and future', *Journal of Folklore Research* 21, 1: 1–18.

Goldstein, K.S. (1964) *A Guide for Field Workers in Folklore*, Hatboro: Folklore Associates Inc. and London: Herbert Jenkins.

Goody, J. (ed.) (1968) *Literacy in Traditional Societies*, London: Cambridge University Press.

Goody, J. (1977) *The Domestication of the Savage Mind*, London: Cambridge University Press.

Goody, J. (1986) *The Logic of Writing and the Organization of Society*, Cambridge: Cambridge University Press.

Goody, J. (1987) *The Interface between the Written and the Oral*, Cambridge: Cambridge University Press.

Goody, J. et al. (1988) 'Selections from the symposium on "Literacy, reading and power"', Whitney Humanities Centre, November 14, 1987', *The Yale Journal of Criticism* 2: 193–232.

Goody, J. and Duly, C. (1981) *Studies in the Use of Computers in Social Anthropology*, London: Unpub. Report to Social Science Research Council.

Goody, J. and Watts, I. (1968) 'The consequences of literacy', in Goody.

Gorfein, D.S. and Hoffman, R.R. (eds) (1987) *Memory and Learning: the Ebbinghaus Centennial Conference*, Hillsdale N.J.: Erlbaum.

Görög, V. (1981) *Littérature orale d'Afrique noire: bibliographie analytique*, Paris: Maisonneuve et Larose.

Görög-Karady, V. (ed.) (1982) *Genres, Forms, Meanings: Essays in African Oral Literature*, Oxford: Journal of the Anthropological Society in Oxford (JASO).

Görög-Karady, V. and Seydou, C. (1982) 'Conte, mon beau conte, de tous tes sens, dis-nous quel est le vrai', *Littérature* 45: 24–34.

Gossen, G.H. (1974) *Chamulas in the World of the Sun: Time and Space in a Maya Oral Tradition*, Cambridge Mass: Harvard University Press.

Gourlay, K.A. (1978) 'Towards a reassessment of the ethnomusicologist's role in research', *Ethnomusicology* 22: 1–35.

Graham, J.F. (1989) 'Translation, theories of', in Barnouw, vol. 4: 259–61.

Graham, W.A. (1987) *Beyond the Written Word: Oral Aspects of Scripture in the History of Religion*, Cambridge: University Press.

Gramsci, A. (1971) *Selections from the Prison Notebooks*, English trans., London: Lawrence and Wishart.

Gravel, P.B. and Ridinger, R.B.M. (1988) *Anthropological Fieldwork: an Annotated Bibliography*, New York: Garland (Garland Reference Library of Social Science, 419).

Greenway, J. (1964) *Literature among the Primitives*, Hatboro: Folklore Associates.

Grele, R.J. et al. (1985) *Envelopes of Sound. The Art of Oral History*, Chicago: Precedent Publishing, 2nd edition.

Grillo, R. (1989a) *Dominant Languages: Language and Hierarchy in Britain and France*, Cambridge: Cambridge University Press.

Grillo, R. (ed.) (1989b) *Social Anthropology and the Politics of Language*, Sociological Review Monograph 36.

Grolnick, S. A. (1986) 'Fairy tales and psychotherapy', in Bottigheimer 1986b.

Gumperz, J.J. and Hymes, D. (eds) (1972) *Directions in Sociolinguistics: the Ethnography of Communication*, New York: Holt, Rinehart & Winston.

Gunner, E. (1989) 'Orality and literacy: dialogue and silence', in Barber and Farias.

Gupta, S.S. (1967) *A Bibliography of Indian Folklore and Related Subjects*, Calcutta: Indian Publications (Indian Folklore Series 11).

Gurevich, A. (1988) *Medieval Popular Culture: Problems of Belief and Perception*, Eng. trans., Cambridge: Cambridge University Press.

Hall, E.T. (1966) *The Hidden Dimension*, New York: Doubleday.

Hall, E.T. (1974) *Handbook for Proxemic Research*, Washington: Society for the Anthropology of Visual Communication.

Hall, S. (1973) 'Encoding and Decoding in the Media Discourse', stencilled paper No. 7, Birmingham: Centre for Contemporary Cultural Studies.

Hall, S. (1981) 'Notes on deconstructing "the popular" ', in Samuel.

Hall, S. (1985) 'Religious ideologies and social movements in Jamaica', in Bocock and Thompson.

Hall, S., Critcher, C., Jefferson, T., Clarke, J. and Roberts, B. (1978) *Policing the Crisis*, London: Macmillan

Hall, S. and Jefferson, T. (1976) *Resistance Through Rituals: Youth Subcultures in Post-War Britain*, London: Hutchinson.

Hall, S. and Whannel, P. (1964) *The Popular Arts*, London: Hutchinson.

Hammersley, M. and Atkinson, P. (1983) *Ethnography, Principles in Practice*, London: Tavistock.

Hanks, W.F. (1989) 'Text and textuality', *Annual Review of Anthropology*, 18: 5–127.

Hannerz, U. (1987) 'Bush and Beento: Nigerian popular culture and the world', unpub. paper, American Anthropological Association Nov. 1987.

Hannerz, U. (1989) 'Notes on the global ecumene', *Public Culture* 1, 2: 66–75.

Harari, J.V. (ed.) (1979) *Textual Strategies: Perspectives in Post-Structuralist Criticism*, Ithaca: Cornell University Press.

Hare, A.P. and Blumberg, H.H. (1988) *Dramaturgical Analysis of Social Interaction*, New York: Praeger.

Haring, L. (1972) 'Performing for the interviewer: a study of the structure of context', *Southern Folklore Quarterly* 36: 383–98.

Haring, L. (1982) *Malagasy Tale Index*, Helsinki: Folklore Fellows Communications 231.

Haring, L. (1985) 'Malagasy riddling', *Journal of American Folklore* 98: 163–90.

Harries, J. (1977) 'Pattern and choice in Berber weaving and poetry', in Lindfors.

Hatto, A.T. (ed.) (1980) *Traditions of Heroic and Epic Poetry*, vol. 1. *The Traditions*, London: Modern Humanities Research Association.

Haywood, C (1961) *A Bibliography of North American Folklore and Folksong*, 2 vols, 2nd edition, New York: Dover.

Henige, D. (1974) *The Chronology of Oral Tradition: Quest for a Chimera*, Oxford: Clarendon Press.

Henige, D. (1982) *Oral Historiography*, Harlow: Longman.

Henige, D. (1988) 'Oral, but oral what? The nomenclatures of orality and their implications', *Oral Tradition* 3, 1/2: 229–38.

Henley, P. (1985) 'British ethnographic film', *Anthropology Today* 1, 1: 5–17.

Hernadi, P. (ed.) (1978) *What is Literature?*, Bloomington: Indiana University Press.

Herndon M. and McLeod, N. (1983) *Field Manual for Ethnomusicology*, Norwood PA: Norwood Editions.

Herskovits, M.J. (1961) 'The study of African oral art', *Journal of American Folklore* 74: 451–6.

Herzfeld, M. (1985) 'Interpretations from within: metatext for a Cretan quarrel', in Alexiou and Lambropoulos.

Hill, J.D. (ed.) (1988) *Rethinking History and Myth: Indigenous South American Perspectives on the Past*, Urbana: University of Illinois Press.

Hill, J.H. and K.C. (1986) *Speaking Mexicano: Dynamics of Syncretic Language in Central Mexico*, Tucson: University of Arizona Press.

Hobbs, S. (1987) 'The social psychology of a "good" story', in Bennett, Smith and Widdowson.

Hobsbawm, E. and Ranger, T. (eds) (1983) *The Invention of Tradition*, Cambridge: Cambridge University Press.

Hodne, Ø. (1984) *The Types of the Norwegian Folktale*, Oslo: Instituttet for Sammenlignende Kulturforskning.

Holbek, B. (1976) 'Games of the powerless', *Unifol*: 10–33.

Holbek, B. (1977a) 'The social relevance of folkloristics', *Unifol*: 21–43.

Holbek, B. (1977b) 'Formal and structural studies of oral narrative: a bibliography', *Unifol*: 149–93.

Holbek, B. (1982) 'The many abodes of Fata Morgana or the quest for meaning in fairy tales', *Journal of Folklore Research* 22: 19–28.

Holbek, B. (1983) 'Nordic research in popular prose narrative', in Honko and Laaksonen.

Holbek, B. (1987) *Interpretation of Fairy Tales: Danish Folklore in a European Perspective*, Helsinki: Folklore Fellows Communications 239.

Holland, D. and Quinn, N. (eds) (1987) *Cultural Models in Language and Thought*, Cambridge: Cambridge University Press.

Hollis, M. and Lukes, S. (eds) (1982) *Rationality and Relativism*, Oxford: Blackwell.

Honko, L. (1976) 'Genre theory revisited', *Studia Fennica* 20: 20–5.

Honko, L. (1981) 'Four forms of adaptation of tradition', *Studia Fennica* 26, Helsinki: 19–33.

Honko, L. (1984) 'Folkloristic studies on meaning. An introduction', *Arv, Scandinavian Yearbook of Folklore* 40: 35–56.

Honko, L. (1985a) 'Empty texts, full meanings: on transformal meaning in folklore', *Journal of Folklore Research* 22: 37–44.

Honko, L. (1985b) 'Zielsetzung und Methoden der finnischen Erzählforschung', *Fabula* 26: 318–35.

Honko, L. (ed.) (1988) *Tradition and Cultural Identity*, Turku: Nordic Institute of Folklore.

Honko, L. (1989a) 'The final text of the Recommendation for the Safeguarding of Folklore', *NIF [Nordic Institute of Folklore] Newsletter*, 17, 2–3: 3–12.

Honko, L. (1989b) 'Folkloristic theories of genre', in Siikalra 1989.

Honko, L. and Laaksonen, P. (eds) (1983) *Trends in Nordic Tradition Research*, Helsinki: Studia Fennica 27.

Honko, L. and Voigt, V. (eds) (1981) *Adaptation, Change, and Decline in*

Oral Literature, Studia Fennica 26, Helsinki: Suomalaisen Kirjallisuuden Seura [Finnish Literature Society].

Hood, M. (1982) *The Ethnomusicologist*, revised ed., Kent Ohio: Kent State University Press.

Hoppál, M. (1981) 'A case study of adaptation in folk narrative: Tolstoy's tale in the Hungarian oral tradition', in Honko and Voigt.

Hoskins, J.A. (1985) 'A life history from both sides: the changing poetics of personal experience', *Journal of Anthropological Research* 41: 147–69.

Howell, S. (1986) 'Formal speech acts as one discourse', *Man* 21: 79–101.

Huebner, T. (1986) 'Vernacular literacy, English as a language of wider communication, and language shift in American Samoa', *Journal of Multilingual and Multicultural Development* 7: 393–411.

Huizinga, J. (1970) *Homo Ludens: a Study of the Play Element in Culture*, English trans., London: Granada.

Huntsman, J. (1981) 'Butterfly collecting in a swamp: suggestions for studying oral narratives as creative art', *Journal of the Polynesian Society* 90: 209–21.

Hymes, D.H. (1959) 'Bibliography: fieldwork in linguistics and anthropology', *Studies in Linguistics*, 14, 3/4: 82–91.

Hymes, D.H. (1961) 'On typology of cognitive styles in language', *Anthropological Linguistics* 3, 1: 22–54.

Hymes, D.H. (ed.) (1964) *Language in Culture and Society: a Reader in Linguistics and Anthropology*, New York: Harper & Row.

Hymes, D.H. (1974) *Foundations in Sociolinguistics: an Ethnographic Approach*, Philadelphia: University of Pennsylvania Press.

Hymes, D.H. (1975a) 'Folklore's nature and the sun's myth', *Journal of American Folklore* 88, 350: 345–69.

Hymes, D.H. (1975b) 'Breakthrough into performance', in Ben-Amos and Goldstein.

Hymes, D.H. (1977) 'Discovering oral performance and measured verse in American Indian narrative', *New Literary History* 8: 431–57 (also reprinted in Hymes 1981).

Hymes, D.H. (1981) *'In Vain I Tried to Tell You': Essays in Native American Ethnopoetics*, Philadelphia: University of Pennsylvania Press.

Hymes, D.H. (1985) 'Language, memory, and selective performance: Cultee's "Salmon's Myth" as twice told to Boas', *Journal of American Folklore* 98: 391–434.

Hymes, D.H. (1987) 'Tonkawa poetics: John Rush Buffalo's "Coyote and Eagle's Daughter" ', in Sherzer and Woodbury.

Hymes, D.H. (1991) 'Notes toward (an understanding of) supreme fictions', in Ralph Ghen (ed.) *Studies in Historical Change*, Charlottesville: University of Virginia Press.

Ikeda, H. (1971) *A Type and Motif Index of Japanese Folk-Literature*, Helsinki: Suomalainen Tiedeakatemia.

Innes, G. (1974) *Sunjata. Three Mandinka Versions*, London: School of Oriental and African Studies.

Iser, W. (1975) 'The reality of fiction: a functionalist approach to literature', *New Literary History* 7: 7–38.

Ives, E.D. (1980) *The Tape-Recorded Interview. A Manual for Field*

Workers in Folklore and Oral History, Knoxville: University of Tennessee Press, revised edition.

Jackson, A. (ed.) (1987) *Anthropology at Home*, London: Tavistock.

Jackson, B. (1987) *Fieldwork*, Urbana: University of Illinois Press.

Jackson, J.E. (1983) *The Fish People: Linguistic Exogamy and Tukanoan Identity in Northwest Amazonia*, Cambridge: Cambridge University Press.

Jackson, M. (1968) 'Some structural considerations of Maori myth', *Journal of the Polynesian Society* 77: 147–62.

Jackson, M. (1982) *Allegories of the Wilderness: Ethics and Ambiguity in Kuranko Narratives*, Bloomington: Indiana University Press.

Jacobs, M. (1959) *The Content and Style of an Oral Literature*, Chicago: University of Chicago Press.

Jacobs, M. (1966) 'A look ahead in oral literature research', *Journal of American Folklore* 79: 413–27.

Jakobson, R. (1960) 'Concluding statement: linguistics and poetics', in Sebeok.

Jakobson, R. (1970) 'On Russian fairy tales', in Lane (reprinted from *Selected Writings* 4, 1966, The Hague: Mouton).

Jameson, F. (1981) *The Political Unconscious: Narrative as a Socially Symbolic Act*, Ithaca: Cornell University Press.

Jansen, W.H. (1957) 'Classifying performance in the study of verbal folklore', in Richmond.

Jansen, W.H. (1983) 'Ethics and the folklorist', in Dorson.

Järvinen, I-R. (1981) 'Transmission of norms and values in Finnish-Karelian sacred legends', *Arv* 37: 27–33.

Jason, H. (1970) 'The Russian criticism of the "Finnish school" in folktale scholarship', *Norweg: Folkelivsgransking* 14: 215–94.

Jason, H. (1986) 'Genre in folk literature: reflections on some questions and problems', *Fabula* 27: 167–94.

Jason, H. and Segal, D. (eds) (1977) *Patterns in Oral Literature*, The Hague and Paris: Mouton.

Jason H. et al. (1977) 'Content analysis of oral literature: a discussion', in Jason and Segal.

Jefferson, A. and Robey, D. (eds) (1986) *Modern Literary Theory: a Comparative Introduction*, London: Batsford.

Johnson, J.M. (1975) *Doing Field Research*, New York: Free Press.

Johnson, J.W. (1974) *Heellooy Heelleellooy: the Development of the Genre Heello in Modern Somali Poetry*, Bloomington: Indiana University Publications.

Johnson, J.W. (1980) 'Yes, Virginia, there is an epic in Africa', *Research in African Literatures* 11: 308–26.

Johnson, L.A. (ed.) (1982) *Toward Defining the African Aesthetic*, Washington: Three Continents Press and African Literature Association.

Johnston, M. (1976) 'That was your life: a biographical approach to later life' in Munnichs, J.M.A. and van den Heuvel, W.J.A. (eds) *Dependency or Interdependency in Old Age*, The Hague: Nijhoff.

Jordan, R.A. and Kalčik, S.J. (1985) *Women's Folklore, Women's Culture*, Philadelphia: University of Pennsylvania Press.

Junaidu, I. (1988) 'Linguistic analysis of Hausa meter', *Research in African Literatures* 19: 350–64.

Jung, C.G. and Kerenyi, C. (1963) *Essays on a Science of Mythology*, Eng. trans., New York: Harper & Row.

Kapferer, B. (1986) 'Performance and the structuring of meaning and experience', in Turner and Bruner.

Kaplan S.L. (ed.) (1984) *Understanding Popular Culture: Europe from the Middle Ages to the Nineteenth Century*, Berlin and New York: Mouton.

Karp, I. and Bird, C.S. (eds) (1980) *Explorations in African Systems of Thought*, Bloomington: Indiana University Press.

Karpeles, M. (ed.) (1958) *The Collecting of Folk Music and other Ethnomusicological Material: a Manual for Field Workers*, London: International Folk Music Council and Royal Anthropological Institute.

Kaufman, N. (1990) 'Lamentations from four continents, after materials from Europe, Asia, Africa and America', *International Folklore Review* 7: 22–9.

Kaufman, N. and D. (1988) *Pogrebalni i Drugi Oplakvania v Bulgaria [Funeral and Other Lamentations in Bulgaria]*, Sofia: Bulgarian Academy of Sciences.

Kendon, A. (ed.) (1981) *Nonverbal Communication, Interaction, and Gesture*, The Hague: Mouton.

Kendon, A. (1989) 'Gesture', in Barnouw: vol. 2: 17–22.

Key, M.R. and Hoenigswald, H. (eds) (1989) *General and Amerindian Ethnolinguistics: In Remembrance of Stanley Newman*, Berlin and New York: Mouton de Gruyter.

Khan, N. (1976) *The Arts Britain Ignores: the Arts of Ethnic Minorities in Britain*, London: Gulbenkian Foundation and Community Relations Committee.

Kidder, L.H. and Judd, C.M. (1986) *Research Methods in Social Relations*, New York: CBS Publishing Japan, 5th edition.

Kiell, N. (ed.) (1982) *Psychoanalysis, Psychology, and Literature: A Bibliography*, 2nd ed., 2 vols, Metuchen N.J. and London: Scarecrow Press.

Kimmel, A. J. (1988) *Ethics and Values in Applied Social Research*, Newbury Park: Sage.

Kiparsky, P. (1973) 'The role of linguistics in a theory of poetry', *Daedalus* 192: 231–44.

Kiparsky, P. (1976) 'Oral poetry: some linguistic and typological considerations', in Stoltz and Shannon.

Kirkland, E.C. (1966) *A Bibliography of South Asian Folklore*, The Hague: Mouton (Indiana University Folklore Series 21/Asian Folklore Studies Monographs 4).

Kirtley, B.F. (1971) *A Motif-Index of Traditional Polynesian Narratives*, Honolulu: University of Hawaii Press.

Kligman, G. (1984) 'The rites of women: oral poetry, ideology, and the socialization of peasant women in contemporary Romania', *Journal of American Folklore* 97: 167–88.

Klipple, M.A. (1938) *African Folktales with Foreign Analogues*, doctoral dissertation, Indiana University.

Koelle, S.W. (1854) *African Native Literature: or, Proverbs, Tales, Fables, and Historical Fragments in the Kanuri or Bornu Language*, London.

Koljević, S. (1980) *The Epic in the Making*, Oxford: Clarendon Press.

Koning, J. (1980) 'The fieldworker as performer: fieldwork objectives and social roles in County Clare, Ireland', *Ethnomusicology* 24: 417–29.

Kratz, C. (1989) 'Genres of power: a comparative analysis of Okiek blessings, curses and oaths' *Man*, 24: 636–56.

Krippendorff, K. (1989) 'Content analysis', in Barnouw vol. 1: 403–7.

Krohn, K. (1971) *Folklore Methodology*, Eng. trans., Austin and London: University of Texas Press.

Krupat, A. (1982) 'An approach to Native American texts', *Critical Inquiry* 9: 323–38.

Krupat, A. (1987) 'Post-structuralism and oral literature' in Swann and Krupat.

Küchler, Suzanne (1987) 'Malangan: art and memory in a Melanesian society', *Man* 22: 238–55.

Kuusi, M. (1972) *Towards an International Type-System of Proverbs*, Helsinki: Folklore Fellows Communications 221.

Kuusi, M. (1974) ' "The Bridge and the Church": an anti-church legend', *Finnish Folkloristics* 2, Helsinki: *Studia Fennica: Review of Finnish Linguistics and Ethnology* 18: 37–75.

Labov, W. (1972) *Language in the Inner City: Studies in the Black English Vernacular*, Philadelphia: University of Pennsylvania Press.

Lambrecht, W. (1967) *A Tale Type Index for Central Africa*, doctoral dissertation, University of California, Berkeley.

Lane, M. (ed.) (1970) *Structuralism. A Reader*, London: Cape.

Lawless, E.J. (1987) 'Tradition and poetics: the folk sermons of women preachers', in Foley.

Lawless, E.J. (1988) *Handmaidens of the Lord: Pentecostal Women Preachers and Traditional Religion*, Philadelphia: University of Pennsylvania Press.

Layton, R.(1981) *The Anthropology of Art*, London: Granada Publishing.

Leach, E. (ed.) (1967) *The Structural Study of Myth and Totemism*, London: Tavistock.

Leach, E. (1970a) 'Lévi-Strauss in the Garden of Eden: an examination of some recent developments in the analysis of myth', in Hayes, E.N. and T. (eds) *The Anthropologist as Hero*, Cambridge Mass: MIT Press.

Leach, E. (1970b) *Lévi-Strauss*, London: Fontana.

Leach, M. (ed.) (1949) *Funk and Wagnalls Standard Dictionary of Folklore, Mythology, and Legend*, New York: Funk & Wagnalls.

Lefevere, A. (1986) 'Translation and/in comparative literature', *Yearbook of Comparative and General Literature* 35: 40–50.

Le Page, R.B. and Tabouret-Keller, A. (1985) *Acts of Identity: Creole-Based Approaches to Language and Ethnicity*, Cambridge: Cambridge University Press.

LeRoy, J. (1985) *Fabricated World: an Interpretation of Kewa Tales*, Vancouver: University of British Columbia Press.

Lévi-Strauss, C. (1963) 'The structural study of myth', in *Structural Anthropology*, New York: Basic Books.

Lévi-Strauss, L. (1967) 'The story of Asdiwal', in E. Leach.

Lévi-Strauss, C.(1969–81) *Introduction to a Science of Mythology* (English trans. of *Mythologiques*), 4 volumes [*The Raw and the Cooked* 1969;

From Honey to Ashes 1973; *The Origin of Table Manners* 1978; *The Naked Man* 1981], New York: Harper & Row.

Limón, J.E. (1983) 'Western Marxism and folklore: a critical introduction', *Journal of American Folklore* 96: 34–52.

Limón, J.E. (1984) 'Western Marxism and folklore: a critical reintroduction', *Journal of American Folklore* 97: 337–44.

Limón, J.E. and Young, M.J. (1986) 'Frontiers, settlements, and development in folklore studies, 1972–1985', *Annual Review of Anthropology* 15: 437–60.

Lindfors, B. (ed.) (1977) *Forms of Folklore in Africa: Narrative, Poetic, Gnomic, Dramatic*, Austin and London: University of Texas Press.

List, G. (1963) 'The boundaries of speech and song', *Ethnomusicology* 7: 1–16.

Littleton, C.S. (1982) *The New Comparative Mythology: an Anthropological Assessment of the Theories of Georges Dumézil*, 3rd ed., Berkeley: University of California Press.

Lloyd, A.L. (1952) *Come All Ye Bold Miners: Ballads and Songs of the Coalfields*, London: Lawrence & Wishart.

Lloyd, A.L (1967) *Folk song in England*, London: Laurence & Wishart.

Lomax, A. (1968) *Folk Song Style and Culture*, Washington: American Association for the Advancement of Science.

Lord, A.B. (1960) *The Singer of Tales*, Cambridge Mass: Harvard University Press.

Lord, A.B. (1974) 'Oral poetry', in Preminger: 591–93.

Lord, A.B. (1986a) 'The merging of two worlds: oral and written poetry as carriers of ancient values', in Foley.

Lord, A.B. (1986b) 'Perspectives on recent work on the oral traditional formula', *Oral Tradition* 1: 467–503.

Lord, A.B. (1987a) 'Characteristics of orality', *Oral Tradition* 2, 1: 54–72.

Lord, A.B. (1987b) 'The nature of oral poetry', in Foley 1987b.

Lundell, T. (1986) 'Gender-related biases in the Type and Motif Indexes of Aarne and Thompson', in Bottigheimer 1986b.

Lüthi, M. (1982) *The European Folktale: Form and Nature*, Eng. trans., Philadelphia: Institute for the Study of Human Issues.

Lutz, C.A. and Abu-Lughod, L. (eds) (1990) *Language and the Politics of Emotion*, Cambridge: Cambridge University Press.

Lutz, C. A. and White, G.M. (1986) 'The anthropology of emotions', *Annual Review of Anthropology* 15: 405–36.

Luykx, A. (1989) 'The evocation of the aesthetic: questions of performance and audience in written texts', unpublished seminar paper, University of Texas at Austin, Dec. 1989.

McCall, M.M. (1989) 'The significance of storytelling', *Life Stories/Récits de Vie* 5: 39–47.

Macdonald, D. (1882) *Africana: Or, the Heart of Heathen Africa*, 2 vols, London.

Macdonald, D.A. (1972) 'Fieldwork: collecting oral literature', in Dorson 1972a.

MacDonald, M.R. (1982) *The Storyteller's Sourcebook: a Subject, Title, and Motif Index to Folklore Collections for Children*, Detroit: Neal-Schuman.

McKenzie, D.F. (1986) *Bibliography and the Sociology of Texts*, Panizzi Lecture 1985, London: British Library.

McMath M. and Parima, T. (1990) 'Winged Tangi'ia: a Mangaian dramatic performance', in Finnegan and Orbell.

Magoun, F.P. (1953) 'Oral-formulaic character of Anglo-Saxon narrative poetry', *Speculum* 28: 446–67.

Malinowski, B. (1948) 'Myth in primitive psychology', in *Magic, Science and Religion and Other Essays*, New York: Doubleday.

Mannheim, B. and Tedlock, D. (eds) (1990) *The Dialogic Emergence of Culture*, Philadelphia: University of Pennsylvania Press.

Mapanje, J. and White, L. (eds) (1983) *Oral Poetry from Africa*, New York and Essex: Longman.

Maranda, E.K. (1973) 'Five interpretations of a Melanesian myth', *Journal of American Folklore* 68: 4–13.

Maranda, P. (1967) 'Computers in the bush: tools for the automatic analysis of myths', in Helm, J. (ed.) *Essays on the Verbal and Visual Arts*, Proceedings of the 1966 Annual Spring Meeting of the American Ethnological Society, Seattle: University of Washington Press.

Maranda, P. (ed.) (1972) *Mythology*, Harmondsworth: Penguin.

Maranda, P. and E.K. (eds) (1971) *Structural Analysis of Oral Tradition*, Philadelphia: University of Pennsylvania Press.

Margolis, J. (1989) 'Aesthetics', in Barnouw vol. 1: 27–30.

Mattelart, A. (1989) 'Marxist theories of communication: Third World approaches', in Barnouw, vol. 2: 479–83.

Mayer, A. (1989) 'Anthropological memories', *Man* 24: 203–18.

Medvedev, P.N. [attributed to Bakhtin, M.M.] (1978) *The Formal Method in Literary Scholarship: a Critical Introduction to Literary Poetics*, Eng. trans., Baltimore: Johns Hopkins University Press.

Merriam, A.P. (1964) *The Anthropology of Music,* Evanston: North Western University Press.

Messenger, J.C. (1983) *An Anthropologist at Play: Balladmongering in Ireland and its Consequences*, Lanham: University Press of America.

Messerschmidt, D.A. (ed.) (1981) *Anthropologists at Home in North America: Methods and Issues in the Study of one's own Society*, Cambridge and New York: Cambridge University Press.

Middleton, D. and Edwards, D. (eds) (1990) *Collective Remembering*, London: Sage.

Middleton, R. and Horn, D. (eds) (1981) *Folk or Popular? Distinctions, Influences, Continuities*, Popular Music Yearbook 1, Cambridge: Cambridge University Press.

Mieder, W. (1982) *International Proverb Scholarship: an Annotated Bibliography*, New York: Garland.

Mieder, W. and Dundes, A. (eds) (1981) *The Wisdom of Many: Essays on the Proverb*, New York and London: Garland.

Mitchell, W.J.T. (ed.) (1981) *On Narrative*, Chicago and London: University of Chicago Press.

Mitchell, W.J.T. (ed.) (1986) *Iconology: Image, Text, Ideology*, Chicago and London: University of Chicago Press.

Moerman, M. (1987) *Talking Culture: Ethnography and Conversation Analysis*, Philadelphia: University of Pennsylvania Press.

Moore C.-L. and Yamamoto, K. (1988) *Movement Observation and Analysis*, New York: Gordon & Breach.

Mosher, H.F. (1981) 'Recent studies in narratology', *Papers in Language and Literature* 17: 88–110.

Moyo, S.P.C. (1986) 'The aesthetic structure of oral poetry: the media of a complex form', in Moyo, S.P.C. et al. (eds) *Oral Traditions in Southern Africa*, Lusaka: Institute of African Studies, University of Zambia, vol. 4: 482–515.

Mumin, Hassan Sheikh, trans. Andrzejewski, B.W. (1974) *Leopard among the Women: Shabeelnaagood, a Somali Play*, London: Oxford University Press.

Munn, N. (1973) *Walbiri Iconography: Graphic Representation and Cultural Symbolism in Central Australian Society*, Ithaca, London: Cornell University Press.

Myerhoff, B. et al. (1980) 'Telling one's story', and 'Discussion', *The Center Magazine* 13, 2: 22–40.

Nagy, J.F. (1985) *The Wisdom of the Outlaw: the Boyhood Deeds of Finn in Gaelic Narrative Tradition*, Berkeley: University of California Press.

Nagy, J.F. (1986) Review of Dundes, *Sacred Narrative*, *Western Folklore* 45.

Nagy, J.F. (1989) 'Representations of oral tradition', in DeMaria and Kitzinger.

Nenola, A. and Timonen, S. (eds) (1990) *Louhen sanat. Kirjoituksia kansanperinteen naisista. The Words of Louhi. Articles on Women in Folklore*, Helsinki.

Nenola-Kallio, A. (1982) *Studies in Ingrian Lament*, Helsinki: Folklore Fellows Communications 234.

Nenola-Kallio, A. Malmberg, D., Johnsen, B.H. and Rørbye, B. (1985) *Women's Folkloristics in the Nordic Countries*, Uppsala: Etnologiska Institutionen.

Ngugi, wa Thiong'o (1986) *Decolonising the Mind: the Politics of Language in African Literature*, London: J. Curry.

Nicolaisen, W.F.H. (1988) 'German *Sage* and English *Legend*: terminology and conceptual problems', in Bennett and Smith.

Nicoloff, A. (ed. and trans.) (1979) *Bulgarian Folktales*, Cleveland Ohio: A. Nicoloff.

Nikiforova, I.D. (1987) 'The development and distinctive features of the forms of the novel in African literature', *Research in African Literatures* 18: 422–33.

Niles, S. (1981) *South American Indian Narrative: Theoretical and Analytical Approaches: an Annotated Bibliography*, New York and London: Garland Folklore Bibliographies 1.

Nketia, J.H.K. (1955) *Funeral Dirges of the Akan People*, Achimota [publisher not given].

Norris, C. (1982) *Deconstruction: Theory and Practice*, London: Methuen.

Obiechina, E.N. (1973) *An African Popular Literature: a Study of Onitsha Market Pamphlets*, Cambridge: Cambridge University Press.

Oinas, F.J. (ed.) (1978) *Heroic Epic and Saga*, Bloomington: Indiana University Press.

Oinas, F.J. (1984) *Essays on Russian Folklore and Mythology*, Columbus Ohio: Slavica.

Okpewho, I. (1977) 'Does the epic exist in Africa? Some formal considerations', *Research in African Literatures* 8: 171–200.

Okpewho, I. (1979) *The Epic in Africa: Toward a Poetics of the Oral Performance*, New York: Columbia University Press.

Okpewho, I. (1983) *Myth in Africa: A Study of its Aesthetic and Cultural Relevance*, Cambridge: Cambridge University Press.

Okpewho, I. (ed.) (1990) *The Oral Performance in Africa*, Ibadan: Spectrum Books.

Olrik, A. (1965) 'Epic laws of folk narrative', in Dundes.

O'Neill, P. (1978) 'Responsibilities of the broadcast media', in Rosenberg.

Ong, W. (1982) *Orality and Literacy. The Technologizing of the Word*, London and New York: Methuen.

Oosten, J.G. (1985) *The War of the Gods: The Social Code in Indo-European Mythology*, London: Routledge & Kegan Paul.

Opie, I. and P. (eds) (1951) *The Oxford Dictionary of Nursery Rhymes*, Oxford: Clarendon Press.

Opie, I. and P. (1961) *The Lore and Language of Schoolchildren*, Oxford: Clarendon Press.

Opland, J. (1983) *Xhosa Oral Poetry. Aspects of a Black South African Tradition*, Cambridge: Cambridge University Press.

Opland, J. (1984) 'The isolation of the Xhosa oral poet', in White and Couzens.

Opland, J. (1986) 'World epic: on heroic and epic traditions in oral and written literature', in Shaffer, E.S. (ed.) *Comparative Criticism* 8: 307–20.

Opland, J. (n.d.) *Praise Poetry: a Case Book*, forthcoming.

Oral History Society (1990) 'Popular memory', Special Issue, *Oral History* 18, 1.

Orbell, M. (1974) *A Select Bibliography of the Oral Tradition of Oceania*, University of Auckland: Department of Anthropology Working Papers, 36.

Orbell, M. (1990) ' "My summit where I sit": form and content in Maori women's love songs', in Finnegan and Orbell.

Oring, E. (1987) 'Generating lives: the construction of an autobiography', *Journal of Folklore Research* 24: 241–62.

Ortner, S. (1984) 'Theory in anthropology since the sixties', *Comparative Studies in Society and History* 26: 126–66.

Ortony, A. (ed.) (1979) *Metaphor and Thought*, Cambridge: Cambridge University Press.

Ortutay, G. (1959) 'Principles of oral transmission in folk culture', *Acta Ethnographica* 8: 175–221.

Ostendorf, B. (1975) 'Black poetry, blues, and folklore: double consciousness in Afro-American oral culture', *Amerikastudien* 20: 209–59.

Ó'Súilleabháin, S. (1942) *A Handbook of Irish Folklore*, Dublin: Folklore of Ireland Society.

Pace, D. (1982) 'Beyond morphology: Lévi-Strauss and the analysis of folktales', in Dundes.

Paine, R. (ed.) (1981) *Politically Speaking: Cross-Cultural Studies of Rhetoric*, Philadelphia: Institute for the Study of Human Issues.

Paredes, A. (1969) 'Concepts about folklore in Latin America and the United States', *Journal of Folklore Institute* 6: 20–38.

Paredes, A. (1977) 'On ethnographic work among minority groups: a folklorist's perspective', *New Scholar* 6: 1–32.

Paredes, A. and Bauman, R. (eds) (1972) *Toward New Perspectives in Folklore*, Austin: University of Texas Press and American Folklore Society.

Parkin, D. (1984) 'Political language', *Annual Review of Anthropology* 13: 345–65.

Parks, W. (1987) 'Orality and poetics: synchrony, diachrony, and the axes of narrative transmission', in Foley 1987b.

Parry, A. (ed.) (1971) *The Making of Homeric Verse: the Collected Papers of Milman Parry*, Oxford: Clarendon Press.

Parry, M. and Lord, A.B. (eds) (1954) *Serbo-Croatian Heroic Songs*, vol. 1, *Novi Pazar: English Translations*, Cambridge Mass and Belgrade: Harvard University Press and Serbian Academy of Sciences.

Parry, M., Lord, A.B. and Bynum, D.E. (eds) (1974) *Serbo-Croatian Heroic Songs*, vol. 3, *The Wedding of Smailagić Meho, Avdo Medjedović*, Cambridge Mass: Harvard University Press.

Paulme, D. (1976) *La Mère Dévorante: Essai sur la Morphologie des Contes Africains*, Paris: Gallimard.

Paulme, D. (1977) 'The impossible imitation in African Trickster tales', in Lindfors.

Peacock, J.L. (1968) *Rites of Modernization: Symbolic and Social Aspects of Indonesian Proletarian Drama*, Chicago: University of Chicago Press.

Pentikäinen, J. (1976) 'Repertoire analysis', in Pentikäinen and Juurikka.

Pentikäinen, J. (1978a) *Oral Repertoire and World View: An Anthropological Study of Marina Takalo's Life History*, Folklore Fellows Communications 219.

Pentikäinen, J. (1978b) 'Oral transmission of knowledge', in Dorson.

Pentikäinen J. and Juurikka, T. (eds) (1976) *Folk Narrative Research*, Studia Fennica 20, Helsinki: Finnish Literature Society.

Pepicello, W.J. and Green, T.A. (1984) *The Language of Riddles: New Perspectives*, Columbus: Ohio State University Press.

Perelman, Ch. and Olbrechts-Tyteca, L. (1969) *The New Rhetoric: a Treatise on Argumentation*, Eng. trans., Notre Dame, Indiana: University of Notre Dame Press.

Perić-Polonijo, T. (1988) 'Criteria for classification of oral lyric poetry', in Rajković.

Personal Narratives Group (ed.) (1989) *Interpreting Women's Lives: Feminist Theory and Personal Narratives*, Bloomington: Indiana University Press.

Philips, S.U. et al. (eds) (1987) *Language, Gender and Sex in Comparative Perspective*, Cambridge: Cambridge University Press.

Philipsen, G. and Carbaugh, D. (1986) 'A bibliography of fieldwork in the ethnography of communication', *Language in Society* 15: 387–97.

Pickering, M. (1982) *Village Song and Culture: a Study based on the Blunt*

Collection of Song from Adderbury, North Oxfordshire, London: Croom Helm.

Pickering, M. and Green, T. (1987) *Everyday Culture: Popular Song and the Vernacular Milieu*, Milton Keynes and Philadephia: Open University Press.

Pond, W. (1990) 'Wry comment from the outback: songs of protest from the Niua Islands, Tonga', in Finnegan and Orbell.

Pool, I. de S. (ed.) (1959) *Trends in Content Analysis*, Urbana: University of Illinois Press.

Poyatos, F. (1983) *New Perspectives in Nonverbal Communication: Studies in Cultural Anthropology, Social Psychology, Linguistics, Literature, and Semiotics*, Oxford and New York: Pergamon.

Poyatos, F. (ed.) (1988) *Literary Anthropology: a New Interdisciplinary Approach to People, Signs and Literature*, Amsterdam and Philadelphia: John Benjamins.

Preminger, A. (ed.) (1974) *Princeton Encyclopedia of Poetry and Poetics*, Princeton: Princeton University Press.

Preston, D.R. (1982) ' "Ritin" fowklower daun 'rong: folklorists' failures in phonology', *Journal of American Folklore* 95: 304–26.

Preston, D.R. (1983) 'Mowr bayud spellin': a reply to Fine', *Journal of American Folklore* 96: 330–9.

Priebe, R. (1978) 'Popular writing in Ghana: a sociology and rhetoric', *Research in African Literatures* 9: 395–432.

Prince, G. (1982) *Narratology: the Form and Functioning of Narrative*, Berlin, New York and Amsterdam: Mouton.

Prince, G. (1987) *A Dictionary of Narratology*, Lincoln and London: University of Nebraska Press.

Prince, G. (1989) 'Narrative', in Barnouw: vol. 3, 161–4.

Propp, V. (1968) *The Morphology of the Folktale*, Eng. trans., 2nd ed., Austin: University of Texas Press.

Puhvel, J. (1987) *Comparative Mythology*, Baltimore: Johns Hopkins University Press.

Quine, W.V.O. (1960) *Word and Object*, New York and London: Wiley.

Radice, W. and Reynolds, B. (eds) (1987) *The Translator's Art: Essays in Honour of Betty Radice*, Harmondsworth: Penguin.

Raffel, B. (1986) 'The manner of Boyan: translating oral literature', *Oral Tradition* 1: 11–29.

Rajković, Z. (ed.) (1988) *Contributions to the Study of Contemporary Folklore in Croatia*, Special Issue, 9, Zagreb: Institute of Folklore Research.

Ranke, K. (1977–) *Enzyklopädie des Märchens: Handwörterbuch zur historischen und vergleichenden Erzählforschung*, Berlin and New York: de Gruyter (several volumes – in progress).

Ray, B. (1980) 'The story of Kintu: myth, death, and ontology', in Karp and Bird.

Reder, L.M. (1987) 'Beyond associations: strategic components in memory retrieval', in Gorfein and Hoffman.

Renoir, A. (1988) *A Key to Old Poems: The Oral-Formulaic Approach to the Interpretation of West-Germanic Verse*, University Park and London: Pennsylvania State University Press.

Renwick, R. de V. (1980) *English Folk Poetry, Structure and Meaning*, Philadelphia: University of Pennsylvania Press.

Rice, P. and Waugh, P. (eds) (1989) *Modern Literary Theory: a Reader*, London: Edward Arnold.

Richmond, W.E. (ed.) (1957) *Studies in Folklore*, Bloomington: Indiana University Press.

Ricoeur, P. (1971) 'The model of the text: meaningful action considered as text', *Social Research* 38: 529–62.

Riley, M. (1990) 'The dangerous mime: historical photographs, narratives and cultural representations', *Collectanea: Papers in Folklore, Popular and Expressive Culture*, 1: 85–107.

Rivière, J.C. (1979) *Georges Dumézil: à la découverte des Indo-Européens*, Paris: Copernic.

Rivière, P. (1989) 'New trends in British social anthropology', *Cadernos do Noroeste* 2, 2/3: 7–24.

Roberts, H.H. (1989) 'Spiritual or revival hymns of the Jamaica Negros', *Ethnomusicology* 33: 409–74.

Röhrich, L. (1984a) 'Märchen – Mythos – Sage', in Siegmund, W. (ed.) *Antiker Mythos in unseren Märchen*, Veröffentlichungen der Europäischen Märchengesellschaft, 6, Kassel: Roth.

Röhrich, L. (1984b) 'The quest of meaning in folk-narrative research: what does meaning mean and what is the meaning of mean', *Arv* 40: 127–38.

Rollwagen, J.R. (ed.) (1988) *Anthropological Filmmaking*, New York: Harwood.

Rooth, A.B. (1951) *The Cinderella Cycle*, Lund: Gleerup.

Rooth, A.B. (1974) 'On the difficulty of transcribing synchronic perception into chronological verbalisation', Uppsala: Etnologiska Institutionens Småskriftsserie, 15.

Rooth, A.B. (1975) 'Myths – aetia or animal stories?' *Arv* 31: 2–16.

Rooth, A.B. (1976) *The Importance of Storytelling: a Study based on Field Work in Northern Alaska*, Uppsala: Studia Ethnologica Upsaliensia, 1.

Rooth, A.B. (1979) 'Pattern recognition, data reduction, catchwords and semantic problems: an epistemological study', Uppsala: Etnologiska Institutionens Småskriftsserie, 21.

Rooth, A.B. (1980) 'Quantities and qualities. Number and dignity for pattern recognition of tales and myths', Uppsala: Etnologiska Institutionens Småskriftsserie, 29.

Rosenberg, B.A. (1970) *The Art of the American Folk Preacher*, New York: Oxford University Press.

Rosenberg, B.A. and Smith, J.B. (1974) 'The computer and the Finnish historical-geographical method', *Journal of American Folklore* 87: 149–54.

Rosenberg, N.V. (ed.) (1978) *Folklore and Oral History*, St John's Newfoundland: Memorial University of Newfoundland.

Rosmarin, A. (1985) *The Power of Genre*, Minneapolis: University of Minnesota Press.

Rothenberg, J. and D. (eds) (1983) *Symposium of the Whole. A Range of Discourse Toward an Ethnopoetics*, Berkeley, Los Angeles and London; University of California Press.

Rowe, K.E. (1986) 'To spin a yarn: the female voice in folklore and fairy tale', in Bottigheimer 1986b.

Royal Anthropological Institute (1951) *Notes and Queries on Anthropology*, 6th edition, London: Routledge & Kegan Paul.

Russell, I. (ed.) (1986) *Singer, Song and Scholar*, Sheffield: Sheffield University Press.

Russo, J. (1976) 'Is "oral" or "aural" composition the cause of Homer's formulaic style?' in Stolz and Shannon.

Ryan, P. (ed.) (1981) *Memory and Poetic Structure*, London: Middlesex Polytechnic.

Samuel, R. (ed.) (1981) *People's History and Socialist Theory*, London: Routledge.

Samuel, R. (1988) 'Myth and history', *Oral History* 161: 15–18.

Samuel, R. and Thompson, P. (eds) (1990) *The Myths We Live By*, London and New York: Routledge.

Sándor, I. (1967) 'Dramaturgy of tale-telling', *Acta Ethnographica* 16: 305–38.

Sapir, E. (1922) *Language: An Introduction to the Study of Speech*, London: Milford.

Schechner, R. (1985) *Between Theater and Anthropology*, Philadelphia: University of Pennsylvania Press.

Schechner, R. (1988) *Performance Theory*, revised ed., New York and London: Routledge.

Schechner, R. and Appel, W. (eds) (1990) *By Means of Performance: Intercultural Studies of Theatre and Ritual*, Cambridge: Cambridge University Press.

Schegloff, E.A. (1982) 'Discourse as an interactional achievement: some uses of "uh huh" and other things that come between sentences', in Tannen 1982b.

Scherer, K.R. and Ekman, P. (eds) (1982) *Handbook of Methods in Nonverbal Behavior Research*, Cambridge: Cambridge University Press.

Scheub, H. (1971) 'Translation of African oral narrative-performances to the written word', *Yearbook of Comparative and General Literature* 20: 8–36.

Scheub, H. (1975) *The Xhosa Ntsomi*, Oxford: Clarendon Press.

Scheub, H. (1977a) 'Body and image in oral narrative performance', *New Literary History* 8: 345–67.

Scheub, H. (1977b) *African Oral Narratives, Proverbs, Riddles, Poetry and Song*, Boston: G.K. Hall.

Scheub, H. (1985) 'A review of African oral tradition and literature', *African Studies Review* 28, 2/3: 1–72.

Schieffelin, E.L. (1985) 'Performance and the cultural construction of reality', *American Ethnologist* 12, 4: 707–24.

Schmitt, J.-C. (1983) *The Holy Greyhound: Guinefort, Healer of Children since the Thirteenth Century*, Eng. trans, Cambridge: Cambridge University Press.

Scholes, R. and Kellogg, R. (1966) *The Nature of Narrative*, London: Oxford University Press.

Schousboe, K. and Larsen, M.T. (eds) (1989) *Literacy and Society*, Copenhagen: Akademisk Forlag.

Schulte, R. (1987) 'Translation theory: a challenge for the future', in Schulte and Kratz 1–2.

Schulte, R. and Kratz, D. (1987) *Translation Theory*, Special Issue, *Translation Review* 23.

Schwartz, E.K. (1956) 'A psychoanalytic study of the fairy tale', *American Journal of Psychotherapy* 10: 740–62.

Scribner, S. and Cole, M. (1981) *The Psychology of Literacy*, Cambridge Mass and London: Harvard University Press.

Scullion, J.J. (1984) '*Märchen, Sage, Legende*: towards a clarification of some literary terms used by Old Testament scholars', *Vetus Testamentum* 34, 3: 321–36.

Searle, J.R. (1969) *Speech Acts: an Essay in the Philosophy of Language*, Cambridge: Cambridge University Press.

Sebeok, T.A. (ed.) (1960) *Style in Language*, Cambridge Mass: MIT Press.

Seeger, A. (1986) 'Oratory is spoken, myth is told, and song is sung, but they are all music to my ears', in Sherzer and Urban.

Seitel, P. (1980) *See So that We may See. Performances and Interpretations of Traditional Tales from Tanzania*, Bloomington: Indiana University Press.

Sekoni, R. (1990) 'The narrator, narrative-pattern and audience experience of oral narrative-performance', in Okpewho.

Seydou, C. (1982) 'Comment définir le genre épique? un exemple: l'épopée africaine', in Görög-Karady.

Sharp, C. (1932) *English Folk Songs from the Southern Appalachians*, 2 vols, London: Oxford University Press.

Shaw, R.D. (1987) 'The translation context: cultural factors in translation', in Schulte et al. 1987: 25–9.

Sherfey, J., transcribed by Titon, J. and George, K. (1977) 'Dressed in the armor of God', *Alcheringa* 3, 2: 10–31.

Sherzer, J. (1974) '*Namakke, sunmakke, kormakke*: three types of Cuna speech event', in Bauman and Sherzer.

Sherzer, J. (1983) *Kuna Ways of Speaking: an Ethnographic Perspective*, Austin: University of Texas Press.

Sherzer, J. (1987a) 'A discourse-centered approach to language and culture', *American Anthropologist* 89: 295–309.

Sherzer, J. (1987b) 'A diversity of voices: men's and women's speech in ethnographic perspective', in Philips et al.

Sherzer, J. (1989) 'The Kuna verb: a study in the interplay of grammar, discourse, and style', in Key and Hoenigswald.

Sherzer, J. (1990) *Verbal Art in San Blas*, Cambridge: Cambridge University Press.

Sherzer, J. and Urban, G. (eds) (1986) *Native South American Discourse*, Berlin: Mouton de Gruyter.

Sherzer, J. and Wicks, S.A. (1982) 'The intersection of music and language in Kuna discourse', *Latin American Music Review* 3, 2: 147–64.

Sherzer, J. and Woodbury, A.C. (eds) (1987) *Native American Discourse: Poetics and Rhetoric*, Cambridge: Cambridge University Press.

Shils, E.A. (1984) *Tradition*, Chicago: University of Chicago Press.

Shuman, A. (1986) *Storytelling Rights: the Uses of Oral and Written Texts by Urban Adolescents*, Cambridge: Cambridge University Press.

Siikala, A.-L. (1980) 'The personality and repertoire of a story-teller: an attempt at experimental fieldwork', *Arv* 36: 165–74.

Siikala, A.S. (ed) (1989) *Studies in Oral Narrative*, Studia Fennica 33, Helsinki: Finnish Literature Society.

Simmel, G. (1959) 'The adventure', in Wolff, K.H. (ed.) *Georg Simmel, 1858–1918: A Collection of Essays*, Columbus: Ohio State University Press.

Singer, Milton (1972) *When a Great Tradition Modernizes: an Anthropological Approach to Indian Civilization*, New York: Praeger.

Smith, B.H. (1968) *Poetic Closure: a Study of How Poems End*, Chicago and London: University of Chicago Press.

Smith, B.H. (1978) *On the Margins of Discourse: the Relation of Literature to Language*, Chicago and London: University of Chicago Press.

Smith, B.H. (1981) 'Narrative versions, narrative theories', in Mitchell (1st published *Critical Inquiry* 7: 213–36, 1980).

Smith, E.W. and Dale, A.M. (1920) *The Ila-speaking peoples of Northern Rhodesia*, 2 vols., London: Macmillan.

Smith, J.D. (1977) 'The singer or the song: a reassessment of Lord's oral theory', *Man* 12: 141–53.

Smith, J.D. (1981) 'Words, music and memory', in Ryan.

Smith, M.L. and Damien, Y.M. (1981) *Anthropological Bibliographies: a Selected Guide*, South Salem N.Y.: Redgrave.

Smith, P. (ed.) (1984) *Perspectives on Contemporary Legend*, Sheffield: Sheffield Academic Press.

Sokolov, Y.M. (1971) *Russian Folklore*, Eng. trans., Detroit: Folklore Associates.

Spencer, P. (ed.) (1985) *Society and the Dance: the Social Anthropology of Process and Performance*, Cambridge: Cambridge University Press.

Spradley, J.P. (1980) *Participant Observation*, New York: Holt, Rinehart & Winston.

Stahl, S.K.D. and Dorson, R. (eds) (1977) *Stories of Personal Experiences*, Special Double Issue, *Journal of the Folklore Institute* 14.

Stanford, W.B. (1964) *The Ulysses Theme: a Study in the Adaptability of a Traditional Hero*, 2nd ed., New York: Barnes and Noble.

Stewart, K. (1988) 'Nostalgia – a polemic', *Cultural Anthropology* 3: 227–41.

Stewart, S. (1979) *Nonsense: Aspects of Intertextuality in Folklore and Literature*, Baltimore: Johns Hopkins University Press.

Stock, B. (1983) *The Implications of Literacy. Written Language and Models of Interpretation in the Eleventh and Twelfth Centuries*, Princeton: Princeton University Press.

Stoeltje, B.J. (ed.) (1988) *Feminist Revisions in Folklore Studies*, Special Issue, *Journal of Folklore Research* 25, 3.

Stoeltje, B.J. (1989) 'Festival', in Barnouw vol. 2: 161–6.

Stoller, P. (1989) *The Taste of Ethnographic Things: the Senses in Anthropology*, Philadelphia: University of Pennsylvania Press.

Stolz, B.A. and Shannon, R.S. (eds) (1976) *Oral Literature and the Formula*, Ann Arbor: Center for the Coördination of Ancient and Modern Studies, University of Michigan.

Stone, K.F. (1986) 'Feminist approaches to the interpretation of fairy tales', in Bottigheimer 1986b.

Stone, R.M. (1982) *Let the Inside be Sweet. The Interpretation of Music Event among the Kpelle of Liberia*, Bloomington: Indiana University Press.

Stone, R.M. (1988) *Dried Millet Breaking: Time, Words, and Song in the Woi Epic of the Kpelle*, Bloomington: Indiana University Press.

Stone, R.M. and Stone, V.L. (1981) 'Event, feedback and analysis: research media in the study of music events', *Ethnomusicology* 25, 2: 215–25.

Street, B.V. (1984) *Literacy in Theory and Practice*, Cambridge: Cambridge University Press.

Suojanen, P. (1989) 'The spontaneous sermon: its production and performance', in Siikala.

Swann, B. and Krupat, A. (eds) (1987) *Recovering the Word: Essays on Native American Literature*, Berkeley: University of California Press.

Sweeney, A. (1980) *Authors and Audiences in Traditional Malay Literature*, Berkeley: Center for South and South East Asian Studies, University of California.

Sweeney, A. (1987) *A Full Hearing: Orality and Literacy in the Malay World*, Berkeley: University of California Press.

Szwed, J.F. (1981) 'The ethnography of literacy', in Whiteman.

Szwed, J.F. and Abrahams, R.D. (1978) *Afro-American Folk Culture: an Annotated Bibliography of Materials from North, Central, and South America, and the West Indies*, Philadelphia: Institute for the Study of Human Issues.

Tannen, D. (ed.). (1982a) *Spoken and Written Language: Exploring Orality and Literacy*, Norwood N.J.: Ablex.

Tannen, D. (ed.) (1982b) *Analyzing Discourse: Text and Talk*, Washington: Georgetown University Press.

Tannen, D. (ed.) (1984) *Coherence in Spoken and Written Discourse*, Norwood N.J.: Ablex.

Tannen, D. (1989) *Talking Voices: Repetition, Dialogue, and Imagery in Conversational Discourse*, Cambridge: Cambridge University Press.

Taylor, A. (1928) 'Precursors of the Finnish method in folk-lore study', *Modern Philology* 25: 481–91.

Tedlock, B. (ed.) (1987) *Dreaming: Anthropological and Psychological Interpretations*, Cambridge: Cambridge University Press.

Tedlock, B. and D. (1986) 'Text and textile: language and technology in the arts of the Quiché Maya', *Journal of Anthropological Research* 41: 121–46.

Tedlock, D. (1971) 'On the translation of style in oral narrative', *Journal of American Folklore* 84: 114–33.

Tedlock, D. (1972) *Finding the Center: Narrative Poetry of the Zuni Indians*, New York: Dial.

Tedlock, D. (1977) 'Toward an oral poetics', *New Literary History*, 8: 507–19.

Tedlock, D. (1979) 'The analogical tradition and the emergence of a dialogical anthropology', *Journal of Anthropological Research* 35: 387–400.

Tedlock, D. (1983) *The Spoken Word and the Work of Interpretation*, Philadelphia: University of Pennsylvania Press.

Tedlock, D. (1985a) 'Learning to listen: oral history as poetry', in Grele.

Tedlock, D. (trans.) (1985b) *Popul Vuh: The Definitive Edition of the Mayan Book of the Dawn of Life and the Glories of the Gods and Kings*, New York: Simon and Schuster.

Tedlock, D. (1989) 'Ethnopoetics', in Barnouw: vol. 2: 116–17.

Tempels, P. (1959) *Bantu Philosophy*, Paris: Présence africaine.

Thomas. A. and Tuia, I. (1990) 'Portrait of a composer: Ihaia Puka, a *polotu* of the Tokelau Islands', in Finnegan and Orbell.

Thomas, R. (1989) *Oral Tradition and Written Record in Classical Athens*, Cambridge: Cambridge University Press.

Thompson, E.P. (1977) 'Folklore, anthropology, and social history', *Indian Historical Review* 3: 247–66.

Thompson, P. (1978) *The Voice of the Past. Oral History*, Oxford: Oxford University Press. (2nd ed. 1988).

Thompson, S. (1946) *The Folktale*, New York: Holt, Rinehart & Winston.

Thompson, S. (1955–8) *Motif-Index of Folk-Literature: a Classification of Narrative Elements in Folktales, Ballads, Myths, Fables, Mediaeval Romances, Exempla, Fabliaux, Jest-Books and Local Legends*, revised and enlarged edition, 6 vols, Bloomington: Indiana University Press.

Thompson, S. and Balys, J. (1958) *The Oral Tales of India*, Bloomington: Indiana University Press.

Thoms, W. (1846) Letter in *The Athenaeum* 982, Aug. 22.

Titon, J.F. (1985) 'Stance, role, and identity in fieldwork among folk Baptists and Pentecostals', *American Music* 3, 1: 16–24.

Todorov, T. (1975) *The Fantastic: a Structural Approach to a Literary Genre*, Ithaca: Cornell University Press.

Todorov, T. (1977) *The Poetics of Prose*, Eng. trans., Ithaca: Cornell University Press.

Todorov, T. (1986), 'Structural analysis of narrative', in Davis.

Toelken, B. (1979) *The Dynamics of Folklore*, Boston: Houghton Mifflin.

Tonkin, E. (1974) 'Implications of oracy: an anthropological view', *Oral History* 3.1: 41–9.

Tonkin, E. (1982) 'The boundaries of history in oral performance', *History in Africa*, 9: 273–84.

Tonkin, E. (1991) *Narrating our Pasts: the Social Construction of Oral History*, Cambridge: Cambridge University Press.

Tual, A. (1986) 'Speech and silence: women in Iran', in Dube, L., Leacock, E. and Ardener, S. (eds) (1986) *Visibility and Power: Essays on Women in Society and Development*, Delhi: Oxford University Press.

Turner, V.W. (1982) *From Ritual to Theatre. The Human Seriousness of Play*, New York City: Performing Arts Journal Publications.

Turner, V.W. and Bruner, E.M. (eds) (1986) *The Anthropology of Experience*, Urbana: University of Illinois Press.

Urban, G. (1986) 'Ceremonial dialogues in South America', *American Anthropologist* 88: 371–86.

Urban, G. (1988) 'Ritual wailing in Amerindian Brazil', *American Anthropologist* 90: 385–400.

Urban, G. (1989) Personal Communication.

Utley, F. L. (1978) 'The folktale: life history vs. structuralism', in Dundes, A. (ed.) *Varia Folklorica*, The Hague: Mouton.

Van Maanen, J. (1988) *Tales of the Field: on Writing Ethnography*, Chicago and London: University of Chicago Press.

Vander, J. (1988) *Songprints: the Musical Experience of Five Shoshone Women*, Urbana: University of Illinois Press.

Vansina, J. (1965) *Oral Tradition: A Study in Historical Methodology*, London: Routledge.

Vansina, J. (1985) *Oral Tradition as History*, London: James Currey, Nairobi: Heinemann.

Vavilov, V.N. (1987) 'Prose genres in the making of African English-language literature', *Research in African Literatures* 18: 434–46.

Vincent, D. (1989) *Literacy and Popular Culture: England 1750–1914*, Cambridge: Cambridge University Press.

Von Franz, M-L. (1972a) *Problems of the Feminine in Fairytales*, Dallas: Spring Publications.

Von Franz, M-L. (1972b) *Patterns of Creativity Mirrored in Creation Myths*, Zurich: Spring Publications.

Von Sydow, C.W. (1948) *Selected Papers on Folklore*, Copenhagen: Rosenkilde and Baggers.

Waites, B., Bennet, T. and Martin, G. (eds) (1982) *Popular Culture: Past and Present*, London: Croom Helm.

Wallis, R. and Malm, K. (1984) *Big Sounds from Small Peoples: The Music Industry in Small Countries*, London: Constable.

Waterman, C.A. (1988) 'Asiko, sakara and palmwine: popular music and social identity in inter-war Lagos, Nigeria', *Urban Anthropology* 17: 229–58.

Waterman, P.P. (1987) *A Tale-Type Index of Australian Aboriginal Oral Narratives*, Helsinki: Folklore Fellows Communications 238.

Watt, I. (1964) 'Literature and society' in Wilson.

Wax, M.L. and Cassell, J. (eds) (1979) *Federal Regulations: Ethical Issues and Social Research*, Boulder, Colorado: Westview Press for American Association for the Advancement of Science.

Webber, R.H. (ed) (1987) *Hispanic Balladry Today*, Special Issue, *Oral Tradition* 2, 2/3.

Weber, R.P. (1985) *Basic Content Analysis*, London: Sage.

Weerasinghe, L. (ed.) (1989) *Directory of Recorded Sound Resources in the United Kingdom*, London: British Library, National Sound Archive.

Weigle, M. (1982) *Spiders and Spinsters: Women and Mythology*, Albuquerque: University of New Mexico Press.

Weigle, M. (1989) *Creation and Procreation: Feminist Reflections on Mythologies of Cosmogony and Parturition*, Philadelphia: Pennsylvania University Press.

Wellek, R. and Warren, A. (1949) *Theory of Literature*, Harmondsworth: Penguin.

White, L. and Couzens, T. (eds) (1984) *Literature and Society in South Africa*, Harlow: Longman.

Whiteman, M.F. (ed.) (1981) *Writing: The Nature, Development, and Teaching of Written Communication*, vol. 1. *Variation in Writing: Functional and Linguistic-Cultural Differences*, Hillsdale, N.J.: Lawrence Erlbaum Associates.

Whorf, B.L. (1956) *Language, Thought, and Reality. Selected Writings*, ed. J.B. Carroll, Cambridge Mass: MIT Press.

Whybray, R.N. (1987) *The Making of the Pentateuch. A Methodological Study*, Sheffield: Sheffield Academic Press.

Wilgus, D.K. (1959) *Anglo-American Folksong Scholarship since 1898*, New Brunswick: Rutgers University Press.

Wilgus, D.K. (1973) 'The text is the thing', *Journal of American Folklore* 86: 241–52.

Wilgus, D.K. (1983) 'Collecting musical folklore and folksong', in Dorson.

Williams, R. (1973) *The Country and the City*, New York: Oxford University Press.

Williams, R. (1977) *Marxism and Literáture*, Oxford: Oxford University Press.

Williams, R. (1983) *Keywords: a Vocabulary of Culture and Society*, revised ed., New York: Oxford University Press.

Willis, R.G. (1981) *A State in the Making: Myth, History, and Social Transformation in Pre-Colonial Ufipa*, Bloomington: Indiana University Press.

Wilson. R.N. (ed.) (1964) *The Arts in Society*, Englewood Cliffs: Prentice-Hall.

Wilson, W.A. (1973) 'Herder, folklore, and romantic nationalism', *Journal of Popular Culture* 6: 819–35.

Wingfield, A. (1981) 'Memory since Bartlett: schemata, scripts, and story grammars', in Ryan.

Wingfield, A. and Byrnes, D.L. (1981) *The Psychology of Human Memory*, New York: Academic Press.

Wolff, J. (1983) *Aesthetics and the Sociology of Art*, London: Allen and Unwin.

Yai, O. (1989) 'Issues in oral poetry: criticism, teaching and translation', in Barber and Farias.

Yankah, K. (1985) 'Risks in verbal art performance', *Journal of Folklore Research* 22: 133–53.

Yates, F.A. (1966) *The Art of Memory*, Chicago: Chicago University Press.

Zan, Y. (1982) 'The text/context controversy: an explanatory perspective', *Western Folklore* 41: 1–27.

Zeitlin, S.J. et al. (1982) *A Celebration of American Family Folklore*, New York: Pantheon.

Zipes, J. (1979) *Breaking the Magic Spell: Radical Theories of Folk and Fairy Tales*, Austin: University of Texas Press.

Zipes, J. (1983) *Fairy Tales and the Art of Subversion: the Classical Genre for Children and the Process of Civilization*, New York: Methuen.

Zipes, J. (1984) 'Folklore research and Western Marxism: a critical replay', *Journal of American Folklore* 97: 329–37.

Zolberg, V.L. (1990) *Constructing a Sociology of the Arts*, Cambridge: Cambridge University Press.

Zumthor, Paul (1983) *Introduction à la Poésie Orale*, Paris: Editions du Seuil.

Zumwalt, R.L. (1988) *American Folklore Scholarship: a Dialogue of Dissent*, Bloomington: Indiana University Press.

Name index

Aarne, A.A. 163, 165
Abercrombie, J.R. 182
Abrahams, R.D. 40, 98, 128, 137, 142, 150, 154, 155, 156, 176
Abu-Lughod, L. 107
Akeroyd, A.V. 216, 220, 221, 223, 226, 227
Albrecht, M.C. 33
Alcheringa-Ethnopoetics 16, 45, 132, 204
American Journal of Folklore 231
Andrzejewski, B.W. 8, 49, 115, 116, 139, 179, 189, 201
Archive of Folk Song 210
Asturias, Miguel Angel 190
Atkinson, P. 18
Azzolina, D.S. 163, 164

Babalola, A. 168
Babcock, B.A. 172
Babcock-Abrahams, B. 98
Bakhtin, M.M. 18, 72, 98, 137, 138, 156, 158, 184
Barber, K. 16, 103, 131–2, 183, 201
Barnes, D.R. 148
Barnes, J.A. 221
Barthes, R. 39
Bartlett, F.C. 114–15
Bascom, W.R. 10, 146–9
Basso, K.H. 20, 130, 176, 183
Bateson, G. 116
Battaglia, D. 116
Baum, W.K. 47
Bauman, R. 7, 13, 19, 40, 59, 92, 101, 102, 137, 150, 172, 176, 185, 232

Bäuml, F.H. 120
Baxter, P.T.W. 188
Becker, H.S. 51, 130
Béhague, G.H. 111
Beissinger, M.H. 140
Ben-Amos, D. 136, 142, 149, 174, 207
Bennett, G. 110, 148, 161, 176
Berndt, R.M. 198
Berry, J. 17
Best, E. 174
Birdwhistell, R.L. 106, 203–4
Blackburn, S.H. 13
Blacking, J. 106, 107, 108
Bloch, M. 207
Blumberg, H.H. 91
Bohannan, L. 73
Bolter, J.D. 182
Bornat, J. 128
Bottigheimer, R.B. 129
Bowden, B. 160
Brandon-Sweeney, B. 106
Brenner, L. 115
Briggs, C.L. 13, 59, 175, 185, 206, 232
Brower, R.A. 187, 188
Brunvand, J.H. 11, 17, 148, 162
Burgess, R.G. 53
Burke, K. 91
Burke, P. 15, 178
Burns, A.F. 9
Burton, R.F. 9

Cahiers de Littérature Orale 9
Calame-Griaule, G. 40, 68, 131, 162, 203, 207

Subject index

accidental audience 99
acoustic media of performance 104–5; of presentation 207–9; in style 177; *see also* audio
aesthetics 130, 131–4, 141–2; *see also* ethnoaesthetics; functions; style
age 95, 123, 126
aims of research: and ethical issues 215–19; and processing texts 212–13, 229; and dissemination 200, 232
allegorical aspects 129–30
alliteration 175
amateur 16, 96, 124
anonymity 226; *see also* ownership; intellectual property rights; individual creativity
anthropology, current trends in xv, 1–3, 20, 23–4, 50–2; ethics in 225–6
appeal to tradition: as aid to researcher 74; as mark of performance 102; in relation to identity 128
archetype 30–1, 33, 161–3
archive collections: deposit of records 210–12; importance of consulting 60
archive research: effect of collecting processes for 72, 82–3; ethical issues 214, 220 and chapter 10 *passim*; implications of transcription problems for 199; importance in early studies 27–8,

30–1; relevance of recording technology for 53, 71; relevance of performance for 94, 111; settings for recording 82–3; working with existing texts xvi, 2, 56, 158, 159–60 and chapter 8 *passim*; *see also* deposit of records
art, sociology of 34; versus non-art 141–2, 173
'artificial' settings 77–80, 82
assonance 175
atmosphere: conveyed through performance 108; lost in translation 192
audience behaviour 108–11; *see also* audiences
audiences 97–100; importance for 'meaning' 93, 184, 185; in performances 93–4, 95–100 *passim*, 109–11; in settings for recording 77, 79, 81: interaction with other participants 108, 109–11, 203; for publication and presentation 199, 200, 212; for translations 193–4
audio: as means of recording 62–5, 69, 109; as component in performance 104–5, 107; and oral history 48; permissions for audio recording 87, 226–9, 232; as form of presentation 207–9; *see also* acoustic; oral; music; recording
aural 16
authorship, attribution of 200–1, 223, 227; *see also* composition;